CON

Cover design by Jennifer Thomson, Edinburgh.

Pastime Publications Ltd gratefully acknowledge the assistance of The Scottish Tourist Board, Area Tourist Boards, The Royal and Ancient Golf Club of St. Andrews and the United States, The Scottish Cyclists' Union, The Forest Enterprise and others in compiling this guide.

Published by Pastime Publications, 32-34 Heriot Hill Terrace, Edinburgh EH7 4DY.
Telephone: 031-556 1105/0057.

Typesetting by Newtext Composition.
Printed and Bound in the U.K.

UK distribution by AA Developments Ltd

Worldwide distribution by The British Tourist Authority.

Please mention this Pastime Publications guide.

ADVERTISERS' INDEX

2

THE COUNTRY CODE

Wherever you go, please remember to follow the Country Code:

Guard against all risk of fire.

Fasten all gates.

Keep dogs under proper control.

Keep to the paths across farm land.

Avoid damaging fences, hedges and walls.

Leave no litter.

Safeguard water supplies.

Protect wild life, wild plants and trees.

Go carefully on the country roads.

Respect the life of the countryside.

CHILDREN'S HOLIDAYS

Organised Groups only
Rock Lea's qualified staff and highly acclaimed facilities are available for non-residential instruction for groups of 12 to 60 youngsters. All our activities can be tailored to meet the needs of groups of young people aged from 9 to 19. Come for half a day, a couple of days or a fortnight.

Wide choice of tried and tested camping sites, camping barns, and hostels within a one mile radius of the centre itself.

Please phone to discuss your detailed requirements. Prices from £15 per day + VAT each.

Rock Lea Activity centre,
Station Road, Hathersage, Peak National Park,
via Sheffield S30 1DD.
Tel/Fax: (0433) 650345.
(See advertisement on inside back cover)

CAVING/POTHOLING

2-6 nights caving & potholing courses designed for beginners. You can't beat Derbyshire's unique cavern systems to learn or develop the most up-to-date techniques and equipment. Open all year. Suitable ages 18-45+. Groups or youngsters by arrangement.

All equipment provided. Expert tuition. As featured on BBC. From £99 full board for fully inclusive weekend. BAHA founder member.

Rock Lea Activity Centre,
Station Road, Hathersage, Peak National Park,
via Sheffield S30 1DD.
Tel/Fax: (0433) 650345.
(See advertisement on inside back cover)

Scotair Balloons

TEL. 0899 21122

Mountain Tots

Quality breathable water proof and fleece clothing for the under-fives - handmade in Scotland.

S.A.E. please to:
Dalbreck Farm,
Strachan,
by Banchory AB31 3LU.
Tel: 033 045 311

"The only gear the discerning toddler wants to wear"

LANDWISE

On Rothiemurchus Estate in Aviemore, Landwise will take you off-road driving with the reassurance of an expert instructor. We have recently introduced a new series of Master Classes for the advanced off-road driver - not for the faint-hearted!

Landwise is run by Mr. Frank Spencer, an Agricultural Training Board Approved Instructor, with 25 years of competition driving experience.

In the interests of conservation, routes are regularly changed.

Landwise also offer laser clay pigeon shooting and during winter months alternative ski-ing - booking essential.

Mr. & Mrs. Frank Spencer,
Landwise (4 X 4),
Tigh Na Feorag,
Kinchurdy Road,
Boat of Garten PH24 3BP.
Tel: 0479 83 609.

Skye
- the Land and People

One of the many Courses based at Sabhal Mor Ostaig, the Gaelic College of Further Education in South Skye.

Skye is renowned for its wide variety of scenery and wildlife. This 5-day Course is led by tutors who live on Skye and who have a wide knowledge of the Island and the Highlands. The week is spent out and about exploring the environment, archaeology, local history, island life and culture. Accommodation is in local Hotels or B. & B. Courses in April, May, June, August and October.

For full details and information on other Courses, throughout the year, in Gaelic, Fiddle, Clarsach, Hebridean and Cape-Breton Dance, Accordion, Piping and Gaelic Song,

contact **THE SHORT COURSES ADMINISTRATOR,**
SABHAL MOR OSTAIG, AN TEANGA,
ISLE OF SKYE, IV44 8RQ
Telephone 04714 373 - Fax: 04714 383

S E L F   C A T E R I N G

SKI-ING

The Scottish Ski Council now issues yellow diamond skier figure with campaign logo for symbol of the commitment to skier safety.

The Scottish National Ski Council continues its promotion of the campaign to alert skiers to their responsibilities, to themselves and those around them on pistes. The Be Aware Ski With Care campaign and logo incorporates and symbolises the internationally recognised Code of Conduct for Skiers.

The SNSC campaign logo can be seen at local equipment retailers and dry ski slopes, as a sign of their attention and commitment to skier safety and responsible skiing.

You can demonstrate your personal dedication to ski safety by getting a yellow diamond sticker of your own from the Scottish National Ski Council, Caledonia House, South Gyle, Edinburgh EH12 9DQ. (Larger versions, suitable for display by commercial operators in the ski industry can also be obtained). Earlier this year the SNSC published their ski safety manual Ski Safe, still enjoying considerable popularity, even on an international scale. Copies of the manual are available from the SNSC.

Please mention this Pastime Publications guide.

Hillend Ski Centre. Still a great place to come if you don't like skiing.

At Hillend Ski Centre, the largest of its kind in Europe, you'll find a fully operational 400m long chairlift waiting to take you up where you belong.

Hardy hill walkers can use it to rise to the challenge of the upper Pentlands. While the less energetic can sit back and enjoy views of Edinburgh and the Lothians which will take your breath away without leaving them breathless!

And if all that fresh air works up an appetite, "The Inn on the Hill" restaurant offers good food, drink and company all day long. Plus a lift back down to ground level on your own personal chair!

For more information you can write to us at Hillend Ski Centre. Biggar Road, Edinburgh. Or call us on 031-445 4433.

HILLEND

mountains of fun

SAILING

First-timers can try sailing, canoeing, windsurfing and cable-water-skiing, climbing and mountain biking in a single weekend. Open all year. Excellent staff: pupils ratios.

Most guests come alone, but couples, families and group enquiries also welcome.

Adults-only breaks from £99 for 2 nights full board, fully inclusive of all equipment, expert tuition, insurance, shared-rooms and all meals. Room upgrades also available. BAHA founder member.

Rock Lea Activity Centre,
Station Road, Hathersage, Peak National Park,
via Sheffield S30 1DD.
Tel/Fax: (0433) 650345.
(See advertisement on inside back cover)

WINDSURFING/WATER SKIING

First-timers can try sailing, canoeing, windsurfing and cable-water-skiing, climbing and mountain biking in a single weekend. Open all year. Excellent staff: pupils ratios.

Most guests come alone, but couples, families and group enquiries are welcome.

Adults-only breaks from £99 for 2 nights full board, fully inclusive of all equipment, expert tuition, insurance, shared-rooms and all meals. Room upgrades also available. BAHA founder member.

Rock Lea Activity Centre,
Station Road, Hathersage, Peak National Park,
via Sheffield S30 1DD.
Tel/Fax: (0433) 650345.
(See advertisement on inside back cover)

ACTIVITY HOLIDAYS
A PASTIME PUBLICATION

I/We have seen your advertisement and wish to know if you have the following vacancy: —

Name_____

Address_____

_____

_____

Dates from pm _____

Please give date and day of week in each case

To am _____

Number in Party _____

Detail of Children _____

Please remember to include a stamped addressed envelope with your enquiry.

ACTIVITY HOLIDAYS
A PASTIME PUBLICATION

I/We have seen your advertisement and wish to know if you have the following vacancy: —

Name_____

Address_____

_____

_____

Dates from pm _____

Please give date and day of week in each case

To am _____

Number in Party _____

Detail of Children _____

CUT ALONG HERE

CUT ALONG HERE

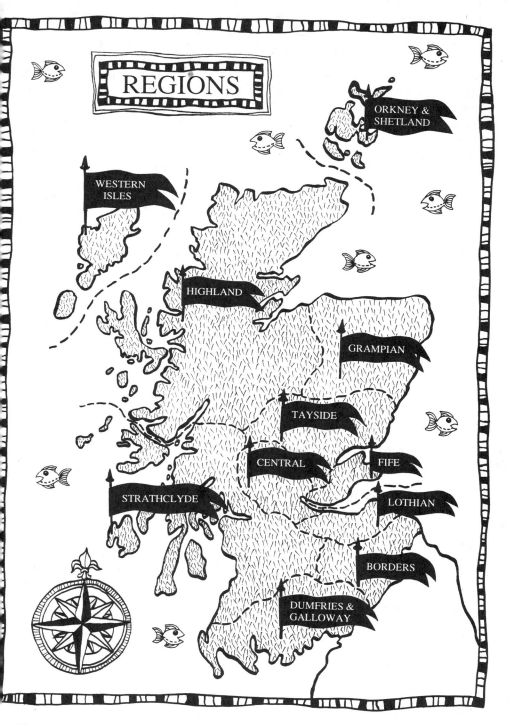

REGIONS

ORKNEY & SHETLAND

WESTERN ISLES

HIGHLAND

GRAMPIAN

TAYSIDE

CENTRAL

FIFE

STRATHCLYDE

LOTHIAN

BORDERS

DUMFRIES & GALLOWAY

WALKS AND TRAILS

All over Scotland there are walks and trails on a wide variety of terrain – from city parks to forest roads to wild moorland.

Now you can follow these walks and trails using this book, which tells you about the walks and how to get there. Most of the walks are designed for a leisurely few hours or less, so you won't require specialist equipment and can bring children along. Often there are helpful signposts and guide books on sale.

You can find out more about local walks from one of the many Tourist Information Centres which can be found all over Scotland.

THE COUNTRY CODE

Wherever you go, please remember to follow the Country Code:

Guard against all risk of fire.

Fasten all gates.

Keep dogs under proper control.

Keep to the paths across farm land.

Avoid damaging fences, hedges and walls.

Leave no litter.

Safeguard water supplies.

Protect wild life, wild plants and trees.

Go carefully on the country roads.

Respect the life of the countryside.

RANGER SERVICES

There are over 100 full-time Rangers in Scotland, employed by a number of organisations to meet and help visitors. Staff on duty at Information or Visitor Centres on each property will be able to give information on where to camp, fish, climb, see birdlife, visit places of interest and also give details of other properties which you might like to visit.

Further information is available from:
The Countryside Commission for Scotland,
Battleby House,
Redgorton,
Perth PH1 3EW.
Tel: Perth (0738) 27921.

CLIMBING

Superb weekend and 6 night beginners introductory rock climbing breaks in the heart of the beautiful Peak National Park. Centre is adjacent to several famous Gritstone crags. Open all year. Adults only; excellent staff: pupil ratios.

Most people come alone, but group enquiries also welcome.

From £99 for 2 nights full board, fully inclusive. From £299 for 6 nights from Saturday, full board, fully inclusive. Room upgrades also available. BAHA founder member.

Rock Lea Activity Centre,
Station Road, Hathersage, Peak National Park,
via Sheffield S30 1DD.
Tel/Fax: (0433) 650345.
(See advertisement on inside back cover)

WALKING

Walking & rambling breaks for adults. Rock Lea is a small and friendly base in the charming Hope Valley where the White Peak's green dales meet the Dark Peak's rugged gritstone uplands.

Easy and harder walks available. Expert guides.

Minibus used to travel to more unusual and interesting walks. Open all year. Fixtures include winter walking & navigation breaks. Weekends from £69 fully inclusive; 6 night breaks from £199. BAHA founder member.

Rock Lea Activity Centre,
Station Road, Hathersage, Peak National Park,
via Sheffield S30 1DD.
Tel/Fax: (0433) 650345.
(See advertisement on inside back cover)

DUMFRIES & GALLOWAY

AE FOREST WALKS
2 miles/3.2km from Ae village on unclassified road, 7½ miles/12km N of Dumfries on A701, between Ae Bridge and Loch Ettrick.
Contact: Forest Enterprise, 55 Moffat Road, Dumfries DG1 1NP. Tel: 0387 69171.
All walks pass through extensive woodland. Riverside walk (yellow) – 1½ miles/2.4km; Craigshiels walk (red) – 2½ miles/4km; Greenhill walk (blue) – 4 miles/6.4km (¾ hour; 1¼ hours; 2 hours to complete).
Stout footwear recommended.
Open all year. Car park. Picnic area. Guide book available – free.

COWTHAT GLEN/BURNSWARK
Ecclefechan (sign at Haggs Playing Field Pavilion). N of village, which lies directly on A74.
Contact: Hoddom & Ecclefechan Community Council, The Surgery, Ecclefechan, Dumfriesshire DG11. Tel: 05763 208.
Wild woodland in the glen, Roman and Iron Age remains on Burnswark. 2 miles/3.2km and 7 miles/11.2km (¾ hour and 2½ hours).
No dogs on Burnswark.
Open all year. Car park. Picnic areas. Information board.

DRUMLANRIG WOODLAND TRAILS
Drumlanrig Castle, 4 miles/6.4km N of Thornhill, 1 mile/1.6km W of A76 on minor road.
Contact: Visitor Services Manager, Drumlanrig Castle, Thornhill, Dumfries DG3 4AG. Tel: 0848 31555/30248.
Woodland walks to lochs and burns. Interesting varity of trees, plants and animals. Victorian heather summer houses, viewpoint. 1-3 miles/1.6-4.8km (1-3 hours).
Open with Castle or by prior arrangement. Open 30 April to 21 August. Car park. Toilets. Picnic areas. Information Centre. Ranger service (guided walks). Adventure woodland. Nature trail for disabled along loch side, with wheelchair access to bird hide.

GALLOWAY FOREST PARK
Contact: Forest Enterprise, Creebridge, Newton Stewart, Dumfries & Galloway DG8 6AJ. Tel: 0671 2420.
Stroan Bridge Forest Trail
Stroan Bridge car park. A75 to Newton Stewart, A714 to Bargrennan Village, follow signs to Loch Trool.
Walk through conifer woodland, viewpoints over Water of Minnoch and Southern Uplands. Choice of four trails: 5 miles/8km, 4½ miles/7.2km, 2½ miles/4km, and 1½ miles/2.4km (3, 2½, 1½ and ½ hour respectively).
Good footwear essential. Observe Country Code. No fires. No litter. Dogs under control at all times.
Open all year. Car park. Picnic areas. Leaflet available.

Talnotry Forest Trail
Talnotry Campsite. A712 Queensway, 7 miles/11.2km NE of Newton Stewart.
Trail climbing past Murray's Monument to afford excellent views over the Palnure Valley to Cairnsmore-of-Fleet and southwards over Cree estuary. Selection of three trails – 3¼ miles/5.2km, 3 miles/4.8km, 2 miles/3.2km (2½, 2 and 1½ hours respectively).
Good footwear essential. Observe Country Code. No fires. No litter. Dogs under control at all times.
Open all year. Car park. Toilets. Picnic areas. Information centre.

GREY MARE'S TAIL
Car park. Off A708, 10 miles/16km NE of Moffat.
Contact: National Trust for Scotland, Hutchesons' Hall, 158 Ingram Street, Glasgow G1 1EJ. Tel: 041-552 8391.
Spectacular 200ft waterfall with wild flowers and herd of wild goats. Seasonal ranger service offers guided walks in summer. 1-3 miles/1.6-4.8km (½-2 hours).
Dangerous slopes: keep to the two paths provided. Dogs on lead during lambing.
Open all year. Car park.

HODDOM
Hoddom Bridge Visitors' Lodge. 2 miles/3.2km SW of Ecclefechan. B723.
Contact: Duncan Ford, Hoddom & Kinmount Estates, Hoddom, Lockerbie, Dumfries & Galloway DG11 1BE. Tel: 05763 244.
Walks: woodland, scenic hill, riverside and farmland. Approx. ½-1½ hours.
Dogs on lead on golf course and near livestock.
Open all year. Car park. Toilets. Picnic areas. Information Centre. Leaflet available showing all walks.

KELHEAD
3 miles/4.8km WNW of Annan on the A75.
Contact: Duncan Ford, Countryside Ranger, Hoddom & Kinmount Estates, Hoddom, Lockerbie, Dumfries & Galloway DG11 1BE. Tel: 05763 244.
Old lime kiln, picnic area, coarse fishing, lochside and woodland walk. ¼ mile/0.75km (30 minutes).
No fires. No boating.
Open all year. Car park. Toilets. Picnic areas. Information board.

KIRROUGHTREE FOREST TRAILS

Kirroughtree Visitor Centre. 1 mile/1.6km off A75 at Palnure village, 3½ miles/5.6km E of Newton Stewart.
Contact: Forest Enterprise, Creebridge, Newton Stewart, Dumfries & Galloway DG8 6AJ. Tel: 0671 2420.
Good views over Cairnsmore-of-Fleet and River Cree estuary. Old woodland as well as replanted landscape. Varied selection of flora and fauna. Selection of several trails from 1½-5 miles/2.4-8km (1-4 hours).
Observe the Country Code. No fires. No litter. Dogs under control at all times.
Open all year. Car park. Toilets. Picnic areas. Information Centre. Leaflet available.

LOCH TROOL FOREST TRAIL

Caldons Campsite. A75 to Newton Stewart, A714 to Bargrennan village. Follow signs to campsite.
Contact: Forest Enterprise, Creebridge, Newton Stewart, Dumfries and Galloway DG8 6AJ. Tel: 0671 2420.
Walk around Loch Trool passing through campsite, old conifer plantations, along scree slopes, affording good views particularly on the latter part of trail alongside Bruce's Stone. 5½ miles/8.8km (3-4 hours).
Good footwear essential. Observe Country Code. No fires. No litter. Dogs under control at all times.
Open all year. Car park. Toilets. Picnic areas. Information Centre (Caldons Campsite).

MABIE FOREST TRAILS

On A710, 4 miles/6.4km from Dumfries on the New Abbey road.
Contact: Forest Enterprise, Ae Village, Parkgate, Dumfries DG1 1QB. Tel: 038786 247.
Walks through woodlands. Chinny Field walk (red) – 1 mile/1.6km (1 hour); Marthrown walk (blue) – 2 miles/3.2km (2 hours); Dalshinnie walk (white) – 3 miles/4.8km (3 hours); Bauldies Brae walk (yellow) – 4 miles/6.4km (4 hours). Children's adventure trail. Conservation trail. Disabled routes (suitable for wheelchairs incl. disabled).
Stout footwear advised.
Open all year. Car park. Toilets (incl. disabled). Picnic areas. Barbecues. Information board. Guide map available – free.

PENNINGHAME FOREST TRAIL

Forest car park near Glenrazie House. A75 Newton Stewart, 2 miles/3.2km, A714 to Challoch Church, turn left on B7027 for 1½ miles/2.4km.
Contact: Forest Enterprise, Creebridge, Newton Stewart, Dumfries & Galloway DG8 6AJ. Tel: 0671 2420.
Walk through conifer and broadleaved woodlands with good views over Cree Valley and Southern Uplands. 1½ miles/2.4km (¾-1 hour).
Observe Country Code. No fires. No litter. Dogs under control at all times.
Open all year. Car park.

ROCKCLIFFE JUBILEE PATH

Rockcliffe. Off A710, 7 miles/11.2km S of Dalbeattie.
Contact: Peter Norman, Ranger/Naturalist, Threave Garden, Castle Douglas DG7 1RX. Tel: 0556 2575.
Walk through delightful coastal scenery. 2 miles/3.2km (1 hour).
Open all year. Car park. Toilets. Picnic areas.

THREAVE COUNTRYSIDE TRAIL

Threave Garden, off A75, 2 miles/3.2km SW of Castle Douglas.
Contact: Peter Norman, Ranger/Naturalist, Threave Garden, Castle Douglas DG7 1RX. Tel: 0556 2575.
Walk through mixed woodland planted for amenity and shelter. Extensive views over surrounding Galloway countryside. ¾ mile/1.2km (¾ hour).
Open all year. Car park. Toilets. Picnic areas. Information Centre (manned March to October). Admission (includes Threave Gardens): Guide book available.

WOOD OF CREE NATURE TRAIL (RSPB)

From car park at mid-point of wood. 4miles/6.4km NW of Newton Stewart on minor road along E side of River Cree, from Minnigaff to Loch Trool.
Contact: Paul N. Collin, RSPB Warden, Gairland, Old Edinburgh Road, Minnigaff, Newton Stewart, Wigtownshire DG8 6PL. Tel: 0671 2861.
Through woodland and along burnsides and moorland. More than 1 mile/1.6km.
Dogs to be kept on leash.
Open all year. Car park. Picnic areas.

BORDERS

BOWHILL WOODLAND NATURE TRAILS
Bowhill House, Selkirk. 3 miles/4.8km W of Selkirk on A708.
Contact: House Manager, Bowhill, Selkirk TD7 5ET. Tel: 0750 20732.
Trail through woodland to Yarrow Water and two lochs. Trail along riverside to ruin of Newark Castle. Extensive animal and plant life. 1¾-3 miles/2.7-4.8km (1-4 hours).
Open May to August daily (12.00-17.00). Car park. Toilets. Picnic areas. Guide book and trail leaflets available.

CARDRONA TRAILS
Kirkburn car park, off Traquair Road. 4 miles/6.4km from Peebles on B7062.
Contact: Forest Enterprise, Lothian & Tweed Forest District Office, Greenside, Peebles EH45 8HS. Tel: 0721 20448.
Three walks on old tracks through extensive woodlands. Points of interest include Cardrona Tower, Roman fort and views of Tweed Valley. 1-4 miles/1.6-6.4km (1-3½ hours).
Observe Forestry Commission bye-laws.
Open all year. Car parks. Picnic areas.

CRAIK FOREST WALK
Forest Enterprise, Craik picnic site car park. Take the B711 Hawick-Tushielaw Road, at Roberton Church take Borthwick Water road for 7 miles/11.2km.
Conact: Forest Enterprise, Ladylaw Centre, Bath Street, Hawick, Roxburghshire. Tel: 0450 77001.
Pleasant streamside walk along paths through extensive woodland to Wolfcleuchhead Waterfall. 3 miles/4.8km (2 hours).
Stout footwear recommended. Dogs to be kept under control.
Open all year. Car park. Toilets. Picnic areas. Information from Hawick Office.

GLENTRESS FOREST TRAILS
2 miles/3.2km E. of Peebles on A72.
Contact: Forest Enterprise, Lothian & Tweed Forest District Office, Greenside, Peebles EH45 8JA. Tel: 0721 20448.
A wide selection of walks of varying lengths on forest roads and woodland tracks providing a diversity of interest and scenery. Between ½ mile/0.8km and 5¾ miles/9.2km (½ to 4 hours).
Observe Forest Enterprise bye-laws.
Main car park. Open all year. Additional in-forest car parks open weekends. Toilets. Picnic areas. Small car park charge. Free leaflet.

LINDINNY WOOD TRAIL
Car park, 100m E of Yair Bridge. 4 miles/6.4km from Selkirk on A707 Selkirk to Peebles road.
Contact: Forest Enterprise, Lothian & Tweed Forest District Office, Greenside, Peebles, Borders EH45 8HS. Tel: 0721 20448.
A waymarked walk illustrating aspects of the long-term development of the area into a broadleaved wood. Under 1 mile/1.6km (1 hour).
Observe Forest Enterprise bye-laws.
Open all year. Car park. Picnic areas.

ST. ABBS HEAD NATURE RESERVE
Steading car park, Northfield Farm. Signposted off B6438 Coldingham-St. Abbs Road.
Contact: Kevin Rideout, National Trust for Scotland, Ranger's Cottage, Northfield, St. Abbs, Eyemouth, Berwickshire TD14 5QF. Tel: 08907 71443.
Cliff walk giving views of breeding sea-birds, returning beside small loch. Rich in wildlife – birds, plants and insects. 3½ miles/5.6km (3 hours).
Open all year. Car park. Toilets. Picnic areas. Information Centre.

TWEED WALK
Hay Lodge Park, Peebles. A72 W of Peebles.
Contact: Borders Regional Council, Planning Department, Regional Headquarters, Newtown St. Boswells, Roxburghshire TD6 0SA. Tel: 0835 23301.
Riverside walks partly on former railway line with impressive bridges. 1½ miles/2.4km; 2½ miles/4km; 6 miles/9.6km (1-3 hours).
Open all year. Car park. Leaflet available.

WOODLAND WALKS
The Woodland Centre, Ancrum, Jedburgh, Roxburghshire TD8 6VQ. A68, 4 miles/6.4km N of Jedburgh.
Contact: Dr. R. Evans (Lothian Estates), The Woodland Centre, Ancrum, Jedburgh, Roxburghshire TD8 6VQ. Tel: 08353 306.
Four walks through mainly mixed woodland, with wide variety of trees, plant life and birds. Access to base of Waterloo Monument, with panoramic views. From 1 mile/1.6km to 3½ miles/5.6km (30 minutes to 2 hours).
Open Easter to end October (yellow walk all year round). Car park. Toilets. Picnic areas. Information Centre. Access to tearoom and shop free of charge.

LOTHIAN

ALMONDELL & CALDERWOOD COUNTRY PARK

North entrance – off A89, 10 miles/16km W of Edinburgh; south entrance – at East Calder on B7015, off A71, 10 miles/16km W of Edinburgh. Calderwood entrance at Mid Calder on B7015, off A71, 12 miles/19.3km W of Edinburgh.

Contact: Visitor Centre, Almondell Country Park, by Broxburn, West Lothian EH52 5PE. Tel: 0506 882254.

River valley, woodland walks. Rich plant life. 4½ miles/7.2km of footpaths in Almondell, footpaths not so well defined in Calderwood. Unrestricted walking.

No cars allowed but restricted vehicle access at N entrance for disabled parties or individuals by arrangement (telephone number above).

Open all year. Car park. Picnic areas. Barbecue site (booking necessary – small charge). Toilets. Information Centre with displays of local water life and tape/slide programme. Guided walks available in summer – free.

BEECRAIGS COUNTRY PARK

2 miles/3.2km S of Linlithgow (signposted from the town). 5 miles/8km N of Bathgate (signposted from town).

Contact: West Lothian District Council, Park Centre, Beecraigs Country Park, near Linlithgow, West Lothian EH49 6PL. Tel: 0506 844516.

Several waymarked routes throughout the Country Park, mainly through coniferous woodland of various ages. One trail goes round 20-acre loch. Red deer farm and trout farm can also be visited. Woodland and loch walk – 2¼ miles/3.7km (1 hour); Woodland walk – 1¼ miles/2km (30 minutes); Cockleroy walk – 1¼ miles/2km (30 minutes).

Forestry operations may occasionally close some paths.

Open all year. Car park. Toilets. Picnic areas. Information Centre. General guide available.

DALKEITH PARK NATURE TRAILS

Main gate at N end of Dalkeith High Street, off A68, 7 miles/11.2km S of Edinburgh.

Contact: Buccleuch Recreation, Smeaton Lodge, Dalkeith, Midlothian EH22 1BY. Bookings – Tel: 031-663 5684.

Woodland and riverside walks beside the Rivers North Esk and South Esk. Trails pass an Adam Bridge, Dalkeith House (c. 1708), 300-year-old trees, man-made caves and tunnels. Up to 4½ miles/7.2km.

Dogs not allowed before 13.00, thereafter must be kept on lead.

Open late March to late October daily (11.00-18.00 or dusk if earlier); also weekends

in November. Car park. Picnic areas. Toilets. Information Centre. Guide book available. Adventure play area.

EDINBURGH – HERMITAGE OF BRAID

Information Centre, off Braid Road. Between Blackford Hill and the Braid Hills, near Morningside Station.

Contact: Countryside Ranger, Hermitage House, Hermitage of Braid, Braid Road, Edinburgh EH10 6JF. Tel: 031-447 7145.

Walk through mixed woodland along the banks of the Braid Burn to the summit of Blackford Hill with its fine views. 2½ miles/4km (1½ hours).

Keep dogs under control.

Open all year. Car park. Toilets. Picnic areas. Information Centre. Partly suitable for disabled.

EDINBURGH – NEW TOWN

Contact: Edinburgh New Town Conservation Centre, 13a Dundas Street, Edinburgh EH3 6QG. Tel: 031-556 7054.

Commencing at the Conservation Centre, a choice of four walks through the Georgian New Town of Edinburgh, with details of architecture and interesting historical facts on well-known individuals described in the guide book. 2 miles/3.2km (1½-2 hours).

Guide book available. Conservation Centre open all year – Monday to Friday (09.00-13.00/14.00-17.00). Exhibitions of conservation and architecture. Conservation reference library. Guided evening walks on Wednesdays (June to August), including visits to 2 private houses and wine (limited to 25 – booking advisable). Guided walks for groups up to 25 with house visit and wine by special arrangement.

EDINBURGH – RIVER ALMOND WALKWAY

Mouth of River Almond at Cramond or Strathalmond Road, off Queensferry Road. A90 N of Edinburgh.

Contact: Edinburgh District Council Planning Department, 1 Cockburn Street, Edinburgh EH1 1BJ. Tel: 031-225 2424.

Walk follows E bank of River Almond along attractive wooded river valley. 1¾ miles/2.8km (45 minutes).

Extensive flight of steps to be negotiated half-way along route.

Open all year. Car park. Picnic areas.

EDINBURGH – WATER OF LEITH

Contact: Edinburgh District Council, Planning Department, 1 Cockburn Street, Edinburgh EH1 1BJ. Tel: 031-225 2424, ext. 6570.

Edinburgh's own waterway has a walkway along it from Leith at the mouth of the Water of Leith to Balerno near the Pentland Hills. On the edge of the countryside, the wooded valley route in part follows a former railway branch line. There are interesting industrial archaeological sites – former mill buildings, etc. – as well as a surprising variety of wildlife, even within the city. Up to 10 miles/16km.
Open all year. Car park. Picnic areas.

HOPETOUN HOUSE NATURE TRAIL
Unclassified road, 2 miles/3.2km W of South Queensferry. Signposted from A904.
Contact: The Administrator, Hopetoun House, South Queensferry EH30 9SL. Tel: 031-331 2451/1546.
Trail in 14 stages through mixed woodland, overlooking deer park and River Forth with fine views. Sea-shore and burn mouth. General natural history and local history interest. 2½ miles/4km (2½ hours).
Dogs must be kept on lead.
Open Easter, then 30 May to 19 September (daily 11.00-17.30). Car park. Picnic areas. Toilets. Exhibition room. Ranger on duty 13.00-18.00, offering guided walks. Leaflet available. Most of trail suitable for disabled.

HOUSE OF THE BINNS WOODLAND WALK
Car park off unclassified road to Blackness, off A904, 15 miles/24.1km W of Edinburgh.
Contact: National Trust for Scotland, Cramond House, Kirk Cramond, Edinburgh EH4 6NS. Tel: 031-336 2157.
Walk through woodland with fine views over the Forth and surrounding farmland. ¾ mile/1.2km (20 minutes).
Open all year. Car park. Picnic areas.

JOHN MUIR COUNTRY PARK, CLIFFTOP TRAIL
Dunbar Harbour, or Shore Road car park in Belhaven, W of Dunbar.
Contact: John Muir Country Park Ranger, Ranger's House, Tyninghame, Dunbar, East Lothian EH42 1XL. Tel: 0620 860556.
Coastal cliff walk with interesting geology and coastal plants. Some nesting seabirds at Dunbar Harbour. 1½ miles/2.4km (2 hours).
Care should be taken with young children near cliffs.
Open all year. Car park. Information Centre (Dunbar). Guide Book available.

KINNEIL ESTATE
Car parks. Off B904 Grangemouth to Bo'ness road.
Contact: Falkirk District Council, Leisure Services Department, Kilns House, Falkirk. Tel: 0324 24911.
Various woodland walks and parkland. Various lengths.
Open all year. Car park. Toilets. Picnic areas. Information Centre. Suitable for disabled.

LINLITHGOW HERITAGE TRAIL
The Cross, Linlithgow, town centre. A904, approximately 17 miles/27.3km W of Edinburgh.
Contact: Forth Valley Tourist Board, Burgh Halls, The Cross, Linlithgow, West Lothian EH49 7AH. Tel: 0506 844600.
Walk through historic royal burgh of Linlithgow. Approximately 1 mile/1.6km (1 hour).
Open all year. Car park. Toilets. Picnic areas. Information Centre. Booklet available.

MUIRAVONSIDE COUNTRY PARK
Car park, farm or Visitor Centre – off B825. Signposted off A801 Bathgate-Grangemouth road.
Contact: Falkirk District Council, Leisure Services Department, Kilns House, Falkirk. Tel: 0324 24911.
Various woodland, farm, river and meadow walks – all around 170-acre park. Varied lengths and times.
Open all year. Car park. Toilets. Picnic areas. Information Centre. Suitable for disabled.

PENICUIK TO BONNYRIGG WALKWAY
Runs for about 5 miles through beautiful countryside, under tunnels and over bridges and a viaduct. Access points include Penicuik, Harper's Brae, Auchendinny, Roslin Glen, Rosewell and Bonnyrigg.
Contact: Midlothian District Council, 1 Eskdaill Court, Dalkeith. Tel: 031-663 2881.

YELLOWCRAIG NATURE TRAIL
Car park. A198 Edinburgh-North Berwick, turn off N at E end of Dirleton village.
Contact: A. Mathieson, Countryside Ranger, Craigielaw Cottages, Aberlady, East Lothian EH32 0PY. Tel: 08757 265.
Woodland, dune grassland, volcanic plug, seashore birds (woodland and sea), plants, seashore life. 1 mile/1.6km (1 hour plus stops).
Open all year. Car park. Toilets. Picnic areas. Guide book available.

STRATHCLYDE

ADD PONDS CONSERVATION AREA
Next to the River Add at the north west end of Loch Glashan in the centre of Kilmichael Forest.
Contact: Forest Enterprise, Loch Awe Forest District, Whitegates, Lochgilphead, Argyll PA31 8RS. Tel: 0546 602518.

AVICH FALLS
1½ miles – 45 mins.
Starts from Barnaline car park which has a large picnic and play area. Follows the forest road a short way and strikes off on a path closely following the River Avich.
Contact: Forest Enterprise, Loch Awe Forest District, Whitegates, Lochgilphead, Argyll, PA31 8RS. Tel: 0546 602518.

AYR GORGE
On B743 Mauchline/Failford road – begins at the hamlet of Failford.
Contact: Scottish Wildlife Trust. Tel: (0290) 52668.
SWT will arrange walks with advance notice during summer months.

BALLOCH CASTLE COUNTRY PARK NATURE TRAIL
From the main entrance at the South Lodge, follow road signs for Country Park.
Contact: Dumbarton District Countryside Ranger Service, Balloch Castle Country Park, Balloch, Dunbartonshire. Tel: 0389 58216.
Walk through woodland and grassland along the banks of the River Leven, with views of Loch Lomond. 1½ miles/2.4km (1 hour).
Open all year. Car park. Visitor Centre. Picnic areas. Toilets.

BARON'S HAUGH WALK
North Lodge Avenue, Motherwell. Take Hamilton Road – Airbles Road – Leven Street – North Lodge Avenue.
Contact: Russell G. Nisbet, RSPB Warden, 9 Wisteria Road, Carluke ML8 5TB. Tel: 0555 70941.
Through woodland, along river bank and around water body with much wildfowl. 2-3 miles/3.2-4.8km (1-1½ hours). Open all year. Car park.

BENBEOCH HILL
By road side, High Pennyvenie. Take B741 from Dalmellington and head through Pennyvenie to High Pennyvenie.
Contact: Ayrshire Valleys Tourist Board, Dalmellington Tourist Information Centre, Ayr Road, Dalmellington, Ayrshire. Tel: 0292 550145.

Head in a NW direction from High Pennyvenie across moorland for about 1 mile/1.6km towards Benbeoch (uphill). Interesting geological feature of hexagonal basalt columns. Good views of surrounding area including Kyle Forest. 1-1½ miles/1.6-2.4km (1-1½ hours).
Stout footwear needed; tends to be snow-bound in winter.
Open all year (but not advisable in winter). Car park. Information Centre (Dalmellington Tourist Information Centre).

BEN LORA WALKS
Car park at Benderloch, 7 miles/11.2km N of Oban, across the Connel Bridge on A828.
Contact: Forest Enterprise, Lorne Forest District, Millpark Road, Oban, Argyll PA34 4NH. Tel: 0631 66155.
Steep walks through plantations giving extensive views to Mull and Morvern. Longer walk gives access to Beinn Lora (1,010 ft/308m) which is an excellent viewpoint. Lower walk (red) – 1 mile/1.6km (50 minutes); Summit walk (blue) – 2¾ miles/4.4km (2¼ hours).
Open all year. Car park. Picnic areas.

CAIRN TABLE
Muirkirk Centre. Turn right off A70 at hotel to Cairn Table.
Contact: Mauchline Tourist Information Centre, National Burns Memorial, Mauchline, Ayrshire. Tel: 0290 51916.
Panoramic view to Ayr and Arran. 3 miles/4.8km (1½ hours).
Open all year. Car park. Information Centre (Cumnock).

CARRADALE FOREST
W end of Carradale village on B879; Grianain Gate on B842, 3 miles/4.8km N of Carradale (15 miles/24.1km NE of Campbeltown).
Contact: Forest Enterprise, Kintyre Forest District, Whitegates, Lochgilphead, Argyll PA31 8RS. Tel: 0546 602518.
Four walks.

Seneval Walk
Hillside track through young plantation with many wild flowers. Fine views. 2 miles/3.2km (1¼ hours).
Stout footwear advised.
Open all year. Car park. Leaflet available.

Sally's Walk
Short secluded and sheltered walk with a variety of ornamental shrubs and trees. 1 mile/1.6km (¾ hour return).
Open all year. Car park. Leaflet available.

Grianain Walk
On forest track on a hillside. Deer can sometimes be seen. 3 miles/4.8km (2 hours + return).
Stout footwear advised.

Shore walk
Through varied forest with extensive views of Arran. About half the walk is along the shore of Kilbrennan Sound. 3 miles/4.8km (2 hours + return).
Stout footwear advised.
Open all year. Car park. Picnic areas.

CHATELHERAULT COUNTRY PARK
Visitor Centre. A74 1½ miles/2.4km S of Hamilton.
Contact: Ranger Service, Chatelherault Country Park, Ferniegair, Hamilton ML3 7UE. Tel: 0698 426213.
Through ancient parkland and gorge woodland rich in wildlife and historic features. Several routes totalling up to 10 miles/16km (½-4 hours).
Open all year. Car Park. Toilets. Picnic areas. Information Centre. Admission charge for Centre.

CULZEAN COUNTRY PARK
The Visitor Centre, off A719, 12 miles/19.3km S of Ayr.
Contact: National Trust for Scotland, The Visitor Centre Office, Culzean Country Park, Maybole, Ayrshire KA19 8LE. Tel: 06556 269.
Four walks.

Silver Avenue/Piper's Brae
Silver firs and beeches, past Camellia House and Swan Pond.

Cliff Walk
To N end of Maidens Bay, with seabirds, flora (especially Spring), good views.

Happy Valley and Swinston Ponds
Variety of well-established trees, nature and plant interest.

The Old Railway
Park at Kennelmount. Plants, birds, good views. In addition there are many other footpaths of interest which lead to the beaches etc.
Open all year. Car park. Picnic areas. Visitor Centre. Toilets. Admission to park is free for pedestrians. Guide book available. Ranger-naturalist service offers guided walks in summer. The country park is run by the NTS for the District Councils of Kyle and Carrick, Cumnock and Doon Valley, and for Strathclyde Regional Council.

CUMNOCK WALK
Craigens Road, Cumnock. A76, 1 mile/1.6km S of Cumnock. Turn right, follow Craigens Road to Loganhill Road, turn left to Glenmuir Water Road.
Contact: Mauchline Tourist Information Centre, National Burns Memorial, Mauchline, Ayrshire. Tel: 0290 51916.
3½ miles/5.6km (2 hours).
Open all year. Car park. Information Centre (Cumnock).

CUMNOCK & DOON VALLEY DISTRICT
A convenanting Trail.
Contact: Mauchline Tourist Information Centre, National Burns Memorial, Mauchline. Tel: (0290) 51916.
Follows covenanting history throughout the area.

CUMNOCK HERITAGE TRAIL
Woodrow Park, Cumnock.
Contact: Local History Librarian, Cumnock & Doon Valley District Council, Council Office, Lugar, Cumnock. Tel: (0290) 22111.
Shows history and development of Cumnock.
Takes approx. 1-1½ hours.
Toilets. Available all year.

DALAVICH OAKWOOD TRAIL
Barnaline picnic area. 15 miles/24.1km S of Taynuilt on W side of Loch Awe.
Contact: Forest Enterprise, Loch Awe Forest District, Whitegates, Lochgilphead, Argyll PA31 8RS. Tel: 0546 602518.
Walk through oak and conifer woodland. 1¾ miles/3km (1 hour).
Open all year. Car park. Picnic areas. Information Centre.

DALMELLINGTON TO LOCH DOON
Cathcartston Interpretation and Visitor Centre, A713 Ayr – Dalmellington road.
Contact: A. Joss, 2 Ayr Road, Dalmellington, Ayrshire KA6 7SJ. Tel: 0292 550339.
Country tracks, woodland, moorland, lochs and uplands scenery. 3 miles/4.8km each way (2½ hours).
Open all year. Car park. Information Centre (Cathcartston).

DALMELLINGTON TOWN TRAIL
Contact: Cathcartston Visitor Centre, Dalmellington. Tel: (0292) 550633.
Starts at Catchartston Visitor Centre where you listen to the weavers family talking before you set off and imagine what life was like in the 1800's.

DUNARDRY
2½ miles – 1½ hours. Waterproof footwear advisable.
Car park situated about 100 yards into the forest, waymarked off the B841 approx. ½ mile west of Cairnbaan.

The walk rises at an even gradient along the forest road above the Crinan Canal with fine views. Going downhill, leave the tarmac road on the west side of the Dunardry Burn. The walk then proceeds through Douglas fir trees, onto a broad track with views along the Crinan Canal and to Cairnbaan.
Contact: Forest Enterprise, Loch Awe Forest District, Whitegates, Lochgilphead, Argyll, PA31 8RS. Tel: 0546 602518.

DUN CORRACH
1¾ miles – 45 mins. Waterproof footwear advisable.
Starts across the main road from the Arinechtan car park and goes up 'Viewpoint Road'. The top of the walk gives good views to Loch Awe and Eredine forest. Descent to the public road is rather steep and difficult in parts.
Contact: Forest Enterprise, Loch Awe Forest District, Whitegates, Lochgilphead, Argyll PA31 8RS. Tel: 0546 602518.
Picnic area beside car park.

DUNDONALD TOWN TRAIL
Dundonald Church, Main Street, Dundonald. A759 from Kilmarnock to Troon. Cut off for Dundonald or take A77 from Ayr to Kilmarnock and cut off at B730 to Dundonald.
Contact: Kilmarnock Tourist Information Centre, 62 Bank Street, Kilmarnock. Tel: 0563 39090.
Historic town trail and woodland area. Approximately 1½ miles/2.4km for initial walk, but up to 4 miles/6.4km up through woodland area. (Approx. 1½ hours; 3 hours for full trail). Wellington boots needed in damp weather.
Open all year. Car park. Leaflet available from Ayrshire Valleys Tourist Board.

DUN NA CUAICHE WOODLAND WALK
Inveraray Castle car park, A83.
Contact: Argyll Estates Office, Cherry Park, Inveraray, Argyll PA32 8XE. Tel: 0499 2203.
Three walks of varying distance. The longest route leads to the top of the hill called Dun Na Cuaiche with excellent views over Loch Fyne. Interesting specimen conifer trees and deciduous wood. 1-2½ miles/1.6-4km (1¼-3 hours).
Open all year. Car park. Picnic areas.

ELLERIC/BALLACHULISH
Forest Enterprise car park at Elleric in Glen Creran. A828 to the head of Loch Creran, turn off onto unclassified road.
Contact: Forest Enterprise, Lorne Forest District, Millpark Road, Oban, Argyll PA34 4NH. Tel: 0631 66155.
Long walk to Ballachulish Village, rough track climbing to 1300ft/395m. This is not a circular walk. 7 miles/11.2km (3½ hours + return).
Open all year. Car park.

FALLS OF CLYDE NATURE RESERVE
New Lanark, 1 mile/1.6km S of Lanark.
Contact: Ranger Naturalist, Scottish Wildlife Trust, Falls of Clyde Nature Centre, The Dyeworks, New Lanark, Lanarkshire ML11 9DG. Tel: 0555 65262.
Spectacular walk along the sides of a steep-sided gorge. Famous waterfalls at Corra Linn and Bonnington Linn. Nature reserve with primary woodland and a variety of wildlife. Up to 7 miles/11.2km of woodland trails.
Open all year. Car park. Picnic areas. Information Centre. Some disabled access.

FINLAYSTONE WOODLAND WALKS & GARDEN
All walks start from car park. On A8 W of Langbank. 20 miles/32km W of Glasgow.
Contact: Mrs. G. MacMillan or Countryside Ranger, Finlaystone, Langbank, Renfrewshire PA14 6TJ. Tel: 047554 505/285.
Choice of five paths through mixed woodland on family estate. On south side of Clyde with four waterfalls. Beautiful gardens. Up to 3 miles/4.8km (up to 45 minutes).
No bicycles. Large groups should book in advance (e.g. more than 15).
Open all year. Car park. Toilets. Picnic areas. Play areas. Information Centre.

GARTOCHARN
Car park on N side of village of Gartocharn, off A811.
Contact: Countryside Ranger Service, Dumbarton District Council, Balloch Castle, Dunbartonshire. Tel: 0389 58216.
Circular walk to the banks of Loch Lomond. 3½ miles/5.6km (2 hours).
Dogs on lead at all times. Important to keep to shore path.
Open all year. Car park. Information Centre at Balloch (seasonal).

Duncryne Hill
Car park N side of Gartocharn village off A811. A walk to the indicator at the top of Duncryne Hill, spectacular views N to Loch Lomond and mountains. 2 miles/3.2km (1½ hours).
Open all year. Car park.

GLASHAN BURN
1½ miles – 45 mins.
The Glashan Burn car park is reached by a tarmac forest road off the main A83, half a mile north of Lochgair.
The path follows the burn upstream through a delightful oak woodland until it reaches the forest road below the hydro-electric dam. Turn left along the road below the dam and then right to the Loch Glashan viewpoint with access to the lochside.
Contact: Forest Enterprise, Loch Awe Forest District, Whitegates, Lochgilphead, Argyll PA31 8RS. Tel: 0546 602518.

GLENCOE LOCHAN TRAIL

Located near the Glencoe Hospital off the A82 in Glencoe village.
Contact: Forest Enterprise, Lorne Forest District, Millpark Road, Oban, Argyll PA34 4NH. Tel: 0631 66155.

GLEN DUBH FOREST WALK

Sutherland's Grove on A828. 8 miles/12.8km N of Connel Bridge.
Contact: Forest Enterprise, Lorne Forest District, Millpark Road, Oban, Argyll PA34 4NH. Tel: 0631 66155.
Circular walk of easy gradient and length in the oldest part of the forest. Impressive stand of Douglas fir trees planted in 1870. Walk: Red markers (1½ miles/2.4km) (45 minutes).
Open all year. Car park. Picnic areas.

GLEN NANT FOREST TRAIL

Car park across bridge 2 miles/3.2km S of Taynuilt on the B845.
Contact: Forest Enterprise, Lorne Forest District, Millpark Road, Oban, Argyll PA34 4NH. Tel: 0631 66155.
Nature trail which lies in part of Glen Nant Forest Nature Reserve. Woodland plant life and extensive vegetation including former charcoal hearths. Strenuous walk. 2½ miles/4km (2 hours). Also short walk for disabled along bank (15 minutes).
Open all year. Car park. Information boards.

KILMARNOCK TOWN TRAIL

Start at Laigh Kirk Church, Kilmarnock.
Contact: Kilmarnock Tourist Information Centre, 62 Bank Street, Kilmarnock. Tel: (0563) 39090.
Tour the historic core of Kilmarnock's Covenanters and Robert Burns Trail.
Open all year. Car park. Toilets. Suitable for disabled. Booklet available from Kilmarnock Tourist Information Centre.

KILMAURS & STEWARTON TOWN TRAILS

Contact: Kilmarnock Tourist Information Centre, 62 Bank Street, Kilmarnock. Tel: (0563) 39090.
Kilmaurs town trail begins at Kilmaurs Museum and follows various points of interest.
Stewarton town trail begins at Avenue Square and takes in various historical buildings.

KILMORY WOODLAND PARK

Located 2¼ miles from Lochgilphead.
Car parking is available with the co-operation of Argyll & Bute District Council at Kilmory Castle Gardens visitors car park near Lochgilphead. The facilities available include walks, viewpoints and a picnic area.
Contact: Forest Enterprise, Loch Awe Forest District, Whitegates, Lochgilphead, Argyll PA31 8RS. Tel: 0546 603381.

KNAPDALE FOREST

Contact: Forest Enterprise, Kintyre Forest District, Whitegates, Lochgilphead, Argyll PA31 8RS. Tel: 0546 602518.

Loch Coille-Bharr Walk
Car park. 1 mile/1.6km SW of Barnluasgan, on B8025. 10 miles/16km W of Lochgilphead.
Circular tour of loch, via forest roads and lochside paths. Several ancient monuments can be seen on this secluded walk. 3 miles/4.8km (2 hours).
Stout footwear advised.
Open all year. Car park. Picnic areas.

Steps Walk
Car park at Barnluasgan, just off B8025. 9 miles/14.4km W of Lochgilphead.
Ridge-top walk with views over Loch Coille-Bharr. 1 mile/1.6km (¾ hour).
Stout footwear advised.
Open all year. Car park. Picnic areas.

LOCHAN TRAIL

Glencoe Hospital. Off A82 in Glencoe village.
Contact: Forest Enterprise, Lorne Forest District, Millpark Road, Oban, Argyll PA34 4NH. Tel: 0631 66155.
Two walks, with attractive views of Loch Leven, Ardgour Hills and part of Glencoe, varied tree species in woods beside lochan; the lochan circuit is a shorter alternative. Trail – 1¾ miles/2.8km (1 hour). Lochan circuit – 1 mile/ 1.6km (25 minutes).
Open all year. Car park.

LOCH SLOY DAM

Car park opposite Loch Sloy power station on A82.
Contact: Countryside Rangers Department, Dumbarton District Council, Balloch Castle, Dunbartonshire. Tel: 0389 58216.
A pleasant walk along the North of Scotland Hydro-Electric Board road to Loch Sloy dam. 7 miles/11.2km (3 hours).
Dogs not advisable.
Open all year. Car park. Toilets. Information Centre (Tarbert – seasonal).

LOCHWINNOCH R.S.P.B. RESERVE & NATURE CENTRE

½ mile/0.8km E of Lochwinnoch village, beside A760 Paisley-Largs road.
Contact: Royal Society for the Protection of Birds, Largs Road, Lochwinnoch, Renfrewshire PA12 4JF. Tel: 0505 842663.
Wetland reserve including open lochs, marsh and mixed woodland. ¼ mile nature trails allow pleasant access through marsh and woodland to the birdwatching hides. Summer is best for breeding birds and wild flowers – winter brings the greatest abundance of wildfowl. Otter and roe deer also occur.
Open six days a week throughout the year from 10am-5pm (closed all day Thursdays). Groups

by prior arrangement. Car park. Toilets. Picnic area. Disabled facilities.
RSPB members – free. Guide book available. Nature centre. Gift shop. Observation tower. Exhibitions. Refreshments at weekends.

LOUDOUN HILL
At side of single track road approximately ½ mile/0.8km from A71. Head E on A71, turn left onto single track road 3 miles/4.8km past Darvel.
Contact: Kilmarnock Tourist Information Centre, 62 Bank Street, Kilmarnock. Tel: (0563) 39090.
Walk through pleasant countryside and hillside, footpath well trodden. Spectacular view of Irvine Valley and Isle of Arran on a clear day. 1-2 miles/1.6-3.2km (30 minutes-2 hours).
Control children and dogs. Dangerous crags on S and E faces.
Open all year. Car park. Darvel Tourist Information Centre.

MAUCHLINE TOWN TRAIL
The car park Loudoun Street.
Contact: Mauchline Tourist Information Centre, National Burns Memorial, Mauchline. Tel: (0290) 51916.
A variety of walks giving interesting points of Robert Burns' connections with Mauchline.
Leaflet available. Toilets.

OCHILTREE AREA
Ochiltree, Mill Street. Mill Street-Mill Bridge-Mill House-Langholm-South Lodge-Ochiltree.
Contact: Mauchline Tourist Information Centre, National Burns Memorial, Mauchline. Tel: (0290) 51916.
Woodland and riverside walk. 3 miles/4.8km (1½ hours).
Open all year. Car park. Information Centre (Mauchline).

OVERTOUN NATURE TRAIL
From A82 at Milton.
Contact: Dumbarton District Countryside Ranger Service, Balloch Castle Country Park, Balloch, Dunbartonshire. Tel: 0389 58216.
Walk along a picturesque steep-sided glen supporting a wide variety of plant and animal life. 1¼ miles/2km (1 hour).
Open all year. Car park. Picnic areas. Guide book available.

RIVER AYR
Near Mauchline. From Mauchline take A76 for 1 mile/1.6km towards Cumnock. Take first right after Kingencleugh turnoff.
Contact: Mauchline Tourist Information Centre, National Burns Memorial, Mauchline. Tel: (0290) 51916.
Woodland walk, beside the River Ayr, with extensive plant life. 5 miles/8km (3 hours). Children and dogs should not be allowed to wander.
Open all year. Car park. Mauchline Tourist Information Centre.

ROZELLE NATURE TRAILS
Duck pond at Rozelle Mansion House. From Ayr town centre continue along Beresford Terrace, right fork at Monument Road (B7024), signposted Alloway.
Contact: Director of Parks and Recreation, 30 Miller Road, Ayr KA7 2AY. Tel: 0292 281511 ext. 249.

Pond Walk and Nature Trail
Walk round pond and adjoining woodland, with a variety of trees, bushes and plants with water fowl, other birds and small mammals. ½ mile/0.8km (1 hour).

Woodland Walk
Walk through amenity woodland with extensive flora and fauna. 1¾ miles/2.8km (1 hour).
Open all year. Car park. Toilets. Facilities include pony track, pitch and putt course. Rozelle Mansion House. Walk round pond partly suitable for disabled.

STINCHAR BRIDGE
Stinchar Bridge. 20 miles/32.1km S of Ayr on B7045.
Contact: Forest Enterprise, Dalmellington Road, Straiton, Maybole, Ayrshire KA19 7NG. Tel: 06557 637.

Cornish Hill Walk
Upland walk. 4 miles/6.4km (2-3 hours).
Open all year. Car park. Picnic Areas.

Stinchar Falls Walk
Through woodland, rugged conditions in parts. 5 miles/8km (2-3 hours).
Open all year. Car park. Picnic areas.

STONEYMOLLAN
Car park on old Luss road adjacent to A811 in Balloch.
Contact: Countryside Rangers Service, Dumbarton District Council, Balloch Castle, Dunbartonshire. Tel: 0389 58216.
A pleasant walk from Balloch to the wide moorland on the Highland edge affording splendid views of Ben Lomond. 4 miles/6.4km (2 hours).
No dogs.
Open all year. Car park. Information Centre (Balloch – seasonal).

STRATHCLYDE COUNTRY PARK
Leave M74 at junctions 5 and 6.
Contact: Director, Strathclyde Country Park, 366 Hamilton Road, Motherwell, Lanarkshire. Tel: 0698 66155.
A variety of walks through the park – these include the Woodland Walk Nature Trail, the History Trail, Calder Valley, the Willow Trail, Dry Bridge Nature Trail and the Scrubland Trail. Up to 2½ miles/4km (2 hours).
Open all year. Car park. Toilets. Picnic areas. Information Centre. Leaflets available for all walks and the park in general.

CENTRAL

CALLANDER AREA

Car park off A84 adjacent to Information Centre (Leny Road).
Contact: Countryside Ranger Service, Stirling District Council, Stirling. Tel: 0786 7900.
A woodland walk from Callander, taking in the former Callander-Oban railway, Kilmahog and the Loch Venachar dam. 4½ miles/7.2km (2 hours).
Open all year. Car park. Toilets. Information Centre (Callander).

CALLANDER PARK ESTATE

Various parking facilities around estate. Off A9 Edinburgh-Falkirk Road.
Contact: Falkirk District Council, Leisure Services Department, Kilns House, Falkirk. Tel: 0324 24911.
Various walks through park, gardens and coniferous woodland. All walks varied (length and times).
Open all year. Car park. Toilets. Picnic areas. Information Centre. Suitable for disabled.

THE DARN ROAD

Car park in Dunblane, adjacent to Allan Water, off A9.
Contact: Countryside Ranger, Stirling District Council, Stirling. Tel: 0786 79000.
This ancient trail links Dunblane and Bridge of Allan through pleasant wooded parkland. 4 miles/6.4km (2 hours).
Care necessary when walking with children on the banks of the Allan Water.
Open all year. Car park. Toilets. Information Centre (Dunblane-seasonal).

DOLLAR GLEN

N side of Dollar, off A91.
Contact: National Trust for Scotland, Central & Tayside Regional Office, The Old Granary, West Mill Street, Perth PH1 5QP. Tel: 0738 31296.
Spectacular walks through woodland glen; Clackmannan District Council operates ranger service offering guided walks in summer. 1-2 miles/1.6-3.2km (¾-1½ hours).
During or after rain the path can be dangerous – great care is advised. Dogs on lead during lambing season.
Open all year. Car park.

DOUNE PONDS

Much animal, bird and plant life has colonised this reserve since its closure as a sand and gravel pit in the mid 1970's. The nature trail begins at the hide overlooking Central Pond and is about ⅔ mile/1 km long.
To enjoy your visit and see some of the wildlife, allow 45 minutes to an hour on the trail. If you bring your dog, please keep it on the lead to avoid disturbance to the wildlife or other visitors.
Keys for the hides can be obtained from the "SPAR" SHOP, 36 Main Street, Doune. Please record any sightings or observations in the reserve log book and return the keys.
Contact: David Warnock, Senior Countryside Ranger, Stirling D.C., Beechwood House, Stirling. Tel: 0786 79000, Ext. 72154.

GARTMORN DAM COUNTRY PARK & LOCAL NATURE RESERVE

Follow signs from A908 on N side of Alloa.
Contact: Clackmannan District Ranger Service, Clackmannan District Council, Leisure Service Department, Speirs Centre, 29 Primrose Street, Alloa. Tel: 0259 213131.
A walk round the Country Park, which is focused on Scotland's oldest man-made reservoir still in use today. Set against the back cloth of the Ochil Hills, this scenic walk is ideal for all seasons. The route follows the perimeter of the Dam which has been designated a site of special scientific interest, and is renowned for its wildlife, particularly the wildfowl. 3 miles/4.8km (approx. 2 hours).
Open all year. Ranger service. Visitor Centre. Bird hides. Sunken garden. Barbecue and picnic sites.

GLEN GYLE & LOCH KATRINE

Car park at Stronachlachar. Turn right on western junction of the B829.
Contact: Countryside Ranger, Stirling District Council, Stirling. Tel: 0786 79000.
A pleasant, easy walk around the Strathclyde Water Board private road on the banks of Loch Katrine. Up to 10 miles/16km (4-5 hours, in full).
Open all year. Car park. Information Centre. Suitable for disabled.

GLEN OGLE RAILWAY WALK

Car park on A85 opposite watersports centre. ¼ mile/0.4km E of junction of A84 and A85.
Contact: Countryside Ranger, Stirling District Council, Stirling. Tel: 0786 79000.
Spectacular walk along old Caledonian railway line through Glen Ogle, sometimes known as Scotland's "Khyber Pass". 5 miles/8km. (3 hours).
Open all year. Car park. Toilets.

INCHCAILLOCH

From pier on Inchcailloch, one of Loch Lomond's islands. Access from Balmaha

boatyard via ferry. Off B837, 6 miles/9.6km E
of Drymen.
Contact: Nature Conservancy Council Warden,
21 Ardmore Gardens, Drymen. Tel: 0360
60723.
A walk round the island nature reserve
affording spectacular views over Loch Lomond.
2½ miles/4km (2 hours).
Subject to boat access from Balmaha boatyard.
Open all year. Car park at Balmaha. Picnic
areas.

POLMONT WOODS
Car park, off B904 Falkirk – Linlithgow road.
Contact: Falkirk District Council, Leisure
Services Department, Kilns House, Falkirk.
Tel: 0324 24911.
Walks through woodland and extensive
plantings, crossing "Antonine Wall". Walks of
varied lengths and times.
Open all year. Car park. Picnic areas.

Leny Wood Walks
Car park by Leny Falls. A84, 2 miles/3.2km
NW of Callander.
Woodland walks from car parks with views over
Pass of Leny. ¾ mile/1.2km; 1 mile/1.6km; 2¼
miles/3.6km.
Dogs on lead. No fires.
Open all year. Car park.

Callander Crags Walk
Callander – tennis/squash club – W end of
town; or Bracklinn Falls road – E end of town.
Variety of walks – crag tops, middle wood walk
or low wood walk. Mixed tree species and wide
variety of birdlife. Good views from upper
areas.
Dogs on lead. No fires. Obey warning signs.
Open all year. Car park.

Sallochy Walk
Sallochy car park. 4 miles/6.4km N of Balmaha
on E side of Loch Lomond.
Walk through conifer and broadleaved
woodlands past viewpoints and ruined clachans.
1¾ miles/2.8km.
Dogs on lead. No fires.
Open all year. Car park.

Balmaha Walks
Car park at Balmaha. On B837 at Balmaha.
Two walks: Steep walk: climb through forest
with views down to Loch Lomond and Balmaha
Bay. Gentle walk: follows paths and forest
roads along lower afforested slopes. 1½ miles/
2.4km and 1¾ miles/2.8km.
Dogs on lead. No fires.
Open all year. Car park. Toilets.

Gleann Riabhach Walk
Behind Loch Achray Hotel. A821 5 miles/8km
N of Aberfoyle.
Follow bronze ring waymarkers on circular
walk through forest with views of the Trossachs
and Ben A'an. 2 miles/3.2km.
Dogs on lead. No fires.
Open all year. Car park. Information Centre
(David Marshall Lodge, Aberfoyle).

Highland Edge Walk
Forestry Commission car park, Braeval, by
Aberfoyle. 1 mile/1.6km NW of Rob Roy
Motel, Aberfoyle, on A81 Aberfoyle-Stirling
road. Adjacent to golf course.
Mixed woodland walk on the Highland
Boundary Fault edge. Lime Craig provides
breathtaking views of the Highlands and
Lowlands. 5 miles/8km.
Dogs on lead. No fires.
Open all year. Car park. Information Centre
(David Marshall Lodge, Aberfoyle).

Doon Hill and Fairy Knowe Walk
Manse Road car park. Unclassified road S from
Aberfoyle village at junction with B829 and
A821.
Oakwood walk with some conifers through Site
of Special Scientific Interest – lots of birdlife,
bluebells (when in season). 1 mile/1.6km.
Dogs on lead. No fires.
Open all year. Car park. Picnic areas.
Information Centre (David Marshall Lodge,
Aberfoyle).

Highland Boundary Fault Trail
David Marshall Lodge Visitor Centre,
Aberfoyle. 1 mile/1.6km N of Aberfoyle on
A821 Dukes Pass road.
Woodland walk with interpretative panels
explaining the geology and formation of the
area. 2-3 hours.
Stout footwear. Dogs on lead. No fires. Keep
clear of quarry faces.
Open all year. Car park (David Marshall
Lodge). Toilets. Picnics allowed anywhere (no
furniture on route). Information Centre (David
Marshall Lodge): open Easter to late
September (10.00-18.00). Cafeteria. Bookshop.
Leaflet available: Easter to September – David
Marshall Lodge; rest of year from Forest
Office.

Waterfall Trail
David Marshall Lodge Visitor Centre,
Aberfoyle. 1 mile/1.6km N of Aberfoyle on
A821 Dukes Pass Road.
Introductory woodland walk – geology, local
history, forest and woodland development,
natural history, tree species explained on
information panels. Waterfall of the Little
Fawn (55ft/17m high) on route. ¾ hour.
Dogs on lead. No fires.
Open all year. Car park. Toilets. Picnic areas.
Information Centre (David Marshall Lodge).

SOUTH BANTASKINE ESTATE
Visitor's car park. Lochgreen Road off B803 to
Slamannan.
Contact: Falkirk District Council, Leisure
Services Department, Kilns House, Kilns
Road, Falkirk. Tel: 0324 24911.
Various walks through parkland, gardens and
old railway towards Union Canal. Walks varied
lengths and times.
Open all year. Car park. Toilets. Picnic areas.
Information Centre. Suitable for disabled.

STRATHYRE FOREST

Car park and visitor centre, Strathyre. A84, S end of Strathyre village.

Contact: Forest Enterprise, Aberfoyle, Stirlingshire FK8 3UX. Tel: 08772 383.

Woodland walk with extended views of Loch Lubnaig. 5 miles/8km.

Dogs on lead. No fires.

Open all year. Car park. Toilets. Picnic areas. Forest Enterprise Visitor Centre (Easter to October – unmanned).

THE WHANGIE

Car park at Queen's View, 4 miles/6.4km. S. of Drymen at A809.

Contact: Countryside Ranger Service, Stirling District Council, Stirling. Tel: 0786 79000.

A walk around Auchineden Hill to an unusual rock formation. Fine views of Loch Lomond. 3 miles/4.8km (2 hours).

No dogs. Wear sensible footwear.

Open all year. Car park.

NOTES

FIFE

LETHAM GLEN NATURE TRAIL
Nature Centre in Letham Glen, Leven, on A915 at Scoonie roundabout.
Contact: Nature Centre Warden, Kirkcaldy District Council, Leisure & Direct Services Division, Carberry House, Leven, Fife KY8 4JS. Tel: 0333 27890 (Carberry House) or 29231 (Warden).
Trail starts at pets' corner and deer park, passes picnic area into woodland with large selection of trees, birdlife, wildflowers, following burn past mill remains, partly on old drove road. 1 mile/1.6km (¾ hour).
Letham Glen is open daily, all year. Nature Centre open Mon-Fri 12.00-3.00pm, Sat 2-4pm, Sun 2-4.30pm. Car park. Toilets. Picnic Areas. Information Centre. Free guide book available. Partly suitable for disabled.

LOCHORE MEADOWS COUNTRY PARK
On B920, 1½ miles/2.4km N of Lochgelly, signposted from M90 junction 3.
Contact: Ranger Service or Receptionist, Lochore Meadows Country Park, Crosshill, Lochgelly, Fife KY5 8BA. Tel: 0592 860086.

Discover Ancient Lochore
Walk demonstrating historical associations with two major land reclamation schemes, one in 1972, the other 1967-76, and the ancient castle of Inchgall. 1½ miles/2.4km (1-1½ hours).

Round Loch Ore in Summer
Interesting walk round lowland loch with water, bird and plant life all year. This walk can be taken in either direction. 3½ miles/5.6km (½-2 hours).

Breaking the Ground
An area of low grassy hills is explored, visiting several archaeological remains, relating them to present landscape evolution. Summer-time flowers attractive. 2½ miles/4km (1-2 hours).

Visit the Mary Pit
A circuit of a recently reclaimed coal-mining landscape centred on the spectacular remains of the Mary Pit. Attempts to bring out the human side of the mining industry. 1½ or ½ mile/2.4 or 0.8km (option of early return) (1 or ½ hour).
Open all year. Car park. Toilets. Picnic Areas. Information Centre. Guide leaflets available. Guided walks and slide shows by arrangement. Fishing, putting and horse-riding. Suitable for disabled if assisted.

THE COUNTRY CODE

Wherever you go, please remember to follow the Country Code:

Guard against all risk of fire.

Fasten all gates.

Keep dogs under proper control.

Keep to the paths across farm land.

Avoid damaging fences, hedges and walls.

Leave no litter.

Safeguard water supplies.

Protect wild life, wild plants and trees.

Go carefully on the country roads.

Respect the life of the countryside.

TAYSIDE

ARBROATH CLIFFS NATURE TRAIL
N end of promenade – Victoria Park.
Contact: Scottish Wildlife Trust, Angus &
Dundee Branch, Secretary, S. Treger, 2
McGregorsland, Kirriemuir, Angus.
Cliff-top path starting at Whiting Ness,
descending to beach at Carlingheugh Bay.
Lush, natural vegetation; colourful maritime
and non-maritime flowers, attractive butterflies
and moths; rich and varied bird life; interesting
geology. 2 miles/3km (1½ hours).
Keep to path along cliff-top as cliffs are
dangerous. No fires. Do not climb cliffs.
Beware of tides on the beaches.
Open all year. Car park. Toilets. Trail guides
available from Arbroath Tourist Information
Centre and Arbroath Museum.

ARBROATH TOWN WALK
Starting at the harbour.
Contact: Angus District Libraries & Museums
Service, Panmure Place, Montrose, Angus
DD10 8HE. Tel: 0674 73232.
Trail around this historic town, including the
12th-century ruins of Arbroath Abbey and "Fit
o' the Toon" fishing quarter.
Open all year. Toilets. Information Centre.
Suitable for disabled.

BIRKS OF ABERFELDY
From Aberfeldy town centre at Bridgend, or at
Crieff Road (A826), ½ mile/0.8km S of town
centre at car park and picnic area.
Contact: Perth and Kinross District Council,
Leisure & Recreation Department, 3 High
Street, Perth PH1 5JU. Tel: 0738 39911.
Walk through wooded den of the Moness Burn,
with beautiful mixed deciduous woodland and
varied plant and birdlife (nature trail marked).
Three sets of falls, the Top Falls being
spectacular in rocky gorge. Up to 3 miles/4.8km
(up to 1½ hours).
Stout footwear required for upper sections.
Open all year. Car park. Picnic area. Viewing
platform at falls. Guide leaflet available.

BIRNAM HILL
Centre of Birnam, ½ mile/0.8km off A9, path
opposite Birnam Hotel.
Contact: Perth and Kinross District Council,
Leisure & Recreation Department, 3 High
Street, Perth PH1 5JU. Tel: 0738 39911.
Two walks amidst superb hill and woodland
scenery overlooking the River Tay. Circular
walk around Birnam village, along banks of the
Tay and the foot of the wooded slopes of
Birnam Hill 3 miles/4.8km (1½ hours). Walk
can be extended up SE slope of Birnam Hill to
summit, descending on N side through woods, 5
miles/8km (2½ hours).

Open all year. Car park. Free map available
from Tourist Information Centre in Dunkeld.

BLACK WOOD OF RANNOCH GUIDES WALKS
Forest Ranger led guided walks in an ancient
Caledonian Pinewood. Only available through
reservations made at Queens View Centre. 5
miles west of Pitlochry on the B8019.
Contact: Forest Enterprise, Queens View
Centre. Loch Tummel, Perthshire. Tel: 0796
473123.

CRAIGOWER HILL, DUNMORE TRAIL
Car park off A924, 1½ miles/2.4km N of
Pitlochry.
Contact: National Trust for Scotland, Central
& Tayside Regional Office, The Old Granary,
West Mill Street, Perth PH1 5QP. Tel: 0738
31296.
Through conifer woodland and open heather to
the summit of a 1,300 ft beacon hill, offering
splendid views of the surrounding district. 3½
miles/5.6km (2 hours).
Open all year. Car park. Ranger/naturalist
service offers guided walks and illustrated talks
during summer: details from Killiecrankie
Visitor Centre. Guide book available. Part of
the network of Garry – Tummel Walks.

CRIEFF NATURE TRAIL
Culcrieff Farm, ¾ mile/1.2km W of Crieff on
A85; turn right onto farm road at 30mph sign.
Contact: Crieff Hydro Hotel, Crieff,
Perthshire. Tel: 0764 2401.
Open and wooded walk with panoramic views
on upper stretch. Varied plant life. 1½ miles/
2.4km (1-2 hours to complete).
Not suitable for children in pushchairs.
Open all year. Car park. Picnic areas. Guide
book available.

DEN OF ALYTH
From N end of Alyth, 5 miles/8km NE of
Blairgowrie, off A926.
Contact: Perth and Kinross District Council,
Leisure & Recreation Department, 3 High
Street, Perth PH1 5JU. Tel: 0738 39911.
Easy walk through wooded den beside Alyth
Burn. Good wide path. Varied flora and fauna
with points of geological interest. 2½ miles/4km
(1½ hours).
Open all year. Car park. Picnic areas. Guide
leaflets available.

FALLS OF BRUAR
Bruar Falls Hotel car park, on B8079, 3 miles/
4.8km W of Blair Atholl on A9.
Contact: Countryside Ranger Service, Leisure

& Recreation Department, Perth & Kinross District Council, 3 High Street, Perth PH1 5JU. Tel: 0738 39911.

Walk up the wooded den of the Bruar Water with coniferous woodland and varied plant and birdlife. Three sets of falls in spectacular rocky gorge, all seen from waymarked path system. 1 mile/1.6km (1 hour).

Stout footwear is recommended and care should be taken – steep banks.

Open all year. Car park. Toilets. Picnic area. Information board. Guide leaflet available.

GARRY – TUMMEL WALK

Pitlochry Hydro Dam, Garry Bridge car park (B8019) or Killiecrankie Visitor Centre. Off A9 N of Pitlochry.

Contact: Countryside Ranger Service, Leisure & Recreation Department, Perth & Kinross District Council, 3 High Street, Perth PH1 5JU. Tel: 0738 39911.

The walk gives a complete circuit of Loch Faskally using waymarked paths and country roads, passing through mature woodland and by loch and riverside. Points of interest include the Pitlochry Dam, the Linn of Tummel, the Soldier's Leap at Killiecrankie and Clunie Memorial Arch. Up to 11 miles/17.7km (3-4 hours).

Open all year. Car parks. Toilets. Picnic areas. Information Centres.

GLEN DOLL PICNIC SITE

From B955, 17 miles/27.3 km NW of Kirriemuir, along unclassified road in Glen Doll.

Contact: Forest Enterprise, Tay Forest District, Inverpark, Dunkeld, Perthshire PH8 0JR. Tel: 0350 727284/727285.

Jock's Road: walk through woodland on old drovers' road with variety of plant life and birds. 1½ miles/2.4km (1-1½ hours).

Capel Track: walk through woodland with interesting birdlife. 1¼ miles/2km (1 hour).

Open all year. Car park. Picnic areas. Toilets.

GLEN LEDNOCK CIRCULAR WALK

Laggan Park or Monument Road car parks. Comrie Village, 7 miles/11.2km W of Crieff.

Contact: Countryside Ranger Service, Leisure & Recreation Department, Perth & Kinross District Council, 3 High Street, Perth PH1 5JU. Tel: 0738 39911.

From Comrie Village, through mixed woodland and up valley of River Lednock to open grassland, set among mountains, returning on other side of valley, again through woodland. Access to fine viewpoints on both banks, notably the Melville Monument on Dun More. Varied plant and animal life. Signposted. 4 miles/6.4km (2-3 hours).

Open all year. Car park. Guide leaflet available.

HERMITAGE FOREST WOODLAND TRAIL

Lower car park, off A9, 2 miles/3.2km W of Dunkeld.

Contact: National Trust for Scotland, Central & Tayside Regional Office, The Old Granary, West Mill Street, Perth PH1 5QP. Tel: 0738 31296.

Walk through woodland with Douglas firs and Scots pine, near the River Braan. Passes the Hermitage, a picturesque folly built in 1758. 1½ miles/2.4km (1 hour).

Open all year. Car park. Picnic areas. Ranger/naturalist service offers guided tours in summer – details from the Ell Shop in Dunkeld or Killiecrankie Visitor Centre. Guide book available. Special route for disabled vehicles gives access to the folly.

KINDROGAN FIELD CENTRE

On A924, 10 miles/16km E of Pitlochry.

Contact: Scottish Field Studies Association, Kindrogan Field Centre, Enochdhu, Blairgowrie, Perthshire PH10 7PG. Tel: 025081 286.

Hill Trail

Path through mainly Forest Enterprise woodland to viewpoint on Kindrogan Hill. Fine scenery and extensive wildlife. 3 miles/4.8km (2-2½ hours).

Open all year. Car park. Toilets. Picnic Areas. Guide book available.

Kindrogan in Victorian Times

Path through Kindrogan grounds and woodland. Landscape history with particular reference to the Victorian estate. 1 mile/1.6km (1 hour).

Open all year. Car park. Toilets. Picnic areas. Guide book available.

KINNOULL HILL TRAIL

Corsiehill Road, 1 mile/1.6km E of Perth city centre across road bridge.

Contact: Perth and Kinross District Council, Countryside Ranger Service, Leisure & Recreation Department, 3 High Street, Perth PH1 5JU. Tel: 0738 39911.

Walk through mixed deciduous and coniferous woodland, with several alternative paths, to summit of Kinnoull Hill (222m), providing superb views. Nature trail and bridle path, and links with Jubilee car park and Deuchny Wood. Up to 4 miles/6.4km (1-2 hours).

Open all year. Car parks. Toilets. Picnic areas. Guide booklet available. Suitable for disabled from Corsiehill (Jubilee car park).

THE KNOCK

From James Square up Hill Street and Knock Road, Crieff, 12 miles/19.3km W of Perth on A85.

Contact: Countryside Ranger Service, Leisure & Recreation Department, Perth & Kinross District Council, 3 High Street, Perth PH1 5JU. Tel: 0738 39911.

Steep, short walk from centre of Crieff through deciduous woods to an indicator and panoramic views across Strathearn and towards the Grampians. 3 miles/4.8km (1½-2 hours).

Open all year. Car park. Toilets. Picnic areas. Information Centre.

LINN OF TUMMEL TRAILS

From car park at Tummel Bridge, A9/B8019. 3 miles/4.8km N of Pitlochry.

Contact: National Trust for Scotland, Central & Tayside Regional Office, The Old Granary, West Mill Street, Perth PH1 5QP. Tel: 0738 31296.

Through attractive mixed woodland by the rivers Garry and Tummel. 2½ miles/4km (1 hour) or 1¼ miles/2km (½ hour).

Please observe the Country Code.

Open all year. Car park. Information Centre (Killiecrankie), 1 mile/1.6km north, accessible by path, open Easter to September. Ranger/ naturalist service offers guided walks, talks and films, details from Information Centre. Guide book available. Part of the network of Garry – Tummel Walks.

RIVER ERICHT WALK

From Wellmeadow, Blairgowrie town centre.

Contact: Blairgowrie Tourist Association, Wellmeadow, Blairgowrie, Perthshire PH10 6AS. Tel: 0250 2960.

Good path along the wooded west bank of the River Ericht, overlooking a dramatic rocky gorge in places. Deciduous woodland with mixed vegetation and wildlife. Interesting old jute mills at Oakbank. 3 miles/4.8 km (1½ hours).

Extension possible along country road to 12th century ruins of Glascune Castle, and return to Blairgowrie by country road. Total 5½ miles/8.8 km (3 hours).

Open all year. Car park. Picnic areas. Toilets (at start). Leaflet guide available. Basic walk suitable for disabled.

TUMMEL FOREST PARK

Contact: Forest Enterprise, Tay Forest District, Inverpark, Dunkeld, Perthshire PH8 0JR. Tel: 0350 727284/727285. No restrictions on entry to any walks.

Queens View Centre
4 miles west of Faskally on B8019 on the north shore of Loch Tummel. Spectacular viewpoint. Disabled access along 250m surfaced path. Refreshments. Forest shop and exhibition. Toilets. Car/coach park. Information. Open Easter – September. Viewpoint open all year round.

Allean Forest Walks
½ mile/0.8km west of Queens View Centre, Loch Tummel.
Mixed conifer woodlands with views over Tummel Valley. 2 miles/3.2km (1 hour). Restored 17th century Clachan on walk circuit. Walks open all year.
Car park. Toilets.

Tummel Bridge Forest Walks
Car park at side of road at Tummel Bridge.

Birch/conifer woodland walk with high level view of Schiehallion and Tummel Valley.

Carie Forest Walk
4 miles/6.4km west of Kinloch Rannoch on south Loch Rannoch Road.
Atmospheric walk along a major streamside. Native pine and broadleaves, combined with spruces and Douglas Fir. Open space gives views over distant hills.
Three walks: ½ mile/0.8km (½ hour) to 5 miles/ 8km (3 hours).
Open all year. Toilets. Car park. Campsite at adjacent Kilvrecht. Picnic and play area.

Faskally Forest Walks
1 mile/1.6km north of Pitlochry.
Tremendous woodland walks through towering 200 year old Douglas fir, silver fir and broadleaved trees and along the edge of Loch Dunmore. 1½ miles/2.4km (1 hour).
Walks open all year.
Car park. Toilets. Picnic areas.

Drummond Hill Forest Walks
Mains Brae car park ½ mile/0.8km off A827, north of Kenmore (follow sign to Tummel Bridge).
Wide open walks through mature woodlands of mixed conifers and broadleaves. Black Rock viewpoint gives fantastic views of Loch Tay, Kenmore Village and crannogs. 3 miles/4.8km (1½ hours).
Walks open all year.
Toilets close by at Dalerb picnic area on shore of Loch Tay.

Weem Forest Walk
Castle Menzies entrance to car park. 1 mile/ 1.6km north of Aberfeldy on B846, ¼ mile/ 0.4km west of Weem village.
A steep walk through the ancient woodland of Weem, one time policy woods of Castle Menzies. The route follows the hermits path to St. David's Well, an historic ecclesiastic retreat which now reveals a fine viewpoint of the mid Tay Valley.
Open all year.

VANE FARM (RSPB)

Nature Centre, on B9097. 2 miles/3.2km E of M90 near Kinross. Leave M90 at junction 5.

Contact: Jim Stevenson, Warden, Vane Farm Nature Centre, Kinross KY13 7LX. Tel: 0577 62355.

Steep walk through birch woodland to a moorland viewpoint. Extensive views to the Highlands and Firth of Forth. Typical woodland birdlife with interesting flowers in spring and fungi in autumn. 1¼ miles/2km (30 minutes-1 hour).

Open daily, all year (closed Christmas Day to New Year's Day). (April-December 10.00-17.00; January-March 10.00-16.00). Car park. Toilets. Picnic areas. Information Centre. RSPB members – free. Disabled access.

GRAMPIAN

ADEN COUNTRY PARK
Variety of walks and nature trails within Park.
Contact: The Ranger, Aden Country Park, Mintlaw, Aberdeenshire. Tel: 0771 22857.
Through mixed woodland, interesting bird and plant life. 300-400 yds/0.5km to ¾ mile/0.6km.
Open all year. Car Park. Toilets (disabled). Picnic areas.

BANFF, WHITEHILLS & ABERCHIRDER
A variety of short-and-medium-length walks.
Contact: Banff and Buchan Tourist Board, Collie Lodge, Banff AB45 1AU. Tel: 02612 2419.
Leaflet available covering walks.

Banff to Whitehills
A pleasant stroll along the shore, beginning at the Links Hotel in Banff. Fine views along the coast. The route passes the "Red Well" supposed to have remedial properties. 2 miles/3.2km (1 hour + return).
Open all year. Car park. Toilets (May to September). Picnic areas. Information Centre.

Whitehills
From the foot of Seafield Street, walk up the street and out of town on the B9121, onto the tree-lined Portsoy road, then turn downhill after passing Warylip Farm, with the panoramic view of the Moray Firth. Return through the west end of Whitehills, where you pass the original fishermen's houses. 2½ miles/4km (1 hour).
Open all year. Car park. Information Centre.

Bridge of Alvah
A beautiful walk starting from Duff House in Banff, initially along a path lined with a wide variety of trees and bushes, then a track bordered by rhododendrons and brambles. Continuing with the River Deveron far below, you reach the Bridge of Alvah over the river. 2½ miles/4km (1 hour + return).
Open all year. Car park. Picnic areas. Information Centre.

Wrack Woodland Path
Duff House car park, off A98 at E end of Banff. Through woodland on the edge of Duff House Royal golf course. 1 mile/1.6km (30 minutes).
Open all year. Car park.

Cleanhill, Aberchirder
From a lay-by on A97, just south of Aberchirder. Cross road for entrance to walk. Path climbs up hill, then there is a circular track around it, with long avenues of trees and panoramic views of the surrounding farmland. 1 mile/1.6km (30 minutes).
Open all year. Car park. Picnic areas.

The Avenue, Aberchirder
Start in North Street, carry straight over the crossroads and follow the track at the end of the road. Turning left, it heads along a fine tree-covered avenue. Return by the A97. ¾ mile/1.2km. (30 minutes).
Open all year. Car park.

BENNACHIE WALKS
Three car parks sited north, east and south of Bennachie ridge between the B9002 and the River Don north of Monymusk.
Contact: Forest Enterprise, Buchan Forest District, Ordiquhill, Portsoy Road, Huntly, Aberdeenshire AB54 4SJ. Tel: 0466 794161.
A variety of walks through woodland and over open hills with interesting plant and wildlife. Fine views. ½-6 miles/0.8-9.6km (15 minutes-4 hours).
Walks. Car parks. Picnic areas. Open all year.
Toilets (facilities for disabled), seasonal.
Leaflet and guide book available.
These footpaths have been designed solely for the use of the walking public, and are not suitable for cyclists.

THE BIN FOREST WALK
Two miles north west of Huntly on the A96 Huntly-Keith road.
Contact: Forest Enterprise, Buchan Forest District, Ordiquhill, Portsoy Road, Huntly AB54 4SJ. Tel: 0466 794161.

CAMBUS O' MAY
4km east of Ballater on the A93 North Deeside road.
Contact: Forest Enterprise, Kincardine Forest District, Kirkton of Durris, Banchory AB31 3BP. Tel: 033 044 537.

COUNTESSWELLS
2km south of the Kingswells roundabout on the A944, Aberdeen-Westhill road.
Contact: Forest Enterprise, Kincardine Forest District, Kirkton of Durris, Banchory AB31 3BP. Tel: 033 044 537.

CRAIGIEVAR CASTLE WALK
Craigievar Castle, off A980, 6 miles/9.6km S of Alford.
Contact: National Trust for Scotland, Rangers Office, Crathes Castle, Banchory AB31 3QJ. Tel: 033044 651.
Through mixed woodland and farmland, and

along a burn. 1 mile/1.6km (½ hour).
Open all year. Car park. Toilets. Picnic areas.
Admission - donation.

CRATHES CASTLE - WOODLAND TRAILS
Crathes Castle, off A93, 14 miles/22.5km W of
Aberdeen.
Contact: National Trust for Scotland, Rangers
Office, Crathes Castle, Banchory AB31 3QJ.
Tel: 033044 651.
Six walks through a rich variety of woodland,
farmland, pond and riverside. Ranger service
offers guided walks in summer. ¼ mile-7 miles/
0.4km-11.2km (½-3 hours).
Dogs on lead in the precinct of the castle. Open
all year. Car park. Toilets. Picnic areas.
Information Centre. Booklet available.

CULBIN FOREST WALK
Contact: Forest Enterprise, Moray Forest
District, Balnacoul, Fochabers, IV32 7LL. Tel:
0343 820223.

CULLEN TOWN TRAIL
The Square.
Contact: Tourist Information Centre, 20
Seafield Street, Cullen, Banffshire AB56 2SH.
Tel: 0542 40757 (Summer only).
The route takes in the principal features of the
17th-18th-and-19th-century architecture of this
delightful small town. 1½ miles/2.4km (1 hour).
Open all year. Car park. Toilets. Picnic areas.
Information Centre. Suitable for disabled.

DRUM CASTLE
Car park, off A93, 10 miles/16km W of
Aberdeen.
Contact: National Trust for Scotland, Ranger's
Office, Crathes Castle, Banchory AB31 3QJ.
Tel: 033044 651.
Woodland and farmland walks, including
ancient oak woodland. Ranger service offers
guided walks during summer. 1-1½ miles/
1.6-2.4km (½-1 hour).
Open all year (09.30-dusk). Car park. Toilets.
Picnic areas. Admission by donation.

DUFFTOWN GIANT'S CHAIR
From the square in Dufftown take Church
Street S to Mortlach Church.
Contact: Tourist Information Centre, The
Clock Tower, The Square, Dufftown,
Banffshire AB55 4AD. Tel: 0340 20501
(summer only).
A circular route along banks of the Dullan
Water including points of geological and
botanical interest. 2 miles/3.2km (1-1½ hours).
Open all year. Shelter. Seats & benches.

DUFFTOWN SPUR
3½ miles/5½ km.
Leaves the Fiddich Park, Craigellachie in a SE

direction following the old Strathspey Railway
track. Walkers will find the Spur an enjoyable
stroll, rich in wild flowers and birds, along the
wooded River Fiddich Valley to Dufftown with
its ruined Balvenie Castle and seven
Distilleries.
Contact: Moray District Council, 17 High
Street, Elgin IV30 1EG. Tel: 0343 542666.

DANGEROUS BRIDGE – The first stone
bridge over the track which you encounter on
leaving Craigellachie, on the Dufftown Spur, IS
IN A DANGEROUS CONDITION. Use the
'by pass' provided and DO NOT GO UNDER
OR OVER THIS STRUCTURE AT ALL.

DUNOTTAR WOODS
Glashan Bridge Car Park. South of Stonehaven
300 metres east of the junction of the A94 and
the A92 at Inverbervie.
Contact: Forest Enterprise, Kincardine Forest
District, Kirkton of Durris, Banchory AB31
3BP. Tel: 033 044 537.

DRUMTOCHTY
Turn off B974 at Clatterin' Brig on the Cairn o'
Mount road 4km towards Auchenblae.
Contact: Forest Enterprise, Kincardine Forest
District, Kirkton of Durris, Banchory AB31
3BP. Tel: 033 044 537.

ELGIN TOWN TRAIL
Elgin Cathedral or any point on the route.
Contact: Tourist Information Centre, 17 High
Street, Elgin, Moray IV30 1EG. Tel: 0343
542666.
A circular walk around the centre of Elgin,
visiting sites of historic and architectural
interest. 3 miles/4.8km (1½ hours).
Open all year. Car park. Toilets. Information
Centre.

FOCHABERS FOREST WALK
Contact: Forest Enterprise, Moray Forest
District, Balnacoul, Fochabers, IV32 7LL. Tel:
0343 820223.

FOREST OF DEER
At entrance to White Cow Wood on minor
road 2½ miles/4km S of Strichen (signposted),
10 miles/16km W of Peterhead.
Contact: Forest Enterprise, Buchan Forest
District, Ordiquhill, Portsoy Road, Huntly,
Aberdeenshire AB54 4SJ. Tel: 0466 794161.

Red Walk
Waymarked circular walk through conifer
plantations, beginning on a forest road,
continuing on a path. 1 mile/1.6km (1/2 hour).

Yellow Walk
Waymarked circular walk with panoramic
viewpoints, passing the remains of a chambered

cairn. Mainly on forest road. 3 miles/4.8km (11/2 hours).
Open all year. Car park. Picnic areas. Toilets (April to October only - suitable for disabled). Forest road sections of walks suitable for disabled.

FORRES TOWN TRAIL
Tolbooth, High Street, Forres. On A96.
Contact: Tourist Information Centre, Falconer Museum, Tolbooth Street, Forres, Moray IV36 0PH. Tel: 0309 72938 (summer only).
A route visiting places of historic and architectural interest in the town of Forres. 3-4 miles/4.8-6.4km (1-2 hours).
Open all year. Car park. Toilets. Picnic areas. Information Centre. Suitable for disabled.

FYVIE LOCHSIDE WALK
Fyvie Castle car park. Off A947, 8 miles/12.8km SE of Turriff and 25 miles/40km NW of Aberdeen.
Contact: National Trust for Scotland, Ranger's Office, Crathes Castle, Banchory AB31 3QJ. Tel: 033044 651.
Walk through mixed woodland and round a loch. 11/2 miles/2.4km (3/4 hour).
Open all year. Car park. Toilets. Picnic areas. Rangers service, guided walks in summer. Admission - donations.

GARDENSTOWN TO CROVIE
New Ground, Gardenstown, or Crovie.
Contact: Banff & Buchan Tourist Board, Collie Lodge, Banff, Banffshire AB45 1AU. Tel: 02612 2419.
Coastal footpath. Up to 3/4 mile/1.2km (up to 20-30 minutes).
Open all year. Car park.

HADDO COUNTRY PARK
Car park/Visitor Centre. 20 miles/32km N of Aberdeen on A92 to Bridge of Don then B999 until 1 mile/1.6km S of Tarves and turn right.
Contact: Grampian Regional Council Ranger Service, The Stables, Haddo Country Park, Tarves, Ellon, Aberdeenshire AB41 0EQ. Tel: 06515 489.

Tree Trail
Walk through woodland and parkland with 15 named trees and booklet on their uses. 11/4 miles/2km (45 minutes).

That's Life
Walk through woodland, grassland and round the lake. Leaflet shows the different habitats and their wildlife. 21/2 miles/4km (11/2 hours).

People's Path
Walk through Haddo House garden, parkland and to lake. Leaflet shows how landscape has

been changed and influenced by man. 11/2 miles/2.4km (1 hour).
Open all year. Car park. Toilets. Picnic areas. Partly suitable for disabled. Leaflets available (May to September).

HAUGHTON COUNTRY PARK
Visitor Centre. 26 miles/41km NW of Aberdeen A944. Situated on outskirts of Alford.
Contact: The Ranger Service, Haughton House Country Park, Alford, Aberdeenshire. Tel: 09755 62453.
Self guided and ranger led walks around paths and trails of birchwood, parkland and riverside. 11/4 miles/2km (approx. 11/4 hours).
Open all year. Car park. Toilets. Visitor Interpretation Centre. Parkland, picnic and play areas.

HOPEMAN TO CLASHACH
From Hopeman Harbour.
Contact: Tourist Information Centre, 17 High Street, Elgin, Moray IV30 1EG. Tel: 0343 542666.
Coastal path along geologically interesting cliffs, with a variety of plants and birdlife. 2 miles/3.2km each way (11/2-2 hours).
Open all year. Car park. Picnic areas.

KIRKHILL and FOUR HILL WALKS
North and south of the junction off the A96 Aberdeen-Kintore and the B979 Kirkton of Skene road.
Contact: Forest Enterprise, Kincardine Forest District, Kirkton of Durris, Banchory AB31 3BP. Tel: 033 044 537.

LEITH HALL TRAILS
Car park. By Kennethmont on A979, 34 miles/54.7km NW of Aberdeen.
Contact: National Trust for Scotland, Ranger's Office, Crathes Castle, Banchory AB31 3QJ. Tel: 033044 651.
Three walks through woodland and farmland, with ponds, bird-hide and good local viewpoint with indicator. Ranger service offers guided walks during summer. 2 miles/3.2km (1 hour).
Open all year. Car park. Picnic areas.

MILLBUIES COUNTRY PARK
3 miles/4.8km S of Elgin on A941 to Rothes.
Contact: Director of Leisure & Libraries, Moray District Council, District Headquarters, High Street, Elgin, Moray IV30 1BX. Tel: 0343 545121.
Two walks around the Country Park. The "plant trail" points out the many wild plants which can be found, while the "tree trail" reveals many rare and valuable tree species and more than 30 varieties of rhododendrons. 11/2-2 miles/2.4-3.2km (1-11/2 hours).
Open all year. Car park. Toilets. Picnic areas.

PITMEDDEN WOODLAND WALK
Car park at Pitmedden Gardens on outskirts of Pitmedden village, B999, off A92, 14 miles/22.5km N of Aberdeen.
Contact: National Trust for Scotland, Ranger's Office, Crathes Castle, Banchory AB31 3QJ. Tel: 033044 651.
Follows thin strip of mixed woodland round Pitmedden Gardens, past old lime kiln with views over surrounding farmland. 1 1/2 miles/2.4km (3/4-1 hour).
Open all year (09.30-dusk). Car park. Admission - donation. Museum. Ranger/naturalist service offers guided walks in summer.

PORTSOY & SANDEND
Starting points within the villages.
Contact: Banff & Buchan Tourist Board, Collie Lodge, Banff AB45 1AU. Tel: 02612 2419.
A variety of walks around the two villages, including:

Portsoy Historic Walk
Walk through Portsoy streets and around Loch Soy, giving a clear idea of the village history. Covers many interesting architectural and historic features, with fine views. 1 mile/1.6km (1/2 hour).

Coastal Walks from Portsoy
Three walks along the coast, two from the caravan site and one from the Square, proceeding up Cullen Street, passing the cliffs and many interesting caves and inlets. Up to 3 miles/4.8km (3 hours with return).

Sandend Walk
Walk along the cliff-tops from Sandend to Findlater Castle. Care should be taken as the path is rugged in places. 2 1/2 miles/4km (3 hours with return).
Open all year. Car park. Toilets. Picnic areas.

SCOLTY
Just south of Banchory over the Bridge of Dee take entrance to Auchaltie and follow signs.
Contact: Forest Enterprise, Kincardine Forest District, Kirkton of Durris, Banchory AB31 3BP. Tel: 033 044 537.

SHOOTING GREENS
From A93 north Deeside road cross bridge at Potarch and follow Feughside road for 4km.
Contact: Forest Enterprise, Kincardine Forest District, Kirkton of Durris, Banchory AB31 3BP. Tel: 033 044 537.

SPEYSIDE FOREST
Contact: Forest Enterprise, Moray Forest District, Balnacoul, Fochabers, Moray IV32 7EP. Tel: 0343 820223.

Earth Pillars
Small car park and picnic site at public roadside on the Speyside Way. 3 miles/4.8km up unclassified road at the E end of Fochabers - signposted "Police".
Short walk through old Scots pine wood, giving excellent views of the Spey and the geological feature of the Earth Pillars. 1/2 mile/0.8km (10 minutes).
Take care on the steep slopes of the gully.
Open all year. Car park. Picnic areas.

Winding Walks
Car park and picnic site at main roadside. 1 mile/1.6km E of Fochabers on A98.
Various linked walks in a valley of mixed woodlands and rhododendrons. Fine views of the Spey and the Moray coastline. 1/2-3 miles/0.8-4.8km (15 minutes-1 1/2 hours).
No fires.
Car park. Toilets. Picnic areas.

TOMINTOUL COUNTRY WALK
Delnabo Road, Tomintoul.
Contact: Tourist Information Centre, The Square, Tomintoul, Banffshire AB37 9ET. Tel: 08074 285 (summer only).
A walk through beautiful Glen Avon with points illustrating the geology, flora and fauna of the area. 4 miles/6.4km (1 1/2 hours).
Open all year. Car park. Picnic areas.

TORIESTON FOREST WALK
Contact: Forest Enterprise, Moray Forest District, Balnacoul, Fochabers IV32 7LL. Tel: 0343 820223.

FOLLOW THE COUNTRY CODE

HIGHLAND

ACHNASHELLACH WALKS

Achnashellach Station, on the A890, 7 miles/ 11.2km NE of Lochcarron.
Contact: Ross and Cromarty Tourist Board, Information Office, Achtercairn, Gairloch IV21 2DN. Tel: 0445 2130.

Strathconon
Follow the Forest Enterprise road across the River Carron and continue uphill. Pass through the forest fence and continue on the hill track to Glenuaig Lodge, then keep to the track on the north bank of the River Meig to Scardroy Lodge. Minor roads then lead down Strath Conon. Approx. 15 miles/24km (5-6 hours).
Arrangements should be made for the return journey.

Kinlochewe
Follow the Forest Enterprise road 200 yards E of the railway bridge. At cross-roads turn NE uphill and follow road to gate in forest fence. Leaving the main track at Coulin, there are two routes to Kinlochewe, either due N, or NW by the shores of Loch Coulin and Loch Clair, to meet the A896, 3 miles/4.8km W of Kinlochewe. Approx. 10 miles/16km (3-4 hours).
Arrangements should be made for the return journey.

Torridon
Walk into Coire Lair by the track on the E side of the River Lair. The route passes Loch Coire Lair, goes through Bealach Ban and Bealach na Lice and along the N side of Loch an Eion. The track joins the A896, 6 miles/9.6km E of Shieldaig. Approx. 8 miles/12.8km (3-4 hours).
Arrangements should be made for the return journey.
Stout footwear recommended. Open all year. Guide book available.

AFFRIC RIVER WALKS

Car park at far end of Glen Affric, 16 miles/ 25.7km from Cannich. A831 to Cannich, then follow Glen Affric road to end of glen.
Contact: Forest Enterprise, Fort Augustus Forest District, Strathoich, Fort Augustus, Inverness-shire PH32 4BT. Tel: 0320 6322.
Two short but attractive circular walks, lying between Lochs Affric and Beneveian. Fine views along Glen Affric, and to the mountains beyond. ½-1 mile/1-1.6km (15-30 minutes).
No fires, no camping or caravans (camping on caravan site in Cannich).
Open all year. Car park. Picnic site. Information board.

AIGAS FIELD CENTRE NATURE TRAIL

Aigas House, Beauly, Inverness-shire, 5 miles/ 8km SW of Beauly on A831.

Contact: Secretary, Aigas Field Centre, Beauly, Inverness-shire IV4 7AD. Tel: 0463 782443.
Nature trail, trees, birds, flowers, loch, views. Approx. 1 mile/1.6km (1 hour).
Dogs on leads. No radios.
Open April to October (10.30-18.00). Car park. Toilets. Information Centre at Aigas House. Admission charge - (charge for descriptive leaflet).

ALLTAN NA BRADHAN

Car park - Achmelvich. Lochinver to Kinlochbervie Road.
Contact: Highland Regional Council, Libraries & Leisure Services, Kinmylies Building, Inverness IV1 5NX. Tel: 0463 234121, ext. 452.
Coastal life nature trail. 1½ miles/2.4km (1 hour).
Dogs on lead.
Open all year. Car park. Information Centre (seasonal).

ARDESSIE WATERFALLS

Start at Ardessie fish farm by Dundonnell on the A832, 30 miles/48.2km NE of Gairloch.
Contact: Ross and Cromarty Tourist Board, Information Office, Achtercairn, Gairloch IV21 2DN. Tel: 0445 2130.
From the fish farm, take the road towards Dundonnell, past the lower waterfall at the roadside and ascend the steep track to the left of the river. This passes a series of spectacular cascades and waterfalls, eventually following the left-hand side of the river. Return by the same route. 3 miles/4.8km (2 hours).
Open all year. Guide book available.

BALMACARA FOREST WALK

Follow the signs from Balmacara Square which is situated close to the Forest Enterprise Campsite at Balmacara, off the A87.
Contact: Forest Enterprise, Wester Ross Forest District, Balmacara, Kyle of Lochalsh, Ross-shire IV40 8DN. Tel: 059 986 321.

BALMACARA - LOCHALSH WALKS

Lochalsh House, S of A87 about 3½ miles/ 5.6km E of Kyle of Lochalsh.
Contact: National Trust for Scotland, Abertarff House, Church Street, Inverness IV1 1EU. Tel: 0463 232034.
Woodland walks around Lochalsh House (not open to the public). Also 6 short walks and 7 longer walks throughout Lochalsh peninsula. Azaleas, rhododendrons and other exotic plants in grounds. Wide variety of wild flowers near Drumbuie. Up to 7 miles/11.2 km (up to 4 hours).

Open all year. Car park. Please keep to the Country Code. Countryside Interpretation Centre. Ranger/naturalist service offer guided walks and evening talks in summer. Guide book available.

BRODIE CASTLE WOODLAND WALK
Brodie Castle, off A96, 4½miles/7.2km W of Forres.
Contact: National Trust for Scotland, Abertarff House, Church Street, Inverness IV1 1EU. Tel: 0463 232034.
Through deciduous and conifer woodlands and round pond with wildlife observation hide. 1 mile/1.6km (¾ hour).
Open all year (09.30-dusk). Admission - donation. Car park. Adventure playground.

CAPE WRATH WALKS
Only accessible by ferry across Kyle of Durness.
Contact: Sutherland Tourist Board, The Square, Dornoch, Sutherland IV25 3SD. Tel: 0862 810400.
Car park. Information Centre.

CARBISDALE CASTLE
Car park within castle gates. On S side of Kyle of Sutherland, above rail bridge and upstream from main A9 bridge at Bonar Bridge.
Contact: Sutherland Tourist Board, The Square, Dornoch, Sutherland IV25 3SD. Tel: 0862 810400.
Forest walk with fine views across the Kyle of Sutherland (1¼ hours).
Open all year. Car park.

CAWDOR CASTLE NATURE TRAILS
Cawdor Castle Gardens. Situated between Inverness and Nairn on the B9090 off the A96.
Contact: Cawdor Castle (Tourism) Ltd., Cawdor Castle, Nairn IV12 5RD. Tel: 06677 615.
Choice of 4 nature trails through some of the most beautiful and varied woodlands in Britain. Ancient oak and beech, magnificent conifers, waterfalls and deep river gorges. All trails are marked. ¾-5 miles/1.2-8km.
Open daily 1 May to 30 September (10.00-17.30; last admission 17.00). Car park. Toilets. Picnic areas. Admission charge. Red trail suitable for disabled.

CHERRY ISLANDS WALK
Just off the A82 1 mile north of Fort Augustus. Car park available.
Contact: Forest Enterprise, Fort Augustus Forest District, Strathoich, Fort Augustus, Inverness-shire PH32 4BT. Tel: 0320 6322.

DOG FALLS & COIRE LOCH WALKS
Car park at Dog Falls, 4½ miles/7.2km down Glen Affric road from Cannich. A831 to Cannich, then follow road down Glen Affric.
Contact: Forest Enterprise, Fort Augustus Forest District, Strathoich, Fort Augustus, Inverness-shire PH32 4BT. Tel: 0320 6322.
Attractive circular walks along River Affric and through native pine reserve. 1½-3¼ miles/2.4-5.2km (¾-½ hours).
No fires. No camping or caravans (camping and caravan site in Cannich).
Open all year. Car park. Toilets. Picnic areas.

DUNNET BAY
Car park. Dunnet Bay, Pavillion, Caithness.
Contact: Highland Regional Council, Libraries & Leisure Services, Kinmylies Building, Inverness IV1 5NX. Tel: 0463 234121, ext. 452.
Sea-side and woodland walks of various lengths. Open all year. Car park. Information Centre (seasonal).

DURNESS & AREA
Varied series of walks which start from Durness or the craft village at Balnakeil. Follow A838 to Durness.
Contact: Sutherland Tourist Board, The Square, Dornoch, Sutherland IV25 3SD. Tel: 0862 810400.
Spectacular cliff and coastal scenery. Various lengths and times.

FALLS OF DIVACH
Midway between Drumnadrochit and Divach 2 miles/3.2km from A831.
Contact: Forest Enterprise, Fort Augustus Forest District, Strathoich, Fort Augustus, Inverness-shire PH32 4BT. Tel: 0320 6322.
A short walk through open oak wood to fenced platform giving view of Divach Falls, which are spectacular in flood, ¼ mile/0.4km. (15 minutes).
No fires.
Open all year. Car park. Picnic area.

FARIGAIG FOREST TRAIL
Forest Centre, from A862 take Dorest to Farigaig road B852. On E shore of Loch Ness.
Contact: Forest Enterprise, Fort Augustus Forest District, Strathoich, Fort Augustus, Inverness-shire PH32 4BT. Tel: 0320 6322.
Forest trail with a wide variety of tree species, including firs and spruces. Viewpoints offer views of Loch Ness and Inverfarigaig.
Trail. Car park & picnic area open all year. Information centre and toilets open from Easter to October (09.30-18.00).

FLOWERDALE FALLS
From Gairloch Pier.
Contact: Ross & Cromarty Tourist Board, Information Office, Achtercairn, Gairloch IV21 2DN. Tel: 0445 2130.
Follow the tree-lined avenue towards Flowerdale House and on across the Old

Sawmill to Flowerdale Mains Farm. Here the tarred road finishes and the track to the waterfalls can be muddy. At the end of plantations the stream ends with waterfalls. 3 miles/4.8km (1½ hours).
Stout footwear recommended.
Open all year. Car park. Guide book available.

FORT WILLIAM
Contact: Fort William & Lochaber Tourism Ltd., Cameron Centre, Cameron Square, Fort William PH33 6AJ. Tel: 0397 703781.

Ariundle Nature Trail
Approaching the village of Strontian from the Corran ferry, go through the small village of Strontian and cross the old stone bridge. Immediately after the bridge take the road to the right signposted to Polloch and Ariundle. Carry on this road for about one mile before turning right at a junction. Follow this unsurfaced road, of good condition, on to the car park.
The walk starts in a lovely wide open glade, along a forestry road but before long the deciduous trees, predominantly oak, slowly close in. This walk is within a nature reserve and after about ten minutes walking you will come across a notice board giving a brief history of the area. Time 100 minutes. Grade: easy. Leaflet is available.

Glen Nevis/Lower Falls/Upper Falls
Take the A82 Inverness road from centre of Fort William to mini roundabout. Take second exit and drive five miles. Park your car in car park and negotiate a stile. There are two walks.

River Route - Walk along the riverside and at first major bend in river walk diagonally slightly uphill, for ease of walking. When you are roughly one hundred feet above level of the river continue walking on this level until you see to your left a bridge from where you can cross to the Glen Nevis road and return to your car. Time 40 minutes. Grade: easy.

Sgurr a Mhaim - Once you have crossed the stile mentioned above, directly in front of you is a ridge leading to the top of Sgurr a Mhaim. On the right side of this ridge there is a clear distinct stalkers path which leads to a lovely small Lochan nestling under Sgurr a Mhaim and Stob Ban. Lovely views from Lochan. Time 90 minutes. Grade: moderate. Leaflet is available.

Hospital Walk
From Ballachulish take the road through Glencoe village passing the Glencoe and North Lorne Folk Museum, and cross the hump back bridge. Carry on for about 100 metres and take the road to the hospital on your left. Continue on this paved road until the first turn off, to the right, away from the hospital and continue on along the un-tarmacked road to the car park. At the car park you have a choice of two walks.

Lochside - If you go towards the larger of the two gates, the path will meander its way to a point where in the distance you can make out an arch formed by two small trees in front of the Lochan. If you walk on to this point and continue on around the loch in an anti-clockwise direction the path will join up with the altitude route at the far end of the loch.

Altitude Walk - Take the wooden gate situated at the top right hand side of the car park and walk up the gravel covered path. There are rhododendron plants in full bloom from June to your left, and pine trees to your right. This walk to the top has quite a steep incline, but after 100 metres you will come to the first of many benches for resting. The path continues on this steep incline for 150 metres. The next bench has a view almost in line of the ridge of Ben Bhan leading up to Sgurr Dhearg. After ten minutes walking, still on a steep climb, you obtain the first view of the artificial loch which is about 400 metres below. Leaflet available.

Loch Tearnait
About 3 miles before Lochaline on the A884 sign posted Ardtornish Castle and Gardens. Follow this road and carry on around the Kinlochaline Castle towards the gardens. At the turn off on the right carry straight on to the estate yard where you should park your car. Time: 2 hours ambling. Grade: easy.
Follow rough road diagonally opposite office and cross hump backed bridge. Keep to road on right until you come to an old wooden gate. Continue past this gate with the Rannoch river on your right. The start of the walk has a slow steady climb, the path being flanked by small sycamore and oak trees to your right, and open fields to your left. Through the trees you can hear the water cascading through the gorge over to the right. Access to view the gorge is difficult so be careful. After about half a mile you come to an old iron gate. You are now in open countryside and the vegetation of heather, deer sedge and purple grass moorland will remain like this all the way to the loch. Leaflet available.

Mallaig Circular Walk
Follow A82 to roundabout and take third turning off into the town centre. Carry on towards Mallaig Bay to sign saying Main road to East Bay, old road Mallaigvaig, 50 minutes 1¼ miles, pedestrians only.
Take this well kept path which is the original access road for people from Mallaigvaig. After the first 100 metres path veers to the left offering a captivating view showing off Mallaig harbour. Spectacular views en route of Rhum, Eigg, Ardnamurchan, Mallaigvaig and Loch Nevis. Leaflet available.

GLENMORE FOREST PARK
7 miles/11.3km east of Aviemore. Off the B9152.

Contact: Forest Enterprise, Inverness Forest Office, Smithton, Inverness IV1 2NL. Tel: 0463 791575.

Open all year. Over 5,000 acres of pine and spruce woods and mountainside on the north west slopes of the Cairngorms, with Loch Morlich as its centre. Fine area for wildlife, including Red deer, reindeer, wildcat, golden eagle, ptarmigan, capercailzie etc. Remnants of old Caledonian Pinewoods. Well equipped visitor centre, and shop with audio-visual display, caravan and camp site open all year, canoeing, sailing, windsurfing, fishing, swimming, forest trails, hillwalking and forest orienteering course. Toilets, picnic areas, shop and cafe. Car and coach parking available. Facilities for the disabled.

GLEN NEVIS
Highland Regional Council picnic site. 1.3 miles/2.1km into Glen Nevis from the Nevis Bridge roundabout on A82 in Fort William.
Contact: Highland Regional Council, Libraries & Leisure, Kinmylies Building, Inverness IV1 5NX. Tel: 0463 234121, ext. 452.
Nature trail through glen, 3 miles/4.8km (2½ hours).
All dogs on lead.
Open all year. Car park. Picnic areas. Information Centre (seasonal).

INVERTROMIE TRAIL
RSPB car park. 1½ miles/2.4km E of Kingussie on B970 road.
Contact: RSPB Warden, Ivy Cottage, Insh, Kingussie, Inverness-shire PH21 1NT.
Two hides overlooking marshes, through woodland, farmland and botanically rich areas, by fast-flowing river. 2 miles/3.2km (1½-2 hours).
No dogs.
Open all year. Car park. Picnic areas. Information Centre (restricted opening). Donations welcome.

KNOCKAN CLIFF TRAIL
Car park below conspicuous cliff. On A835, 15 miles/24km N of Ullapool.
Contact: Sutherland Tourist Board, The Square, Dornoch, Sutherland IV25 3SD. Tel: 0862 810400.
Marked trail along base and top of interesting geological cliff formation. Superb views over Inverpolly Nature Reserve. (1-2 hours).
Strong footwear advised.
Car park. Information Centre.

LAEL FOREST WALKS
Car parks 10 miles/16km SE of Ullapool. A835 2 miles/3.2km NW of Braemore Junction.
Contact: Forest Enterprise, Inverness Forest District, Smithton, Inverness IV1 2NL. Tel: 0463 791575.
Three circular forest walks from ¾ mile/1.2km (1 hour) to 1¾ miles/2.8km (2 hours). All with

fine views through mixed conifer and deciduous woodland. Also a forest garden with arboretum of many tree and rhododendron species.
Open all year. 2 car parks. Picnic areas. Leaflet available.

LANDMARK HIGHLAND HERITAGE & ADVENTURE PARK
Landmark, Carrbridge. A9, 7 miles/11.2km N of Aviemore.
Contact: Mr. D. Fullerton, Landmark, Carrbridge, Inverness-shire PH23 3AJ. Tel: 047984 613. Fax: 047984 384.
Approximately 1½-2 miles of board walk trails and hard paths through ancient Scots pine forest leading to Pinewood Nature Centre, Nature Trail and Tree Top Trail. Also Scottish Forestry Heritage Park with working Steam Powered sawmill and 20 metre high viewing tower.
Giant adventure playground. Woodland maze. "The Highlander" multi-screen slide show and exhibition.
Open all year: summer - 09.30-20.00; winter - 09.30-17.00. Free car park. Admission charge. Large craft & book shop. Restaurant. Snack bar. Picnic area.

LOCHABER
Contact: Forest Enterprise, Lochaber Forest District, Torlundy, Fort Wiliam, Inverness-shire PH33 6SW. Tel: 0397 702184/5.
Allt Coire Gabhail
Drive through Glencoe from the village of Ballachulish for about five miles. Large boulder on the right hand side of the road is the corner point and marker of a large gravelly area where you should park your car.
Walk towards the Three Sisters, descending into the glen to old road. Turn left and carry on until you come to gravel path on right. Follow the path up and over the stile, from here you can take a choice of two routes. If you take the route to the right of the obvious path, and ascend a tussocky grassed ridge for about thirty feet, you will come upon a path which in fact offers you a gentler walk into the valley. The altnerative route is to follow the well made track, which though in places you are required to have a scramble, you are rewarded especially in spring and autumn, with some lovely views of waterfalls, pools and incredible colours all from the river, which the path follows nearly all the way. Carry on these paths until the upper path meets the lower. From here you have to take care in traversing the river by stepping stones. Once across, walk up the steepish bank to your right towards the green bank with some scree slopes up to the left. Carry on up towards the lip of the summit ahead of you and on into the Lost Valley. Time: 180 minutes. Grade: moderate/difficult. Leaflet available.

Caig Waterfall Walk
From Fort William town centre take A82 towards Inverness. 1 mile after Spean Bridge,

take road to the left B8005 to Gairlochy. Carry on this road passing the Mucomir Dam and Hydro Station and cross the Caledonian Canal. From there take the route to the right along the road to the foresty houses at Clunes. Pass these houses and take a sharp left away from Loch Lochy and proceed along the Mile Dorcha for about 3 miles until you come to car park.

The path leads off to the right and leads to the top of the waterfall. You can then follow the path up through the forest. It is flanked on either side with silver birch which then gives way to Norwegian Spruce. The walk is well protected by the trees so even when it is pouring with rain they provide some splendid shelter. Within the forest you gain, near the summit of the walk, glimpses across to the hills on the other side of the small valley. Highest point at a height of 732 metres. After these occasional clearings the path turns to its right. You are now approaching the end of the uphill section. A flight of steps brings you on to the forest road. Turn right and make your way down the forest road. As on the ascent you have some lovely perpendicular spruce trees on either side. Time: 90 minutes. Grade: easy. Leaflet available.

Strone and Erracht

From Fort William town centre take A82 to Inverness for two miles. At the first major junction, signposted to Mallaig, turn left onto A830 for 1.2 miles. Cross the Caledonian Canal and take road signposted to Banavie, Glenloy and Gairlochy for 3.7 miles to entrance to the Strone Walk car park.

Strone - Follow the signposts and the forest road all the way. Excellent views across the Great Glen towards the North Face of Ben Nevis and Aonach Mhor. Through the gate the road zig-zags up the hill giving good views across Glenloy and up the river Lochy and Caledonian Canal.

Erracht Oakwood - Leave car on left at forest entrance. The route is signposted. After walking for about ten minutes you will come to a sign saying "Forest Walk". Follow this sign. Leaflet available.

Inchree Waterfall

S from Fort William on A82 for 9 miles/14.4km; take Inchree road to car park. Across fields and moorland to an exceptionally fine waterfall which descends 120ft in seven stages. Continuing up the hill to a forest road by which a return is made with fine views across to Ardgour. 1½ miles/2.4km (1½ hours).

Corrychurrachan

Start from the car park opposite a cottage just past the 6-mile/9.6km-stone S of Fort William on A82. Cross the old Wade's Bridge then follow the circular route on forest roads and tracks through replanted conifers. There are extensive views of Loch Linnhe and the Ardgour mountains. 1½ miles/2.4km (1½ hours).

Wade's Road

S from Fort William on A82 for 9 miles/14.4km; take Inchree road to car park. Follow the old Wade's Road through the forest and across a burn and return via a forest road down the ridge above Inchree with spectacular views of the Firth of Lorne. 2 miles/3.2km (2 hours). Open all year except during timber operations. Car park. Guide book available.

Achriabhach - Glen Nevis

Park near the lower falls 6 miles/9.6km from Fort William. The path follows the burn, complete with pools and waterfalls through the forest. Several variations are possible returning down the forest road - maximum 1½ miles/2.4km (1½ hours).

NEWTONMORE

Village Hall, Newtonmore, Inverness-shire. 2 miles/3.2km off A9 Perth-Inverness road. Contact: Highland Regional Council, Libraries & Leisure, Kinmylies Building, Inverness. Tel: 0463 234121, ext. 452.
Walk of local interest. 1-2 miles/1.6-3.2km (1 hour).
Dogs on lead.
Open all year. Car park. Information Centre (seasonal).

PLODDA FALLS WALK

Car park, 3½ miles/5.6km beyond Tomich village, Glen Affric. Turn off A831 just before Cannich, follow signpost for Tomich.
Contact: Forest Enterprise, Fort Augustus Forest District, Strathoich, Fort Augustus, Inverness-shire PH32 4BT. Tel: 0320 6322.
Picturesque walk through impressive conifers with vantage points of falls/river along route. 1½ miles/2.4km (¾ hour).
No fires. No camping or caravans (camping and caravan site in Cannich).
Open all year. Car park.

REELIG GLEN FOREST WALK

Off old A9, 8 miles/12.8km W of Inverness, 4 miles/6.4km E of Beauly.
Contact: Forest Enterprise, Fort Augustus Forest District, Strathoich, Fort Augustus, Inverness-shire PH32 4BT. Tel: 0320 6322.
A walk winding through some fine conifers planted in 1880 and other hard woods. With several grottos, bridges and the remains of an old fort, it is an interesting and beautiful walk. 1,500 yds/1.5km (30 minutes).
No fires.
Open all year. Car park. Picnic areas. Guide book available. First half suitable for disabled.

RIVER OICH WALKS

Near Fort Augustus just off A82. Two car parks are available. Grid reference NH 368 090, NH 352 073.
Contact: Forest Enterprise, Fort Augustus

Forest District, Strathoich, Fort Augustus, Inverness-shire PH32 4BT. Tel: 0320 6322.

SIGNAL ROCK & AN TORR
National Trust Visitor Centre, Glencoe, Argyll. Off A82 just SW of Glencoe village.
Contact: Forest Enterprise, Lorne Forest District, Millpark Road, Oban, Argyll PA34 4NH. Tel: 0631 66155.
Woodland walk with outstanding views of surrounding mountains 1½ miles/2.4km (45 minutes).
Open all year. Car park. Toilets. Picnic areas. Information Centre.

SLAGGAN VILLAGE
Take the Mellon Udrigle road at Laide Post Office on A832, 17 miles/27.3km NNE of Gairloch. Park in layby just past Achgarve road end.
Contact: Ross and Cromarty Tourist Board, Information Office, Achtercairn, Gairloch IV21 2DN. Tel: 0445 2130.
An easy walk to the ruined village of Slaggan. Continuing this along the cliff-top to the headland to the right provides a short walk of spectacular scenery, especially in wild weather when the sea breaks violently on the rocks of Greenstone Point. 5 miles/8km (3 hours return).
Open all year. Guide book available.

SLATTADALE SHORE WALK
Off the A832 overlooking Loch Maree.
Contact: Forest Enterprise, Wester ross Forest District, Balmacara, Kyle of Lochalsh, Ross-shire IV40 8DN. Tel: 059 986 321.

ULLAPOOL
Contact: Ross and Cromarty Tourist Board, Information Office, Achtercairn, Gairloch IV21 2DN. Tel: 0445 2130.

Loch Achall
Leaving the village by the north road follow the sign to Rhidorroch House. The road passes the Ullapool River on the way to the lovely Loch Achall. After walking through the glen you emerge to fine views of Ullapool, Loch Broom and the Summer Isles, and rejoin the main road back to the village. 5 miles/8km (3-4 hours).

Rhue Lighthouse
From Castle Terrace you can see the path down to the river on your left. Following the river almost to the sea, take the path that goes along the shore to Strathan Burn and beyond to the rocky promontory of the lighthouse. Return by the road. 5 miles/8km (3-4 hours).

Glastullich
Leave the village by the north road and climb to the top of Morefield Brae, where a metalled road turns off to the right. This soon reduces to a primitive track, excellent for walking. Shortly before Loch Dubh Beag, a path forks back to the right across the valley, looking over Loch Achall. It will then take you down the Rhidarroch Valley to the little house and sheepfold called Glastullich, where you can rejoin the road back to Ullapool. 6 miles/9.6km (4-5 hours).
Open all year. Guide book available.

VICTORIA FALLS
Located within Slattadale Forest off the A832 adjacent to Loch Maree.
Contact: Forest Enterprise, Wester Ross Forest District, Balmacara, Kyle of Lochalsh, Ross-shire IV40 8DN. Tel: 059 986 321.

SEE MAPS ON PAGES 123–128

AND REGIONAL MAP ON

PAGE 19

SCOTTISH ISLANDS

ARRAN

Contact: Forest Enterprise, Brodick, Isle of Arran KA27 8BZ.

Clauchland Hills
Picnic area on main road mid-way between Lamlash and Brodick.
Outstanding views to N and S from path over Clauchland Hills to Brodick or Lamlash. 3 miles/4.8km (1½ hours).
Open all year. Car park.

Fallen Rocks
North Sannox picnic site. 1 mile/1.6km N of Sannox.
Forest road along coastline beside rugged cliffs and woodland to fallen rocks and back by same route. 3 miles/4.8km (1½ hours).
Open all year. Car park.

Glenashdale Falls
Whiting Bay. Signposts at south side of Whiting Bay.
Circular route from Whiting Bay through broadleaved woodland and coniferous forest to view Glenashdale falls at 40 ft/12m and 90 ft/27m. 2½ miles/4km (1¼ hours).
Open all year. Car park. Picnic areas.
"Seventy Walks on Arran" booklet available from Isle of Arran Tourist Board, Tourist Information Centre, The Pier, Arran KA27 8AU.

BRODICK COUNTRY PARK NATURE TRAILS
Brodick Castle. 2 miles/3.2km N of Brodick, Isle of Arran.
Contact: Administrator, National Trust for Scotland, Brodick Castle, Isle of Arran KA27 8HY. Tel: 0770 2202.
Walks pass through gardens and a variety of woodlands. ¼-3 miles/0.4-4.8km (20 minutes to 2 hours).
Sturdy footwear is required for all walks.
Open all year. Car park. Information Centre. Admission charge.

GIANTS GRAVES
2 miles (steep) 1½ hours. Stout waterproof footwear advisable.
The early stage of this trail starts at Whiting Bay, but then it turns sharply to the left and up a staircase of 265 steps (!!) through the forest. After that the path continues to rise gradually and towards the top there are a number of excellent views over Whiting Bay and Holy Island. The path emerges into a clearing containing the remains of chambered cairns – the so called Giants Graves. The best way back is to retrace one's steps rather than follow one of the unmade routes from the back of the Giants Graves area.

BUTE

ETTERICK BAY
From bus stop at Etterick Bay, 3 miles/4.8km W of Rothesay.
Contact: Buteshire Natural History Society, The Museum, Stuart Street, Rothesay, Isle of Bute.
Coastal road partly through woodland, with excursions off route to shore and up hill. Partly accessible to motorists. 5 or 9 miles/8 or 14.4km (3-5 hours for round journey).
Open all year. Car park. Trail booklet available.

KINGARTH TRAIL, DUNAGOIL & ST. BLANE'S
Kingarth cemetery, 9 miles/14.4km SW of Rothesay.
Contact: Buteshire Natural History Society, The Museum, Stuart Street, Rothesay, Bute.
Farm track on field and foreshore. Motorists could drive as far as Dunagoil Farm. 6 miles/9.6km (4½ hours).
Dogs must be kept on lead between Dunagoil and St. Blane's.
Open all year. Car park. Picnic areas. Trail booklet available.

LOCH FAD & LOCH ASCOG TRAILS
Loch Fad walk from Rothesay Castle. Loch Ascog walk 2¾ miles/4.4km SE of Rothesay.
Contact: Buteshire Natural History Society, The Museum, Stuart Street, Rothesay, Isle of Bute.
Loch Fad, by woodland and farmland road with very little traffic. Loch Ascog by road through farmland. 4½ and 3 miles/7.2 and 4.8km (2 and 1¼ hours).
Open all year. Car park. Toilets. Trail booklet available. Loch Fad part-suitable for disabled.

ROTHESAY WALKS
Starts at Craigmore Pier.
Contact: Buteshire Natural History Society, The Museum, Stuart Street, Rothesay, Isle of Bute.
A choice of three walks within the town, explaining the buildings and places of interest, covering the history of the town. 6 miles/9.6km (approx. 3 hours).
Open all year. Car park. Toilets. Information Centre in town. Trail booklet available. Suitable for disabled.

SOUTH END
Kilchattan Bay, 10 miles/16km S of Rothesay.
Contact: Buteshire Natural History Society,

The Museum, Stuart Street, Rothesay, Isle of Bute.
A walk by narrow paths on foreshore, later through high bracken and fields. 6 miles/9.6km (4 hours).
Dogs must be kept on lead. Stout shoes or boots advised.
Open all year. Car park. Picnic areas. Trail booklet available.

MULL

ARDMORE FOREST WALK
1¼ miles/2 km SE of Glengorm Castle. Take A8073 from Tobermory and turn right on to unclassified road to Glengorm Castle.
Contact: Forest Enterprise, Lorne Forest District, Forest Office, Aros, Isle of Mull, Argyll PA72 6JP. Tel: 06803 346.
Walk through conifer woodland with viewpoints over Sound of Mull to Kilchoan, Ardnamurchan Peninsula with Coll and Tiree to NW. 2½ miles/4km (2 hours).
Car park. Picnic areas (at start of walk).

AROS PARK
Take A848 from Tobermory and turn left through gates into Aros Park after 1 mile/1.6km.
Contact: Forest Enterprise, Lorne Forest District, Forest Office, Aros, Isle of Mull, Argyll PA72 6JP. Tel: 06803 346.
A large number of walks in woodland with loch, sea-views and waterfalls. Also along seashore to Tobermory. Several miles of walks and paths (30 minutes-2 hours).
Old pier now in disrepair.
Open all year. Car park. Toilet. Picnic areas.

TOROSAY WALK
Craignure, 100 yds/90m past garage on left-hand side. On A849 to Bunessan.
Contact: Forest District Manager, Forestry Commission, Forest Office, Aros, Isle of Mull, Argyll PA72 6JP. Tel: 06803 346.
Walk through conifer and broadleaved woodland with superb views up Firth of Lorne to Morvern, Lismore with mountains of Glencoe and Ben Nevis in background. 1¾ miles/2.8km (1 hour).
Open all year. Picnic areas. Information Centre nearby.

ORKNEY ISLANDS

EDAY HERITAGE WALK
Eday Co-op, Island of Eday. Off B9063.
Contact: Dept. of Planning, Orkney Islands Council, Kirkwall, Orkney Islands KW15 1NY. Tel: 0856 3535, ext. 2503.
Signposted with waymarkers and includes interpretation boards and leaflet; through fields, moorland and wood nearby; wildlife, botanical and archaeological interest. 4½ miles/7.2km (4 hours).
Open all year. Car park. Toilets. Information Centre.

KIRKWALL HERITAGE TRAIL
Harbour Street, Kirkwall, Orkney Isles.
Contact: Department of Planning, Orkney Islands Council, Kirkwall, Orkney Islands KW15 1NY. Tel: 0856 3535, ext. 2503.
Trail through town conservation area. ¼ mile/600m (1 hour).
Open all year. Car park. Toilets. Picnic areas. Information Centre. Leaflet available. Suitable for disabled.

OLD MAN OF HOY
Rackwick Village. Ro-Ro ferry from Houton (Orkney mainland) to Lyness. Drive 7½ miles/12km to Rackwick Road along B9047. 3¾ miles/6km along Rackwick Road to Rackwick Village. Or passenger ferry from Stromness to Moness, then walk, taxi, bike to Rackwick, either along footpath through valley (3¾ miles/6km) or road (5 miles/8km) to Rackwick.
Contact: RSPB Warden: K. Fairclough, Ley House, Hoy, Orkney KW16 3NJ. Tel: 085 679 298.
A variety of walks taking in the Old Man of Hoy (a sea-stack) and other examples of fine cliff scenery or to the most northerly native wood in the UK. 3¾-7½ miles/6-12km (2½-5 hours).
Take great care on crumbly cliff edge. Avoid nesting colonies of gulls, skuas, etc.
Open all year. Car park. Toilets. Information Centre (foyer of Hoy Inn).

STROMNESS HERITAGE TRAIL
John Street, Stromness, Orkney Isles.
Contact: Department of Planning, Orkney Islands Council, Kirkwall, Orkney Islands KW15 1NY. Tel: 0856 3535, ext. 2503.
Trail through town conservation area. ⅔ mile/1km (1-1¼ hours).
Open all year. Car park. Toilets. Information Centre. Leaflet available. Suitable for disabled.

WESTNESS WALK
Westness Farm or Midhowe Cairn, Island of Rousay. Off B9064.
Contact: Department of Planning, Orkney Islands Council, Kirkwall, Orkney Islands KW15 1NY. Tel: 0856 3535, ext. 2503.
Signposted with waymarkers and includes leaflet; along coast; wildlife, wild flowers, folk history and archaeological interest. 1 mile/1.6km (45 minutes).
Open all year. Car park.

RAASAY

RAASAY FOREST WALK
Adjacent to the village of Inverarish on the Island of Raasay.
Contact: Forest Enterprise, Wester Ross Forest District, Balmacara, Kyle of Lochalsh, Ross-shire IV40 8DN. Tel: 059 986 321.

SKYE

GLENVARRAGILL WALK
½ mile/0.8km S of Portree on the A850 beside the Aros Heritage Centre.
Contact: Forest Enterprise, Wester Ross Forest District, Balmacara, Kyle of Lochalsh, Ross-shire IV40 8DN. Tel: 059 986 321.
Walk through woodland planted 1956-7, which can be extended to the forest road with views over Portree Bay. ½ or 1 mile/0.8 or 1.6km (20 minutes or 45 minutes).

May be closed during forestry operations or when the fire danger is high.
Open all year. Car park. Picnic areas.

KINLOCH WALK
Off the A851 in South Skye beside Kinloch Lodge Hotel.
Contact: Forest Enterprise, Wester Ross Forest District, Balmacara, Kyle of Lochalsh, Ross-shire IV40 8DN. Tel: 059 986 321.

NOTES

CANAL WALKS

Scotland's canals, Highland or Lowland, provide easy, level walking through some fine scenery with plenty of historical interest.

CALEDONIAN CANAL – TOWPATH
Joining the east to the west coasts and linking Lochs Ness, Oich and Lochy, the banks of the Caledonian Canal offer fine views of the Great Glen at numerous points. Here are two attractive stretches.
Contact: Large groups contact Caledonian Canal Office, Clachnaharry Road, Inverness IV3 6RA. Tel: 0463 233140.

Corpach to Gairlochy
A803 3¹/₂ miles/5.6km N of Fort William. B8004 Gairlochy.
Canal towing path with architectural features – wharf basin and locks at Corpach, Neptune's Staircase (8 locks) at Banavie. Track is on S side of canal. Approx. 8 miles/12.8km (2–3 hours).
No cycles.
Open all year. Car park.

Dochgarroch to Clachnaharry
Via Inverness and Muirtown. A82 6 miles/9.6km SW of Inverness. A862 Muirtown.
Canal towing path on S side of canal past Dochgarroch lock, Tomnahurich Bridge and cemetery, Muirtown Locks (flight of 4), Muirtown Basin, Clachnaharry Works Lock and sea lock. Approx. 7 miles/11.2km (2–3 hours).
No cycles.
Open all year. Car park.

CRINAN CANAL – TOWPATH
Ardrishaig to Crinan. A83 Ardrishaig. Crinan B841. 9 miles/14.4km NW of Lochgilphead.
Contact: Crinan Canal Office, Pier Square, Ardrishaig PA30 8DZ. Tel: 0546 3210.
Canal towpath through conservation area (Bellanoch & Crinan). Superb views at Crinan end. Canal architecture of great charm and character. 10 miles/16km (3 hours).
Open all year. Car park. Picnic areas.

FORTH & CLYDE CANAL
Take Bowling turn-off from A82 out of Glasgow, turn left at "Bowling Pottery" sign, cross railway bridge, bear left into car park or cross drawbridge on foot to gain access to towing path.

Contact: Forth & Clyde Canal Countryside Ranger, British Waterways Board, Canal House, Applecross Street, Glasgow G4 9SP. Tel: 041–332 6936.
Once connecting coast to coast via Bowling on the Clyde and Grangemouth on the Forth, this canal has recently undergone some renovation for recreational usage. Much of the canal offers interesting walking and the 33¹/₂ miles/54km can be explored in convenient sections. These include Bowling-Dalmuir, Glasgow branch-Maryhill, around Cadder and Kirkintilloch, Twechar-Barrhill, Auchinstarry-Craigmarloch near Kilsyth, and other stretches towards Falkirk. Bowling to Kirkintilloch, Castlecary to Falkirk have surfaced towpaths. Features include industrial archaeology, historic monuments, varied plant and animal life, woodlands and the Roman remains along the parallel Antonine Wall (2–3 days).
Open all year. Car park. Picnic areas.

MONKLAND CANAL
Towpaths have now been reinstated from Calderbank to Drumpellier with plans to link with Summerlee Heritage Park.
Contact: Greater Glasgow Tourist Board, 35 St. Vincent Place, Glasgow G1 2ER. Tel: 041–204 4400

UNION CANAL – TOWPATH
The Union Canal once linked Edinburgh with Glasgow, joining the Forth-Clyde Canal at Falkirk. Like the Forth-Clyde Canal it has now been revitalised for recreational usage, though cut in a few places by new roads and other needs. It can be walked in convenient sections – for example Falkirk-Lathallan Road (A801) and then to Linlithgow, Broxburn, Ratho to Wester Hailes in Edinburgh. There is a city section from Wester Hailes to Fountainbridge. In addition to the peaceful rural locations, there is also much of industrial archaeological interest, particularly aqueducts and a tunnel section near Falkirk.
Contact: British Waterways Board, Countryside Ranger, Union Canal, Canal House, Applecross Street, Glasgow G4 9SP. Tel: 041–332 6936.
Canal side, tunnel, open country, contour canal (no locks, no hills). 5¹/₂ miles/9km Falkirk-Lathallen Road (A801) (approx. 3 hours).
Open all year. Car park.

LONG-DISTANCE FOOTPATHS

Scotland's long-distance footpaths are backed by signposting, visitor literature and advice on accommodation. Both the Southern Upland Way and the West Highland Way traverse high ground and walkers are advised to be equipped accordingly.

SOUTHERN UPLAND WAY

Long-distance walkway across the Scottish Borders from Portpatrick in the W to Cockburnspath on the E coast (Britain's first coast to coast long distance footpath).
Contact: Countryside Commission for Scotland, Battleby House, Redgorton, Perth PH1 3EW. Tel: 0738 27921.
The Way runs right across Scotland. It offers opportunities to walkers of varied abilities, from those who aim to walk the whole Way to those who prefer to wander along shorter sections. The route passes through fine and varied countryside with a wealth of local history, literature and wildlife. 212 miles/341km (10–15 days).
Do not attempt longer or more remote stretches of the route unless you are experienced and well equipped.
Open all year. Accommodation on the route, although adequate, should be planned in advance. Detailed guide books for east and west sections are available from HMSO – £5.95 for set of two. Free leaflet available from Countryside Commission for Scotland.

SPEYSIDE WAY

Various access points between Tomintoul and Spey Bay.
Contact: Moray District Council, Director of Leisure & Libraries, District Headquarters, High Street, Elgin IV30 1BX. Tel: 0343 545121.
A long-distance footpath using extensive rights of way, footpaths, and former railway lines. Scenic walk with extensive natural history. Generally it follows the River Spey. 45 miles/72km (2–3 days).
Open all year. Car parks. Toilets. Picnic areas. Ranger service available at Craigellachie Tel: (0340) 881266. Map/leaflet available.

WEST HIGHLAND WAY

Long-distance walkway from Milngavie northwards to Fort William.
Contact: Countryside Commission for Scotland, Battleby House, Redgorton, Perth PH1 3EW. Tel: 0738 27921.
The Way runs from the outskirts of Glasgow, Scotland's largest city, to the foot of Ben Nevis, its highest mountain, following the shores of Loch Lomond. It is a superb walk of varied character through some of the finest scenery in Scotland. Although short sections at the southern end are easy and relaxed walking, farther north the Way can become remote and is unsuitable for inexperienced walkers. 95 miles/152km (6–7 days).
Open all year. Accommodation on the route, although adequate, should be planned in advance. Detailed guide book available from HMSO – £9.95. Free leaflet available from Countryside Commission for Scotland.

SEE MAPS ON PAGES 123–128

AND REGIONAL MAP ON

PAGE 19

NOTES

ACTIVITY HOLIDAYS
A PASTIME PUBLICATION

I/We have seen your advertisement and wish to know if you have the following vacancy: —

Name_____

Address_____

_____

_____

Dates from pm _____

Please give date and day of week in each case

To am _____

Number in Party _____

Detail of Children _____

Please remember to include a stamped addressed envelope with your enquiry.

ACTIVITY HOLIDAYS
A PASTIME PUBLICATION

I/We have seen your advertisement and wish to know if you have the following vacancy: —

Name_____

Address_____

_____

_____

Dates from pm _____

Please give date and day of week in each case

To am _____

Number in Party _____

Detail of Children _____

- - - - - - CUT ALONG HERE - - - - - - - - - - - - - - - - - - CUT ALONG HERE - - - - - -

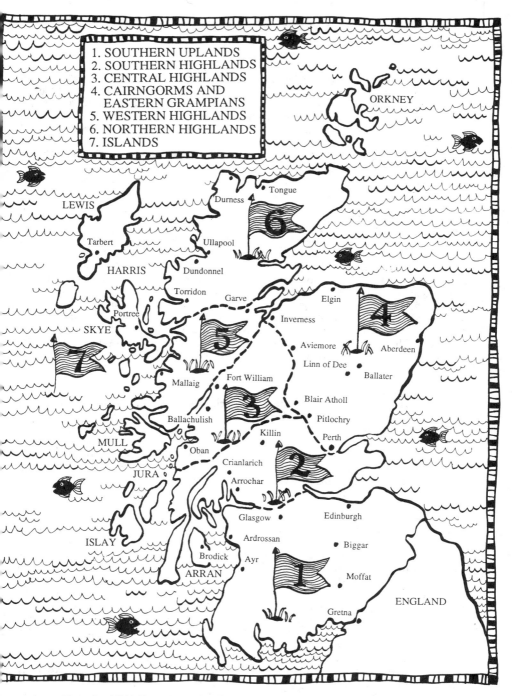

1. SOUTHERN UPLANDS
2. SOUTHERN HIGHLANDS
3. CENTRAL HIGHLANDS
4. CAIRNGORMS AND
   EASTERN GRAMPIANS
5. WESTERN HIGHLANDS
6. NORTHERN HIGHLANDS
7. ISLANDS

r easy reference this map is subdivided into areas corresponding to the divisions made in the Scottish Mountaineering Trust guide books.

HILLWALKING

Introduction

This book is intended to provide information for visitors to Scotland about the country's mountains and the opportunities for hillwalking. Brief descriptions are given of about sixty easy hillwalking and scrambling routes in all parts of the country. It must be emphasised that this is not a comprehensive guidebook, nor is it a manual of climbing. The Scottish Mountaineering Trust publishes a definitive series of guidebooks and several other books about climbing in Scotland are available. It is essential that anyone using this book as a guide for climbing or walking should use it in conjunction with a large scale map.

The most suitable maps for hillwalking are the Ordnance Survey 1:50,000 maps. These show adequate detail and are widely available in many shops.

The routes described

The mountains and routes described in this book have been selected to include the most popular mountains with well-marked tourist routes, and some of the finest mountains from the point of view of their climbing or scenic interest. In the case of the popular peaks like Ben Lomond and Ben Nevis there are well-marked footpaths on these hills, and provided these paths are followed the routefinding difficulties are more or less absent. In the second group are some peaks in Glencoe and the North-West which rank among the finest Scottish mountains. The routes on these peaks are quite steep and the paths narrow or non-existent, and some rock scrambling may be involved. These climbs are suitable for fairly experienced hillwalkers; however, inexperienced hillwakers would be better advised to avoid them.

Scrambles and Climbs

This book is not intended as a guide for rock-climbers, and the standards of difficulty used are intended to be appropriate for hillwalkers and not rock-climbers.

Obviously the difficulty of a climb is relative to a climber's skill and experience, and something that is difficult for an inexperienced walker might be perfectly easy for an experienced climber. As an indication of difficulty, however, the word 'scramble' usually denotes that the climber has to use his hands to maintain balance and assist his upward or downward progress on ground that is fairly steep.

Hillwalking in Scotland

Much of Scotland is hilly, the character varying from smooth, grassy hills and moors in the south to wild and rugged mountains in the north. In this book the country is sub-divided into a number of areas to correspond, for convenience, to the divisions made in the Scottish Mountaineering Trust guidebooks. Most of the boundaries between regions are natural and well defined; it is however easy to move by car or public transport from one region to another and the visiting climber can in a comparatively short holiday sample the climbing in several parts of the country.

By Alpine standards the Scottish mountains are not high; only seven of them exceed four thousand feet (1,200m), and most of them are quite accessible and lie within a short distance of a public road.

Consequently nearly any Scottish hill can be climbed in a single day by anyone with a car who drives to the nearest point on a road. Unlike the Alps where there are many mountain huts, it is unnecessary for the climber to stay in such huts, of which there are few in Scotland. Most climbers either camp in the glens, or stay in hotels, guest houses or youth hostels.

WARNING

Despite their comparatively low altitude, the Scottish mountains are potentially hazardous and are subject to rapid weather changes. Such changes can turn a simple walk up an easy hillside into a serious undertaking requiring a high degree of mountain skill in routefinding, and the arctic weather of the Scottish mountains makes proper clothing and equipment essential.

It is important that all climbers are aware of the potential dangers in the mountains and are properly prepared and equipped to deal with them: alternatively, they should only venture onto very easy climbs in settled weather.

Countryside and Mountain Code

1 Respect private property and keep to paths when going through estates and farmland. Avoid where possible climbing over walls and fences and close gates that you open. Do not leave any litter.

2 Be careful not to disturb sheep in the lambing season (March-May), and avoid deer-stalking and grouse-shooting country during the stalking and shooting season (usually August-October). If in doubt enquire from local farmers or keepers before going on the hills. Keep dogs under control on the hills.

3 In forests keep to paths, avoid smoking and do not light fires. Avoid damaging young trees in newly planted forests.

4 Plan your climb carefully, taking account of the experience and fitness of the party, the prevailing weather and the weather forecast. Allow plenty of time for the climb and plan the route beforehand on a map.

5 Be properly equipped for your climb, and carry adequate food with you.

6 Leave a note in the hotel where you are staying, or with the police or other responsible person, or (failing this) in your car or tent of the names of the party, the objective, the route up and down and the expected time of return.

7 Be prepared to turn back if the weather becomes bad, or if any member of the party is going very slowly or is exhausted. The party should keep together, especially in misty weather.

8 Be particularly careful in the descent, especially if the route is unknown to you. If in doubt go down by your uphill route. Do not run downhill; a sprained ankle might mean a rescue team call-out.

9 In the event of an accident requiring a rescue team at least one person should stay with the injured climber while one or two go down for help. If there are only two in the party the injured climber should be left with all the spare clothing, food, whistle and torch while his companion goes for help. The person descending to the valley should inform the police as quickly as possible.

FOLLOW THE COUNTRY CODE

HILLWALKING

1. SOUTHERN UPLANDS

The southern part of Scotland (south of the low-lying valley between the Firths of Clyde and Forth) is largely a land of broad valleys and rolling, grassy hills. There is a uniform character about much of this country – the valleys dotted with small towns, villages and farms, and above them the land rising in smooth grassy slopes and ridges to high moorland and rounded hilltops. Most of the hill-country is given over to sheep farming, and there is some forestry in the valleys. The main road (A74) from Gretna to Hamilton divides this part of the country in two more or less equal parts. That to the east, known as the Border country, is dominated geographically by the valleys of the River Tweed and its tributaries, and the hills are uniformly smooth and grassy.

To the west, particularly in Galloway, the hills are rather more rugged and akin in character to the Highlands.

None of the hills in the Southern Uplands exceeds 850m, and few of them have the striking features, such as ridge, buttress or corrie, of the northern hills. They are, however, very pleasant for the hillwalker and have the advantage of rather better weather characteristics than the higher mountains to the north.

Merrick and Corserine

Merrick: approx 12m N of Newton Stewart, best approached from A714 by Glen Trool.
Corserine: best approached from A713.

Starting in Galloway, Merrick (843m) is the highest hill in the south of Scotland. It is best approached from Glen Trool where the Forestry Commission administers a Forest Park with facilities for tourists and campers. From a car park on the north side of Loch Trool the path to Merrick is signposted; it follows the west side of the Buchan Burn northwards through the forest and emerges at the ruined house of Culsharg. The route continues by a dyke to Benyellary and then north-east across a grassy dip towards Merrick, leaving the dyke on one's left just after passing the col and heading directly towards the summit.

Five miles (8km) to the east of Merrick there is a long ridge of hills – the Kells Range – of wich Corserine (814m) is the central and highest point. The shortest ascent is from the east where one can leave the Dalry-Carsphairn road (A713) two miles (3km) north of Dalry and drive westwards up the valley of the Polharrow Burn. From the end of the public road continue along the Fore Bush road through the forest to Loch Harrow, and then over North Gairy Top to Corserine.

Lowther Hill and Green Lowther

Off B797 approx. 7m E of Sanquhar.

North-east of Galloway the country is mostly high, featureless moorland, and the next hills of note are Lowther Hills (725m) and Green Lowther (732m) standing a mile (1.5km) apart near the village of Wanlockhead (which is itself the highest village in Scotland). There is a road to these hills from the village, and their summits are disfigured by the masts and aerials of communication equipment. The only point worthy of note is that these are among the most easily climbed hills in Scotland, though one is not actually permitted to drive to their summits by car.

The Border Country

Moving further east to the Border country, the finest group of hills lies north-east of Moffat between the Moffat Water and the headwaters of the River Tweed. These hills are most easily approached from the A708 road from Moffat to Selkirk; this road goes through a fine, narrow glen as it climbs alongside the Moffat Water and crosses the Birkhill Pass to reach the source of the Yarrow and St. Mary's Loch.

A mile and a half (2.5km) on the Moffat side of the pass there is a car park at the foot of the Tail Burn; this burn tumbles down from Loch Skeen and the Grey Mare's Tail, a very beautiful waterfall in a impressively narrow gorge. The area around Loch Skeen and the Grey Mare's Tail is owned by the National Trust for Scotland.

From the car park there are two footpaths, one ascending on each side of the Tail Burn. Both these paths are narrow and cross the very steep sides of the gorge of the burn, and great care should be taken, especially in wet weather. The left hand path (as one looks up from the car park) goes for about half a mile (1km) up the gorge to reach a point from where there is a fine view of the falls; no one without proper footwear should attempt to scramble beyond the end of the path to try to reach the top of the falls.

White Coomb and Hart Fell

Off A708 approx. 7m NE of Moffat.

The other path climbs across the steep hillside on the north-east side of the gorge and continues to Loch Skeen, two miles (3km) from the road. This is a good approach to White Coomb (821m), the highest hill in this group; once one has climbed well above the Grey Mare's Tail and the smaller falls above it, one can cross the burn and climb the eastern shoulder of this hill.

Hart Fell (808m) is the highest hill at the south-west end of this group. It can be climbed from several points – from Moffat by the road to Archbank, from the Devil's Beef Tub along the line of the Peebles-Dumfries county boundary which is marked by a fence, or from Capplegill by the Moffat Water. The Capplegill route leads over Swatte Fell and along a delightful ridge to Hart Fell. Energetic walkers can continue across the undulating plateau to White Coomb and down the Garrifran Burn to reach the road again a mile and a half (2.5km) from the starting point at Capplegill.

Broad Law and Dollar Law
4m E of A701 S of Broughton.
North of the group just described, a narrow public road crosses the hills between Tweedsmuir and St. Mary's Loch, reaching a height of about (450m) at the head of the Meggat Valley. The flooding of this valley to create a new reservoir has changed the landscape; however, the pass at the head of the valley (best reached from the Talla reservoir) is a good starting point for Broad Law (840m), the second highest hill in the South of Scotland. The ascent from the highest point of the road (where one can leave a car) is easy, following a fence all the way to the top of the hill where there is an aircraft radio beacon. An undulating, grassy plateau extends north-east from Broad Law for four miles (6km) to Dollar Law (817m). The walk across this plateau is easy, but one is likely to end up a long way from one's starting point.

The shortest approach to Dollar Law is from Manorhead at the upper end of the Manor Valley, which is approached from Peebles. Alternatively a rather longer route can be made from the Tweed valley; there is a bridge across the River Tweed at Easter Stanhope about four miles (6km) south of Broughton village, and from there one can walk up the Stanhope Burn to reach Dollar Law.

Culter Fell and Tinto
Culter Fell: SE of A702 approx. 3m S of Coulter.
Tinto: S of A73 near Thankerton.
Finally, in this part of the Southern Uplands one notes two more isolated hills - Culter Fell and Tinto. Both are worthy of attention, and because of their isolated positions they command good views of the surrounding country. Culter Fell (748m) is climbed by taking the road from Coulter village to Birthwood and ascending the broad ridge between Kings Beck and Culter Water. Tinto (707m) is most easily climbed by leaving the A73 road at Fallburn (six miles (9km) south-east of Lanark) and taking the minor road to Lochlyock for a quarter of a mile (0.5km), at which point a good track starts for the summit, two miles (4km) away.

Pentland Hills
Approx. 10m SW of Edinburgh off A702.
In concluding this section mention must be made of the Pentland Hills. Not by virtue of their height, but because of the delightful character of these hills and their nearness to Edinburgh they are deservedly popular. Any visitor to Edinburgh in search of a few hours exercise cannot do better than take the bus to Hillend and walk up past the artificial ski-slope to Caerketton. The view across Edinburgh and the Firth of Forth to the hills of Fife is superb, and the walk can be continued to Allermuir and

down to Swanston Village.
Going further afield in the Pentlands, there are some excellent walks across the hills starting at various points on the A702 road from Edinburgh to West Linton, and ending at Balerno or points a few miles south-west of this village on the A70 road. The starting points of these walks are well signposted, and they follow well-marked paths.

The best high-level walk in the Pentlands is the traverse of Carnethy Hill, Scald Law, East Kip and West Kip, an undulating ridge of grassy hills parallel to the A702 road between Glencorse and Nine Mile Burn. Buses run regularly along this road from Edinburgh, so one does not need a car for this expedition.

2. SOUTHERN HIGHLANDS
The Southern Highlands rise north of the Forth-Clyde valley and include the famous Loch Lomond and Trossachs areas, noted for their beauty. On the north the area is bounded by the glens formed by the Rivers Orchy and Tummel, whose headwaters rise in the southern part of the Moor of Rannoch.

Ben A'n
Approx. 5m N of Aberfoyle off the A821.
Loch Achray is in the heart of the Trossachs, and a mile (1.5km) north of the loch rises the prominent rocky peak of Ben A'n (457m) which gives a very pleasant short climb with a fine view from the top. The path up the hill starts from a car park about two hundred meters west of the Trossachs Hotel and leads up through birch woods and conifer forest. Near the top the easy route keeps to the right by a small stream and reaches the summit from the north-east, thereby avoiding the south face of the peak which is very steep and rocky.

Ben Lomond
Approx. 11m NW of Drymen on the E side of Loch Lomond.
Loch Lomond is probably Scotland's most famous loch and Ben Lomond (974m) rises on its east side. A narrow road leads up the east side of the loch as far as Rowardennan. There is a well-established footpath up Ben Lomond starting at Rowardennan Hotel or from the Forestry Commission car park a few hundred metres further north and climbing north-eastwards beside the forest. In one and a half miles (2.5km) the smooth broad south ridge of the mountain is reached and the path follows its crest for a further one and a half miles (2.5km) to the steeper cone of the summit. The ascent takes about three hours and the descent two hours.

The Cobbler
Off A83 approx. 3m W of Arrochar.
One of the best known groups of hills in the Southern Highlands is the Arrochar Alps, a cluster of hills to the north-west of the village of Arrochar at the head of Loch Long. The finest hill in the Arrochar Alps, though not the highest, is The Cobbler (884m), and its strange outline of three rocky peaks is well seen from

Arrochar or from Tarvet on Loch Lomond. Despite its fomidable appearance The Cobbler is easily climbed by the Allt a' Bhalachain (Buttermilk Burn). The usual route starts near the head of Loch Long where the road to Succoth farm joins the main road. Go uphill through the trees by a steep path to reach a 'staircase' formed by the concrete slabs of an old rail-track. At its top follow a horizontal path south-west to reach the Allt a' Bhalachain, and continue up the side of this stream past two huge boulders to a crossing of the stream. Now the route goes due westwards into the upper corrie of The Cobbler enclosed by the three peaks.

The best path goes close under the rocks of the north, or righthand, peak and reaches the col between this peak and the centre peak. The north peak is formed by a spectacular overhanging crag, but the ascent to it from this col is short and easy.

The centre peak is the highest and is easily reached from the col, but the actual summit is formed by a huge block of rock 5 metres high. The ascent of this block calls for some rock climbing, first through a hole or window in the block, then along a narrow ledge and finally up a few metres to the top.

Ben Ime
Off A83 approx. 5m NW of Arrochar.
Ben Ime (1,011m), the highest of the Arrochar Alps, may also be climbed by the Allt a'Bhalachain. From the source of this stream flat ground is crossed northwards and the broad, grassy slopes of Ben Ime are climbed for one mile (1.5km) north-north-west.

Cruach Ardrain
Approx. 3m S of Crianlarich off A82.
Travelling north from Arrochar by Loch Lomond and Glen Falloch, one comes to the village of Crianlarich in the heart of the Southern Highlands.

The most popular climb from Crianlarich is Cruach Ardrain (1,046m), three miles (4.5km) south-south-east of the village. The best route to this mountain starts from the road half a mile (1km) south of the village where a bridge crosses the railway.

The lower slopes of the hill are forested, and a break in the trees should be followed southwards to reach the north-west ridge of Cruach Ardrain which is followed over a few rocky knolls to the final steep, but easy slopes of the mountain.

Ben More and Stobinian
Approx. 3m E of Crianlarich off A85.
Immediately to the north-east of Cruach Ardrain the high twin summits of Ben More and Stobinian dominate this part of the Southern Highlands. Ben More (1,174m) is usually climbed from Benmore Farm, a mile and a half (3km) east of Crianlarich, and the ascent from there is a long, unrelenting climb which becomes quite steep as one nears the summit. Stobinian (1,165m) may also be climbed by the Benmore Burn, but a more pleasant route to this mountain is from the south, starting at the west end of Loch Doine, four miles (7km) west of Balquhidder, and climbing the long south ridge over Stob Invercarnaig to the summit.

Ben Lui
Approx. 5m SW of Tyndrum off A82.
As one goes north-west from Crianlarich towards Tyndrum the splendid peak of Ben Lui (1,130m) is bound to attract attention, on a clear day at least. It is justifiably a popular climb, but the approach from the east along the Cononish River is quite long, and the peak itself is steep so that this is not a climb for the inexperienced. There is a rough road up the Cononish glen, ending a mile (2km) beyond the farm. From there the mountain can best be climbed by one of the two bounding ridges of the steep north-east corrie, in which snow lingers until early summer. It is also possible to climb Ben Lui from the north-west, leaving Glen Lochy near a car park at the foot of the Eas Daimh. This route is shorter, but steeper than the Cononish approach, and one has to cross the River Lochy (no footbridge now) and find a way up through the recently planted forest by narrow paths, at first on the north side of the burn, then crossing and climbing south through a break in the trees.

Ben Lawers
Approx. 6m NE of Killin off A827.
The highest mountain in the Southern Highlands is Ben Lawers (1,214m), which dominates the north-west side of Loch Tay between Killin and Kenmore. Five miles (8km) from Killin a narrow road crosses the western end of the mountain towards Glen Lyon, and two miles (3km) up this road a car park marks the start of a well-marked route to Ben Lawers over the summit of Beinn Ghlas (1,118m). The route follows a broad track on the west side of the Burn of Edramucky for half a mile (1km) and then crosses to the east side of the stream and climbs the south-west side of Beinn Ghlas. From this top the ridge to Ben Lawers drops a few hundred feet and there is a final climb of two hundred metres to the summit. Ben Lawers is noted for its Alpine plants, and the National Trust for Scotland, which owns much of the southern part of the mountain, has created a short nature trail near the car park which points out many features of botanical interest.

Schiehallion
Off B846, approx. 7m NW of Kenmore.
Another well-known mountain in the north-east corner of the Southern Highlands is Schiehallion (1,083m), whose isolated conical peak is well seen from Loch Rannoch and from the lower reaches of the Tummel. A narrow road passes round the north-east side of the mountain and the easiest route of ascent leaves this road at a Forestry Commission car park near Braes of Foss farm. A track leads across the rising moorland south-westwards to reach the east ridge which is followed to the summit.

The top of the mountain is covered with quartzite boulders which makes the walking rather tiresome, but not difficult. The view from the top of Schiehallion is extensive, its finest feature being probably the beautifully wooded strath of Rannoch and Tummel to the north.

Beinn Dorain
Off A82, approx. 4m N of Tyndrum.
Crossing the pass from Tyndrum northwards towards Bridge of Orchy, one is confronted by the steep conical peak of Beinn Dorain (1,076m). The summit of this mountain is a grand viewpoint, and the ascent from Bridge of Orchy is not difficult. Starting from Bridge of Orchy station, one climbs eastwards up a fairly well defined path on the south side of the Allt Coire an Dothaidh to reach the head of this stream and the lowest point of the ridge between Beinn Dorain and Beinn an Dothaidh. From there the ascent to Beinn Dorain is easy and uncomplicated, provided there is good visibility.

3. CENTRAL HIGHLANDS
The Central Highlands are bounded on the south by the Glen Orchy-Rannoch Moor-Tummel line, on the east by the road and railway between Pitlochry and Inverness, and on the west by the faul of the Great Glen from Loch Linnhe in the south-west to Loch Ness in the north-east. This area contains many high and rugged mountains, and for many visitors is the epitome of Scotland's Highland scenery.

Ben Cruachan
Approx. 4m E of Taynuilt off A85 along the Pass of Brander.
In the south-west corner of this area is Ben Cruachan (1,126m), a fine range of peaks overlooking the Pass of Brander between Loch Awe and Loch Etive. On the south side of the range, in the Corrie of the Allt Cruachan, is the reservoir for the Cruachan Hydro-Electric scheme. A private road climbs up to this reservoir and provides easy walking access to the mountain; from the head of the reservoir the highest top is just over a mile (2km) to the north-west.
The usual route strikes westwards from the reservoir to reach the col between Meall Cuanail (a subsidiary top) and Ben Cruachan itself. From this col the last three hundred metres of the climb go northwards up stony slopes to the summit of Ben Cruachan. There is a fairly well-defined path, and the climber is rewarded on a clear day by magnificent views – sea and lochs to the west and mountains to the north and east.

Glen Coe
Along the A82 between Rannoch Moor and Ballachulish.
One of the finest glens in Scotland, Glen Coe was the scene of the massacre of 1692. Now it is one of the principal mountaineering centres in Scotland, and in winter it is also one of

Scotland's three main ski-ing centres, with chairlifts and ski-tows on Meall a'Bhuiridh a few kilometres east of Glen Coe. (Outside main holiday periods, these operate at weekends or by charter only). The mountains of Glen Coe lie near the north-west corner of the Moor of Rannoch, and as the traveller approaches by road along the western edge of the moor he is suddenly confronted by the great rock cone of the Buachaille Etive Mor (1,022m), the outpost of the Glen Coe peaks. The road passes below this peak and drops down into Glen Coe, becoming enclosed by steep and rocky mountains, the long ridge of the Aonach Eagach (967m) on the north, and the projecting spurs of Bidean nam Bian (1,150m) on the south.
These three mountains are more formidable than anything further south; their summits are guarded by huge buttresses and gullies, and there are few easy routes (in a walking sense) to their summits. As a consequence they are not peaks to be undertaken lightly by inexperienced climbers.

Buachaille Etive Mor
Off A82 approx. 2m W of Kingshouse.
The easiest route to the summit of the Buachaille Etive Mor leaves the main road at the cottage called Alltnafeadh, two and a half miles (4km) west of Kingshouse Hotel. Beyond the River Coupall, crossed by a footbridge, a path leads southwards across the moor into the prominent corrie called the Coire na Tulaich. The path is on the west side of the stream and goes straight up to the head of the corrie, where a scree slope leads to a short narrow gully, best climbed by the rocks on its east side (the left hand side facing up).
The main ridge of the mountain is reached half a mile (1km) south-west of the highest point, Stob Dearg, and the going along the ridge is easy although stony, with a faint path marked by cairns. The view from the summit is fine, with a flat expanse of Rannoch Moor to the east (the cone in the distance is Schiehallion) and a panorama of mountains in all other directions from the twin peaks of Ben Cruachan in the south to the flat bulk of Ben Nevis in the north.

Aonach Eagach
On N side of A82 in Glen Coe.
The Aonach Eagach is the mountain enclosing the north side of Glen Coe, its crest being a two-mile (3km) long, jagged, narrow ridge. The traverse of this ridge is a good climb, but it involves a lot of rock scrambling, and once on the ridge the climber is committed to completing the traverse in one direction or the other, as it is inadvisable to attempt to descend the north or south sides of the ridge.
The best ascent and descent routes are (1) the west end where the steep hillside north of Loch Achtriochtan leads to the peak called Sgor nam Fiannaidh, and (2) the east end where the ridge rising above the Meeting of the Three Waters leads to the peak called Am Bodach. (There is a cottage by the roadside at this point, and a

stream flows down a deep gully from the north. The ascent is on the west side of this stream, and there is a faint track in places.)

The Aonach Eagach is a serious climb and should not be attempted by inexperienced climbers or in bad weather.

Bidean Nam Bian
On S side of A82 in Glen Coe.

The highest mountain in Argyll is Bidean nam Bian, whose northern spurs, the Three Sisters of Glen Coe, tower over the glen. High on the north face of Aonach Dubh, the westernmost Sister, is Ossian's Cave, a dark slit like a huge keyhole in the sheer face of the mountain. There are no routes to the summit of Bidean nam Bian that can be described as easy and what tracks there are, are steep and narrow; however, there are two routes which are suitable for experienced hillwalkers.

From the cottage at the west end of Loch Achtriochtan a path leads south into Coire nam Beith (the best path is on the west side of the stream). The path is followed for a mile (1.5km) into the corrie, and the easiest route continues southwards to the west (or right) of the imposing peak of Stob Coire nam Beith. The climb is fairly easy and leads to the main ridge of the mountain just less than a mile (1.5km) north-west of Bidean nam Bian, and there is a fairly well-defined path up the ridge to the summit.

The other route starts at the Meeting of the Three Waters and crosses the River Coe by a footbridge just below the Meeting. On the south side of the river a well marked track bears south-westwards into the Coire Gabhail (the Lost Valley). As the corrie steepens into a narrow ravine the path is well-defined, though very narrow, among the birch trees on the north-west side of the stream. The Lost Valley is a remarkable and beautiful corrie; for several hundred metres the stream disappears under a jumble of huge boulders overgrown with trees and moss, and the path twists hither and thither eventually emerging in the upper corrie.

Beyond a level meadow the path climbs again (on the north-west side of the stream), and is followed until it peters out near the head of the corrie. From here Bidean can be reached either by climbing to the col at the head of the corrie and then up the south-east ridge, or alternatively by ascending westwards to reach the col on the north-east ridge between Bidean and Stob Coire nan Lochan.

Bidean nam Bian is a steep and complex mountain with its many ridges and corries, and in bad weather many parties have mistaken the correct route, particularly on the descent; it is therefore a mountain that calls for good navigation in bad weather.

Beinn A'Bheithir
Off A828 approx. 2m SW of Ballachulish.

Several miles west of Glen Coe, overlooking a new Ballachulish bridge across Loch Leven, are the twin peaks of Beinn a'Bheithir (1,024m). A road which leaves the main road half a mile (1km) west of the bridge leads into Gleann

a'Chaolais. A forest road (not accessible for cars) continues high up into the corrie, and is followed up the west side of the stream before bearing round to the east. The best way from this road through the trees to the hillside above is in the south-east corner of the corrie. A cairn by the roadside marks the start of a path uphill through the forest for a few hundred metres to reach the open corrie which is easily climbed to the lowest point of the ridge between the two peaks of the mountain. From there either Sgorr Dhonuill to the west or Sgorr Dhearg to the east may be climbed without difficulty.

Ben Nevis
Approx. 4m E of Fort William off A82.

Ben Nevis (1,344m), is Scotland's highest mountain and its great bulk looms over Fort William and the surrounding villages. Even the two large industrial complexes at its foot, an aluminium smelter and a pulp mill, are completely dwarfed. From Fort William the Ben appears as a huge rounded hump, and the summit is not well seen; however the traveller coming south from Spean Bridge has a glimpse of the grandeur of the mountain and its precipitous north face as he approaches Fort William.

Needless to say Ben Nevis is one of Scotland's most popular mountains for both rock-climbers and hillwalkers. A very well-made path starts in Glen Nevis at Achintee Farm two miles (3km) from Fort William, and climbs by many zig-zags to the great boulder-strewn summit plateau. (The climb may also be started in Glen Nevis at the Youth Hostel, crossing the river and climbing directly upwards to join the path.) The time for the ascent is likely to be three or four hours, and two for the descent. At the summit there are the remains of an old observatory, and the plateau drops on its northern edge in a series of huge cliffs, gullies and ridges, the highest in Britain.

Snow lingers on the mountain until summer and great care should be taken in approaching the edge of the summit plateau as huge snow cornices may be formed, particularly at the tops of the gullies.

Unfortunately the route up the path does not show the climber the best of Ben Nevis. This can only be seen by going to the north-east side of the mountain from where the grand scale of the cliffs can be appreciated. The route to this side of the mountain follows the ordinary route up the path to the plateau half way up the mountain and then follows a rather faint path over fairly flat ground for almost a mile (1km) northwards. (Lochan Meall an t-Suidhe is on one's left.) The remains of a fence are passed, and the path turns eastwards and descends slightly into the glen of the Allt a'Mhuilinn, reaching this stream near a small climbers' hut. At this point the entire north-east face of Ben Nevis rises above the glen in a grand succession of ridges and gullies.

To reach the summit of the mountain from the Allt a'Mhuilinn, the stream should be followd south-eastwards to its source in the rocky Coire Leis (there is another little shelter in this corrie). Then bearing south into the very head of the corrie a steep climb up boulders and scree leads to the ridge, known as the Carn Mor Dearg Arete, half a mile (0.75km) east of Ben Nevis. The final climb up boulders is marked near the top by several guiding posts. A finer, but more strenuous alternative which gives magnificent views is to climb from the Allt a'Mhuilinn to the summit of Carn Mor Dearg (1,223m), and then follows the delightful narrow ridge, the Carn Mor Dearg Arete, round to Ben Nevis.

The complete traverse of Carn Mor Dearg and Ben Nevis, starting from and returning to Glen Nevis, is a very fine but long expedition suitable for experienced hillwalkers in good, clear weather.

Stob Ban and Sgurr A'Mhaim
Approx. 6m SE of Fort William off A82.
Glen Nevis itself is worth a visit, in particular the fine gorge that separates the lower wooded glen from the desolate upper reaches. There is a good path through the gorge. On the south side of Glen Nevis is a fine chain of mountains, the Mamores. Two of the finest peaks of the Mamores can be easily climbed from the farm at Achriabhach in the glen, six miles (9km) from Fort William. Stob Ban (999m) is two and a half miles (3km) south of the farm and can be climbed by its north ridge or by the path up the Allt Coire a'Mhusgain and its east ridge. Sgurr a'Mhaim (1,099m), which is two miles (3km) south-east of Achriabhach, can be climbed by its north-west ridge directly to the summit.

4. CAIRNGORMS AND EASTERN GRAMPIANS
This group lies to the east of the main road from Perth to Inverness. The best known of these mountains are the Cairngorms, which include four, 1,200m mountains and the largest area of high altitude mountain plateau in Scotland. The climate and flora of this plateau are arctic and severe storms can occur at any time of the year.

The Cairngorms occupy the area between the Rivers Spey and Dee, two of Scotland's finest rivers. South of the Dee are the Eastern Grampians, massive rolling hills crossed by the road from Perth to Braemar over the Cairnwell pass. East of this road there is a high plateau culminating in Lochnagar (1,155m), while to the west there is a large expanse of rolling mountains dominated by Beinn a'Ghlo (1,129m) above Blair Atholl.

Cairn Gorm
Approx. 8m SE of Aviemore off A9, through Coylumbridge and Glen More Forest Park.
The Cairngorms are well known by virtue of the thriving ski centre in the Spey Valley and on Cairn Gorm itself. Cairn Gorm (1,245m) is in fact the most accessible high mountain in the whole of Scotland. A road from Aviemore goes past Loch Morlich to a car park at an altitude of about 670m in Coire Cas, about a mile (1.5km) north-west of the summit. From the car park a chairlift goes to within a few hundred

metres of the summit; alternatively an easy walk takes just over an hour.

In bad weather the walker should be particularly careful not to stray southwards from the top of Cairn Gorm, as the plateau is featureless and beyond it are steep cliffs. In fine weather however there is a good walk south-westwards from Cairn Gorm for two miles (3km) to Cairn Lochan (1,215m) with the cliffs of Coire an t-Sneachda and Coire an Lochain on one's right. From Cairn Lochan the return may be made by the same route; alternatively the walker can continue south-westwards for several hundred metres to the end of the Coire an Lochain cliffs, and then descend northwards to join the stream flowing from the corrie and so back to the car park in a north-easterly direction.

Ben Macdui
Approx. 10m SE of Aviemore off A9.
Ben Macdui (1,309m) is the highest of the Cairngorms and the second highest mountain in Scotland. Any approach involves a long walk, and as good a route as any since the construction of the Cairn Gorm road follows the previous route to Cairn Lochan. Half a mile (1km) before reaching this top the walker should strike south-south-west descending slightly to Lochan Buidhe, a distance of about a mile (1.5km). Finally there is a gentle climb for a mile and a half (2km) south to Ben Macdui. This route crosses a vast, featureless, stony plateau, and although there is a track marked by cairns for most of the way this is only an expedition for experienced hillwalkers in fine settled weather with good visibility.

Access to the Cairngorms from the south is longer as it is not usually possible to take a car beyond the Linn of Dee, and there is a long walk up Glen Derry or the River Dee to reach the mountains. Two very fine walking routes lead through the Cairngorms between Deeside and Speyside. They can be taken equally well in either direction and will be briefly described from south to north.

Lairig Ghru
N end of pass reached from the A9 5m SE of Aviemore.
The Lairig Ghru is the pass west of Ben Macdui which goes through magnificent wild scenery in the heart of the Cairngorms. From the Linn of Dee the way goes either up the River Dee or by Glen Derry and Glen Luibeg and the two routes converge near the Corrour Bothy, a little hut at the foot of the rocky Devil's Point. From there the route is well-defined, northwards through the deep glen ahead with a good path on the east side of the River Dee. Near the top of the pass the going is rough over boulders and past the tiny Pools of Dee, one of the sources of that river.

Once over the summit of the pass the first pine trees of Rothiemurchus Forest are reached in three miles (5km) and the remainder of the walk through the forest to Coylumbridge or Loch Morlich is delightful.

Lairig an Laoigh

S end of pass starts off A93 5m W of Braemar.

The other route, the Lairig an Laoigh, goes from the Linn of Dee to Derry Lodge in Glen Derry and then northwards to the head of this glen and, still northwards, into Glen Avon and round the east side of Bynack More, over the north ridge of this mountain to descend into Strath Nethy and so to Loch Morlich. This pass lacks the grand character of the Lairig Ghru.

Eastern Grampians

On the E side of the A93 between Blairgowrie and Braemar.

The Cairnwell Pass on the road between Perth and Braemar is a good starting point for the hills in this area.

Glas Maol (1,068m) on the east side of the pass is the highest hill in the area and can be easily climbed from the highest point of the road, which is a popular ski-ing area in winter. On the west side of the road there is a chairlift to within a few metres of the summit of Cairnwell (933m).

Lochnagar

Approx 10m SW of Ballater off A93, via Glen Muick.

Lochnagar (1,155m) is probably the most famous mountain in the north-east of Scotland, and its magnificent north-eastern corrie inspired Byron's verses in praise of "the steep frowning glories of dark Lochnagar". It is the highest point of a range of hills forming an almost continuous plateau stretching to Glas Maol nine miles (15km) to the south-west. The usual route to Lochnagar starts in Glen Muick (reached from Ballater in Deeside) at the Spittal, a mile (1.5km) below Loch Muick. A well-defined track leads westwards towards Lochnagar and continues northwards down Glen Gelder. Leaving this track near its highest point one follows a path up to the col between the little conical hill Meikle Pap and Lochnagar itself, and the magnificent north-eastern cliffs come into view. The path climbs to the plateau and continues with the cliffs on one's right hand, to the summit which lies beyond the edge of the corrie at its north-western end.

Beinn a' Ghlo and Ben Vrackie

Beinn a' Ghlo: 9m N of Pitlochry (or 7m NE of Blair Atholl). Ben Vrackie: approx 3m N of Pitlochry off A9.

The south-western corner of the Eastern Grampians is dominated by Beinn a' Ghlo (1,129m), whose three peaks rise above the pass of Killiecrankie north of Pitlochry.

The highest peak is the most remote, being nine miles (15km) from the main road; however Carn Laith, the lowest of the three peaks, can be easily reached from Blair Atholl by the road leading up Glen Fender to Loch Moraig. The climb is about three miles (4.5km) and six hundred metres of ascent over rising moorland to the final steep, but easy slopes.

Six miles (9km) south of Beinn a'Ghlo is Ben Vrackie (841m), a prominent hill overlooking Pitlochry and commanding a magnificent view of the wooded valleys of the rivers Tay, Tummel and Garry. This is a popular short climb and a path up the south side of the hill starts at the village of Moulin, a mile (1.5km) north of Pitlochry.

5. WESTERN HIGHLANDS

To the west of the Great Glen the country is entirely mountainous, intersected by glens and lochs running roughly east to west. Two main roads go through this area, the Fort William to Mallaig road and the road from Invergarry on Loch Oich through Glen Garry, Glen Moriston and Glen Shiel to Loch Duich on the west coast. On the north the area is bounded by the line of the road and railway from Inverness through Garve to Kyle of Lochalsh.

Many of the mountains in this area are quite remote, and few of them have the character of, say, Ben Nevis or Bidean nam Bian. Consequently they are less frequented than the Cairngorms or Central Highlands. Their remoteness, however, gives to them qualities of peace and solitude that are not found among the more popular mountains.

Garbh Bheinn

North of Glen Tarbert off A861 approx. 4m E of Strontian.

At the southern end of the group, Garbh Bheinn (885m) stands proudly above Loch Linnhe, well seen from Ballachulish Bridge. The mountain is approached along the road from Corran Ferry to Strontian through Glen Tarbert. The shortest route to Garbh Bheinn leaves this road at its highest point three miles (5km) west of Loch Linnhe and climbs steeply northwards to the summit, a horizontal distance of only a mile and a half (2km) but rough going. A less steep ascent can be made up the south-east ridge.

Rois-Bheinn

Approx. 3m S of Lochailort off the A861.

The western seaboard at Loch Ailort is dominated by a fine range of hills of which Rois-Bheinn (882m) is the highest. The ascent of this hill on a fine day will be rewarded by one of the finest views of the Highlands; the mainland mountains to the east and in the other direction the western seas and the many islands of the Hebrides. Rois-Bheinn can be climbed either by its long west ridge from Roshven Farm, or by the Alisary Burn where a narrow path, overgrown in places, leads up beside the newly planted forest.

Ladhar Bheinn and Sgurr na Ciche

In Knoydart, approached from Mallaig by ferry to Inverie.

The road from Fort William to Mallaig passes through magnificent mountain and loch scenery in country closely associated with Prince Charles and the ill-fated rising of 1745. Few of the mountains however are high enough to be outstanding, and northwards to Loch Arkaig and Loch Quoich the land is a tangle of lonely peaks and desolate glens. The western seaboard north of Mallaig is indented by magnificent fiord-like sea lochs, of which Loch Nevis and Loch Hourn are the finest. Near the head of these lochs are two very fine mountains, Ladhar Bheinn (1,020m) and Sgurr na Ciche (1,040m). They are both however very remote, and a lot of walking is involved to reach them. Ladhar Bheinn can be most easily climbed from Inverie on the north side of Loch Nevis, accessible by boat from Mallaig. Sgurr na Ciche involves a long approach walk from the head of Loch Arkaig up Glen Dessarry to the pass at its head.

Gleouraich
15m W of Invergarry, on N side of Loch Quoich
One of the most accessible hills in the Western Highlands is Gleouraich (1,035m) on the north side of Loch Quioch. Two and a half miles (4km) west of the Loch Quioch dam a stalkers' path strikes uphill through an overgrown patch of rhododendrons; this path zig-zags up the hillside and eventually ends half a mile (1km) from the summit. There is a faint track up the final ridge.

A'Chralaig and Sgurr nan Conbhairean
Approx. 15m NW of Invergarry, one the N side of Loch Cluanie off A87.
The road from Invergarry to Loch Duich passes through impressive mountains at the head of Glen Moriston and in Glen Shiel. The highest of these are A'Chralaig (1,120m) and Sgurr nan Conbhairean (1,109m), on the north side of Loch Cluanie. Both mountains are easily climbed from the road near the west end of this loch. The best starting point for A'Chralaig is one mile (1.5km) east of Cluanie Inn, and a steep climb north-north-east leads to the south ridge of the mountain which is easily followed to the top. The route to Sgurr nan Conbhairean starts three miles (5km) east of Cluanie Inn and goes directly up the easy south side of the mountain.

Sgurr Fhuaran
Approx 3m SE of Shiel Bridge off the A87.
Probably the best known mountains in this part of the Western Highlands are the Five Sisters of Kintail, a grand range on the north-east side of Glen Shiel, and well seen from Loch Duich a few miles to the west. The highest of the Five Sisters is Sgurr Fhuaran (1,068m), the middle peak of the range. The most direct route up Sgurr Fhuaran is its steep western ridge, starting at a footbridge about half a mile (1km) up the River Shiel from Shiel Bridge. This route is continuously steep, an unremitting climb of over a thousand metres, but it is not difficult and leads directly to the summmit.

Glen Affric, Cannich and Strathfarrar
In the north of the Western Highlands are the long and beautiful glens of Affric, Cannich and Strathfarrar.
These are worth visiting for the beauty of their wooded lower reaches, especially in autumn.
It is not however possible to drive to the heads

of these glens, and the approach to the mountains on foot is quite long. One of the finest expeditions in these hills is the cross-country walk from Glen Affric to Loch Duich. Starting at the Forestry Commission car park at the west end of Loch Beneveian, a good road, then a track leads along the north shore of Loch Affric and up the river of the same name to Alltbeath, where there is a small youth hostel. Beyond Alltbeath there is a choice of routes, either to the north or south of Beinn Fhada, but both routes lead to Croe Bridge at the head of Loch Duich.
This walk is not recommended in wet weather as there are two or three streams to be forded which may be difficult when in flood. The total distance is about eighteen miles (29km).

Carn Eighe and Mam Sodhail
Approx. 15m SW of Cannich off A831.
Carn Eighe (1,183m) and Mam Sodhail (1,181m) are the highest mountains in the Western Highlands, and can both be climbed in a long day starting from Loch Beneveian.
The path up Gleann nam Fiadh is followed for about four miles (6.5km) and the east ridge of Carn Eighe can then be easily reached by climbing north-westwards out of the glen. This ridge is followed for about two miles (3km) to the summit. There is a rather steep drop of 170 metres south-westwards from Carn Eighe, and an equal reascent to Mam Sodhail. The return from Mam Sodhail is best made along the ridge leading east-south-east for two miles (3.5km) to the outlying peak of Sgurr na Lapaich from which a steep but easy descent south-east leads to the wooded shore of Loch Affric. This is a long expedition, for fit climbers only, and will take about nine hours.

6. NORTHERN HIGHLANDS
The Northern Highlands are taken to include the entire mainland north and west of the road and rail line from Inverness through Garve to Kyle of Lochalsh. The area includes many of the finest mountains in Scotland and even some of the comparatively low peaks have great character.
In the south-west of this area, at the head of Loch Torridon, and overlooking Glen Torridon, are three very fine mountains, Ben Alligin (985m), Liathach (1,054m) and Beinn Eighe (1,010m). These are not single peaks, but each is a high ridge with several peaks. Ben Alligin and Liathach are of Torridonian sandstone, and Liathach in particular shows the characteristic stratification of terracing of sandstone mountains on its steep south face overlooking Glen Torridon. The eastern peaks of Liathach are capped with white quartzite, and Beinn Eighe is largely a quartzite mountain, giving it the impression of being permanently snow-covered.
These mountains are very steep and rocky and there are few easy routes of ascent and descent.

Ben Alligin
Approx. 3m NW of Torridon village off A896.
Ben Alligin is probably the easiest of the three

to climb. A good route starts at the road bridge over the stream coming down the Coire Mhic Nobuil two miles (3km) west of Torridon village. From the bridge a line north-west across rather rough and trackless hillside is taken for about a mile (1.5km) to reach the bottom of a little corrie between two steep buttresses. A faint path leads up this corrie ands gradually turns northwards and leads up easy open slopes to Tom na Gruagach, the southern and lower peak of Ben Alligin. The ridge to Sgurr Mor, the highest peak, drops steeply at first and is quite narrow, but there is a faint track and beyond the col the ascent is easy. The easiest descent route back to the day's starting point is to retrace the route of ascent.

For those wishing to complete the traverse, descend steeply eastwards to a col and climb over three small rocky peaks, the Horns of Alligin (some rocky scrambling is involved but this can be avoided by traversing along a narrow path on the south side of the Horns). Finally the descent south-eastwards leads to a good stalkers' path in the corrie.

The direct descent into this corrie from the col just mentioned is very steep and should only be attempted with great caution.

Liathach
Off A896, 2m NE of Torridon village.
Liathach is altogether a more formidable proposition for the climber. Its two highest peaks are separated by a mile and a half (2km) ridge, part of which is very narrow with numerous pinnacles.

The traverse of these pinnacles involves some quite difficult scrambling, although it is possible to avoid most of the difficulties by a narrow path which traverses below the pinnacles on the south side of the ridge. The best route up the western peak, Mullach an Rathain, starts near two small pine woods at the foot of Glen Torridon, and bears more or less directly north to the summit. The route is steep in places and there are bands of sandstone which can for the most part be avoided. The big scree-filled gully descending south-west from the Mullach to Torridon village is not recommended as a route.

It is possible to climb the eastern and highest peak, Spidean a'Choire Leith, from Glen Torridon, starting half a mile (0.75km) east of Glen Cottage. Climb steeply (at first by a path) beside a stream, and continue more or less straight up, bearing right as the ridge is approached, to reach the summit ridge at a col 0.75 mile (1km) east of the summit of Spidean a'Choire Leith. Great care is necessary on the descent of Liathach because of the terracing of the sandstone.

Beinn Eighe
Between Torridon and Kinlochewe off A896.
Beinne Eighe is quite different in appearance from Liathach, its smooth white slopes of quartzite contrasting with the dark terraced walls of its western neighbour. The smooth slopes are deceptive however, and the angular

quartzite rock and scree make ridge walking on Beinn Eighe rough work, but the grandeur of the mountain compensates for this. A fairly easy route leaves Glen Torridon at the ruined cottage at the foot of Coire Dubh and climbs northwards to reach the main ridge; with careful route selection most of the unpleasant quartz screes can be avoided.

Alternatively a start may be made a mile and a half (2km) further east, near Loch Bharranch, and a track followed north-westwards towards a prominent spur, which leads in turn to the main ridge. Once on the main ridge by either of these routes the summit, Ruadh-stac-Mor, is a mile and a half (2.5km) away to the north-west. The intervening ridge is easy, but in bad visibility care is needed to follow the northward running ridge to Ruadh-stac-Mor. Alternatively, once the main ridge is reached it may be followed north-eastwards to Sgurr Ban, and eastwards over another peak and down a broad ridge towards Kinlochewe.

Liathach is in land owned by the National Trust for Scotland, and the eastern end of Beinn Eighe is a nature reserve under the control of the Nature Conservancy Council. Information about these mountains regarding walking and climbing routes, flora and fauna may be had from the Trust warden at Torridon or the NCC warden at Kinlochewe.

Slioch
Approx. 4m NW of Kinlochewe off the A832.
Five miles (8km) north-west of Kinlochewe is the imposing peak of Slioch (980m), rising steeply above Loch Maree. A pleasant walk from Kinlochewe leads to the head of the loch along the north side of the Kinlochewe River, and a good path up the west side of Glen Bianasdail is followed for a mile and a half (2km). A prominent stream is then followed north-westwards up a corrie called the Tuill Bhain to the summit. Slioch is a deer sanctuary and should not be climbed during the stalking season.

An Teallach
Off the A832 approx. 3m S of Dundonnell.
Ten miles (16km) north of Kinlochewe and accessible from the road near Dundonnell at the head of Little Loch Broom is the magnificent mountain An Teallach (1,062m). Like the Torridon mountains, An Teallach is not a single peak, but a complex mountain of several peaks, ridges and corries. One of these corries, the Toll an Lochan, is particularly worth a visit for its superb scenery. The easiest route to the highest peak, Bidein a'Ghlas Thuill, leaves the road half a mile (1km) east of Dundonnell Hotel and follows a path south-eastwards. This path ends high up on a broad stony ridge 1.5 miles (2km) north of Bidein, and the final part of the climb goes south along this ridge over two knolls.

The traverse of the ridge on the south-west side of Toll an Lochan is a very fine climb, but like the traverse of Liathach it involves scrambling. The best approach to this ridge is up the good path which leaves the road three and a half miles (5km) south-east of Dundonnell Hotel. The path is followed for three miles (4km) and a way is then made westwards towards Sail Liath (this route can also be used as an approach to the Toll and Lochan). From Sail Liath the ridge is followed along its rocky crest to Sgurr Fiona, then a steep descent and reascent leads to Bidein a'Ghlas Thuill from where the descent may be made by the route described above.

Stac Pollaidh
Approx. 18m N of Ullapool on the W side of A835.
The country north of Ullapool and east of Lochinver is a wild stretch of desolate moorland studded with lochs, and from it rise several remarkable small mountains of Torridonian sandstone, each one quite isolated from its neighbours. Stac Pollaidh (613m) is easily climbed from the roadside between Drumrunie Lodge and Achiltibuie.
Starting at a car park immediately below the peak, a well-trodden path leads round the eastern end and up gravelly slopes on the north side to reach the summit ridge. This ridge is narrow and crowned by many little pinnacles and towers, and it provides a delightful walk (with occasional scrambling) to the summit which is at the western end.

Cul Beag and Cul Mor
Approx. 18m N of Ullapool on the W side of A835.
To the east of Stac Pollaidh are the twin hills Cul Beag (769m) and Cul Mor (849m), which can be easily climbed by their eastern slopes. The western ends of both peaks are steep sandstone buttresses.

Suilven
4m SE of Lochinver off A837.
Four miles (6km) north of Cul Mor is the remarkable peak of Suilven (731m). Seen from the north or south it appears as a long serrated ridge; however, from Lochinver to the north-west or from Ledmore to the south-east, it appears as a single peak of great steepness. The summit, Caisteal Liath, is at the north-west end of the ridge. The approach from Lochinver involves a walk of about five miles (8km) past Glen Canisp Lodge to the north side of the mountain; then the gully leading to the col east of Caisteal Liath is climbed and once on the ridge the summit is reached by a short and easy climb.

Quinag
Off A837 to the N of Loch Assynt 6m NE of Lochinver.
Several miles north of Suilven, and rising above the northern side of Loch Assynt is Quinag (808m), a fine mountain with three distinct ridges and several tops of which the eastern ones are capped with white quartzite. The easiest approach is from the Inchnadamph to Kylesku road, starting about two miles (3km) north of Skiag Bridge and heading westwards

up easy quartzite slopes to the south-eastern peak, Spidean Coinich.
Continuing north-west for almost a mile (1.5km) over a small top the junction of the three ridges is reached at Point 745m and from there the highest point of Quinag is half a mile (1km) east-north-east along an easy ridge. The northern buttresses of Quinag are very steep, and the west side of the mountain is a long escarpment.

Ben Hope
7m SW of Tongue at the S end of Loch Hope.
In the extreme north of Scotland, in the country of Sutherland and overlooking the wild northern coast, are the outposts of the Scottish Highlands, Ben Hope and Ben Loyal. Roads are few here, but Tongue and Durness are good bases for approaching these mountains by car. Ben Hope (927m) has a steep western face and its north ridge has a short difficult section, so the easiest route starts south-west of the summit about a mile (1.5km) north of the broch at Dun Dornadilla in Strathmore. After the first steep climb the long, broad south ridge is reached and followed easily to the top.

Ben Loyal
Approx. 5m S of Tongue off the A836.
Ben Loyal (764m) is probably best climbed from Ribigill Farm, two miles (3km) south of Tongue, from where it presents a striking appearance. A good track leads south across the moor towards the very steep peak of Chaonasaid, and the climber should head south-eastwards below the foot of this peak to reach easy grassy slopes beyond. It is then possible to climb in a south-westerly direction to reach the summit ridge of Ben Loyal of which Chaonasaid is the northern terminal. The highest peak, A'Chaisteal, is half a mile (1km) south. The west side of Ben Loyal is very steep. The east side is moorland and an easy, but rather uninteresting, ascent can be made on this side starting from Loch Loyal.
Of the other mountain ranges in the Northern Highlands mention may be made of the Fanaichs near the southern edge of this area, the Beinn Dearg group south-east of Ullapool, and the Reay Forest near Ben Hope. Many of the mountains in these groups are quite remote and few of them have the individual characteristics of the mountains just described.

7. ISLANDS
Of Scotland's many islands only a few are mountainous, the most notable being Arran, Mull, Skye and Harris. (The Island of Rhum is also mountainous, but the island is under the control of the Nature Conservancy Council and access to its mountains requires permission.)

Arran
This is the Southernmost of these four mountainous islands, and is easily reached by regular steamer services to Brodick (car ferries from Ardrossan).
The mountains of Arran are in the northern

half of the island, north of Brodick, and two fine glens, Glen Rosa and Glen Sannox, give access to them. The walk up Glen Rosa and down Glen Sannox, crossing the pass between them known as the Saddle is a good walk.

Goatfell, Cir Mhor and A'Chir
Approx. 3m NW of Brodick off A841.
The highest mountain is Goatfell (874m), and it is easily climbed by a path starting near Brodick Castle, a mile and a half (2km) north of Brodick The path is well-defined and climbs the lower moorland in a northerly direction to the eastern shoulder of Goatfell, and so to the top. The ascent can equally well be made from Corrie by a path starting at the south end of the village.

The return may be varied by going northwards along a fine ridge to North Goatfell and then descending north-west to the Saddle. This ridge has some rocky tors, but there is a fair path for most of the way. Cir Mhor (798m) is the beautiful pointed peak at the head of Glens Rosa and Sannox. It may be climbed from either glen by the Saddle and up its steep eastern ridge. If approaching from Glen Rosa, however, it is easier to climb up the left or west side of the peak and climb the easy south-west ridge.

Probably the most pleasant, and certainly the best known climb in Arran, is the traverse of the A'Chir ridge south-west of Cir Mhor. The scramble along the crest of this very narrow ridge is exhilarating, but there are two or three points of difficulty, so it is not for the inexperienced climber.

Mull
Ben More
Approx. 6m S of Salen off B8035.
The island of Mull is reached by steamer from Oban on the mainland, from which it is separated by the Firth of Lorne. Most of the island is rough moorland and low hills. The highest peak is Ben More (966m), which commands a magnificent view of mountains, lochs and islands. The usual route of ascent starts from the side of Loch na Keal about seven miles (10km) south-west of Salen and goes directly up the north-west ridge of the mountain.

Skye
The island of Skye is, of course, famous for the Cuillin mountains. It must be stressed that these are the steepest and the rockiest mountains in Britain and there are only a few summits than can be reached without rock climbing, or at least a good deal of rough scrambling. The mountains are often cloud-covered and the magnetic compass is not reliable, so they should only be climbed in settled, clear weather. Detailed description of the best routes to individual peaks in the Cuillins can be found in the Scottish Mountaineering Club's "Island of Skye" guidebook and the 1:15000 map of the Black Cuillin is also very useful. A few of the easiest and most popular peaks are described below.

Sgurr nan Gillean
Approx. 3m S of Sligachan off A850.
From Sligachan Hotel at the north end of the range Sgurr nan Gillean (965m) is the most prominent peak. The 'tourist route' starts opposite the hotel and crosses the Red Burn by a footbridge. Thereafter the path, which is at times indistinct, crosses the moorland southwards towards the east of the peak and eventually after a steep climb up scree, reaches the south-east ridge of the peak a short distance from the top.

Bruach na Frithe
Approx. 3m SW of Sligachan off A850.
There is a good path from Sligachan past Cuillin Lodge and up the Red Burn to Glen Brittle over a pass called the Bealach a'Mhaim. From the top of the pass Bruach na Frithe (958m) may be quite easily climbed by its north-west ridge. Only the last part of the ridge is narrow and involves some easy scrambling.

Sgurr Dearg
Approx. 5m S of Sligachan off A850. Hills approached from Glen Brittle.
Glen Brittle is the climbing centre of the Cuillins, and there are countless excellent climbs for experienced rock climbers. Sgurr Dearg (986m) can be fairly easily climbed up its west ridge, starting near Glen Brittle House. The Inaccessible Pinnacle is a few metres beyond the Sgurr Dearg cairn and some eight metres higher, but it is a difficult rock climb to reach the top.

Sgurr Alasdair
Approx. 6m S of Sligachan off A850. Hills approached from Glen Brittle.
The well trodden (and usually muddy) path from Glen Brittle to Coire Lagan is the rock climbers' trade route, and th corrie is worth a visit for its magnificent rock scenery. Beyond Loch Coire Lagan the mountains rise in huge cliffs and scree slopes. Sgurr Alasdair (993m) in the south-east corner of the corrie is the highest of the Cuillins, and it can be climbed from Coire Lagan by the long and steep cree gully called the Great Stone Shoot. This is not a particularly pleasant climb and there is some danger from falling stones dislodged by other climbers in the gully.

Loch Coruisk
Best approached by boat from Elgol off A881.
In the centre of the great horseshoe ridge of the Cuillins is Loch Coruisk, probably the wildest and grandest of all Scottish lochs. It may be reached from Glen Brittle by one of several passes over the Cuillin ridge, but none of these is exactly easy. The easiest approach to the loch is either by boat from Mallaig or Elgol, or by walking from Kilmarie in Strathaird by Camasunary and along the side of Loch Scavaig. This is a fine walk, following a rough road at first and then a well-defined footpath above Loch Scavaig with wonderful views of the Cuillins ahead. There is one very short

difficult section near Loch Coruisk where the path crosses a steep slabby buttress by a narrow ledge known as the Bad Step.

Blaven (Bla Bheinn)
3m W of Torrin off A881 at the head of Loch Slapin.
Blaven (928m) is the highest mountain in the group east of the Cuillin main ridge, and like the Cuillins it is a steep and rocky mountain of rough gabbro rock. The ascent from the head of Loch Slapin near the village of Torrin is quite easy. A prominent stream, the Allt na Dunaiche, comes down from Blaven, and a good path goes up the north side of this stream. After about a mile (1.5km) the path ascends south-west into the Coire Uaigneich to reach the broad and rocky south-east face of Blaven which is followed to the top. The view from the Blaven westwards to the complete Cuillin main ridge is quite magnificent.

Trotternish
N of Portree off the A855.
In the north of the island of Skye there are two short but rewardsing climbs in the Trotternisdh peninsula. The Old Man of Storr is a spectacular pinnacle about six miles (9km) north of Portree, and it stands at the foot of the steep cliffs of the Storr (719m).
This is an area of bizarre rock scenery and it can be easily reached from the road between Portree and Staffin, at a point where there is a car park from which a footpath leads up the hillside through recently planted forest. The Storr can be climbed by a steep climb up grassy slopes either north or south of the main cliffs, but these are routes which call for care. The Old Man and other pinnacles shoudl be admired but not climbed as they are very difficult and the rocks are treacherously loose.
Ten miles (16km) further north is the Quiraing, a spectacular group of pinnacles overlooking the village of Staffin. The shortest approach is from a point about a mile and a half (2km) up the road from Staffin to Uig, and a walk north-westwards below the main line of cliffs brings one below the Needle, a spectacular pinnacle. A short steep climb beyond the Needle leads to a strange amphitheatre called the Prison. Here enclosed by cliffs on one side and a line of rock towers on the other, is a raised platform – The Table – covered with grass.
The exploration of the Quiraing is a most interesting walk; there are adequate narrow footpaths, but no attempts should be made to climb the rocks which are dangerously loose.

Harris
Clisham
4m N of Tarbert off the A859.
The Outer Hebrides are for the most part rather low-lying islands. The biggest group of mountains is in the northern part of Harris, and Clisham (799m) the highest of these, is worth climbing for the very fine view from the summit. A start may be made from a point on the road from Tarbert to Stornoway (on Lewis) about a mile and a half (2km) due south of the summit. The climb is quite short and easy over rising moorland to the final steep slopes of the mountain which are probably best taken by the south-east ridge.

OFF-ROAD CYCLING – A CODE FOR SCOTLAND

Preamble

With the advent of the mountain or all-terrain bike more people are cycling off-road, away from busy public roads. Off-road cycling can be fun, but it has its own hazards, and it brings obligations to respect the interest of land managers and owners and to show courtesy to other recreations. This code gives basic advice on access to land in Scotland, on safety and on maintaining goodwill with other users of the countryside.

Access

Access to land in Scotland has long been conducted as a matter of courtesy, tolerance and goodwill. However, there is no legal right to access to land, except on a right-of-way or where access has been specially negotiated.

By law, the off-road cyclist is entitled to use cycle-tracks and those public rights-of-way where a right to cycle exists under common law. The right of the cyclist to cycle on pedestrian rights-of-way is not clear. There are permissive routes (as provided by bodies like the Forestry Commission) and many private and public owners do allow access to cyclists. Many of the traditional tracks through the glens will have right-of-way status for cycles, where use by cyclists has continued over the years, and where the route meets the other tests for a right-of-way. Always be considerate and courteous when taking access, and ask when in doubt.

THE CODE

Think about others

Cycle with consideration for others, always giving way to walkers and horse riders and to farm and forest workers. Give a friendly greeting to people you meet and acknowledge the courtesy of those who give way for you. Watch your speed when close to others.

- Try to avoid places that are heavily used by pedestrians, especially family groups – always walk through congested areas. Don't alarm walkers by coming up silently behind them.
- Respect other land management activities e.g. Don't pass close to forestry operations until told that it is safe to pass, or disturb sheep gathering or game shooting.
- Dismount where necessary to avoid disturbing farm animals.
- Follow the Country Code

Take care of the environment

- Keep to hard tracks and paths, avoiding shortcuts on paths.
- Walk over very soft ground to avoid cutting it up.
- Avoid fierce braking and skids on downhill riding to minimise damage to path surfaces.
- Don't take bikes onto high mountain tops and plateaux where vegetation is easily damaged.
- Leave no impacts in remote areas. In particular, take all litter home.
- Take special care when cycling downhill – this is when most accidents occur. Watch your speed on loose surfaces.
- Upland Scotland can be rough and remote – cycle within your abilities as an accident or a breakdown in a remote place could be serious.

**UNDERSTAND
THE BASICS OF MOUNTAIN SAFETY**

- Take a companion in remote areas.
- Think about weather hazards.
- Remember that crossing burns and rivers in spate can be dangerous.
- Take a map and know how to navigate.
- Carry warm and waterproof clothing, emergency food, a lamp and tools.
- Consider wearing a helmet and protective clothing if riding at speed or in rough country.

ALSO Your bike should be legal for use on the road. And don't arrange competition without the consent of landowners or the guidance of the Scottish Cyclist Union. Seek consent for rallies or large groups.

DUMFRIES & GALLOWAY

CARRICK FOREST
1 mile south of Dalmellington. Off the A713 follow minor public road beside Loch Doon.
Contact: Forest Enterprise, 55 Moffat Road, Dumfries DG1 1NP. Tel: (0387) 69171.
Loch Doon - Barr through route (red markers) - 20 miles moderate on minor roads.

CLATTERINGSHAWS
Start at Clatteringshaws Forest Wildlife Centre, 6 miles west of New Galloway.
Contact: Forest Enterprise, 55 Moffat Road, Dumfries DG1 1NP. Tel: (0387) 69171.
Clatteringshaws Loch Route (green) 14 miles easy
Craignell Hill Route (purple) 15 miles moderate
Deer Range Route (blue) 9 miles demanding
Benniguinea Viewpoint Route (red) 4 miles demanding
Car park. Information centre. Refreshments.

DALBEATTIE FOREST
Start at Richorn car park on B793, south of Dalbeattie.
Contact: Forest Enterprise, 55 Moffat Road, Dumfries DG1 1NP. Tel: (0387) 69171.
Moyle Hill Route (green) 7 miles easy
Ironhash Hill Route (purple) 11 miles moderate
Car park.

FOREST OF AE
2 miles from Ae village on unclassified road. 7.5 miles N of Dumfries on A701 between Ae Bridge and Loch Ettrick.
Contact: Forest Commission, 55 Moffat Road, Dumfries DG1 1NP. Tel: (0387) 69171.
Windy Hill Route (green) 10 miles easy

Greenhill & Whaup Knowe Route (purple) 7.5 miles moderate
Upper Ae Route (red) 15 miles moderate

GLENTROOL FOREST
Start east of Glentrool village, off the A714 at the Stroan Bridge car park between the village and Loch Trool.
Contact: Forest Enterprise, 55 Moffat Road, Dumfries DG1 1NP. Tel: (0387) 69171.
Minniwick Route (red) 5 miles easy
Balunton Hill Route (blue) 7 miles moderate
Palgowan Route (green) 8 miles moderate
Borgan Route (purple) 10 miles moderate
Car park.

KIRROUGHTREE FOREST
Start east of Newton Stewart off the A75 at the Kirroughtree Visitor Centre.
Contact: Forest Enterprise, 55 Moffat Road, Dumfries DG1 1NP. Tel: (0387) 69171.
Palnure Burn Route (blue) 4 miles easy
Larg Hill Route (green) 7 miles moderate
Dallash Route (purple) 10 miles moderate
Old Edinburgh Route (red) 18 miles moderate.
Car park. Visitor Centre.

MABIE FOREST
4 miles south-west of Dumfries off the A710 at the Old Quarry.
Contact: Forest Enterprise, 55 Moffat Road, Dumfries DG1 1NP. Tel: (0387) 69171.
Woodhead Route (green) 4 miles easy
Craigend Hill Route (purple) 8 miles moderate
Lochbank Route (blue) 10 miles moderate
Marthrown Hill Route (red) 3.5 miles demanding
Car park.

BORDERS

There are twelve hundred miles of quiet roads which meander across moors, through forests and along the coast. The area is also criss-crossed by hill tracks and drove roads, which are readily explored by all-terrain bicycles.
Contact: Scottish Borders Tourist Board, Municipal Buildings, Selkirk TD7 4JX. Tel: (0750) 20555.

FOLLOW THE COUNTRY CODE

SET A GOOD EXAMPLE
AND TRY TO FIT IN WITH THE
LIFE AND WORK OF THE COUNTRYSIDE

Please mention this Pastime Publications guide.

LOTHIAN

EDINBURGH - WATER OF LEITH
Contact: Edinburgh District Council, Planning Dept., 1 Cockburn Street, Edinburgh EH1 1BJ. Tel: 031-225 2424, ext. 6570.
From the mouth of the Water of Leith to Balerno, the wooded valley route follows a former railway branch line. 10 miles. Picnic areas.

EDINBURGH
Edinburgh has an extensive network of short and long cycle routes. These can be best explored using the Spokes Cycle Map of Edinburgh or guides produced by Edinburgh District Council or Lothian Regional Council.
Contacts: Edinburgh District Council, Planning Dept., 1 Cockburn Street, Edinburgh EH1 1BJ. Tel: 031-225 2424, ext. 6510.
Lothian Regional Council, Highways Dept., 19 Market Street, Edinburgh EH1 1BL. Tel: 031-229 9292, ext. 4691.
Spokes, St. Martin Church, 232 Dalry Road, Edinburgh EH11 2JG. Tel: 031-313 2114.

HADDINGTON - LONGNIDDRY CYCLEWAY
Using the disused Haddington to Longniddry branch line, offering spectacular views from the elevated embankments. 7km.
Contact: Lothian Regional Council, Highways Dept., 19 Market Street, Edinburgh EH1 1BL. Tel: 031-229 9292, ext 4691.

LINLITHGOW TO SOUTH QUEENSFERRY
Starting at Linlithgow Station, which has regular train services from Edinburgh, Glasgow and Stirling, this 14km route makes use of minor roads.
Contact: Planning Dept., West Lothian District Council. Tel: (0506) 843121.

LIVINGSTON VILLAGE - CRAIGSHILL - MID CALDER
A shared footpath/cycleway of 5km beginning at Old Livingston village, through Almondvale Park and onto Almond Park.
Contact: Livingston Development Corporation. Tel: (0506) 414177.

NEWBRIDGE TO QUEENSFERRY CYCLEWAY
A 7km route constructed on disused railway. Gives excellent views of the Forth rail and road bridges.
Contact: Lothian Regional Council, Highways Dept., 19 Market Street, Edinburgh EH1 1BL. Tel: 031-229 9292, ext 4691.

PENCAITLAND RAILWAY ROUTE
12km disused railway from West Saltoun, through Pencaitland and Ormiston to Crossgatehill. Picnic areas.
Contact: Lothian Regional Council, Highways Dept., 19 Market Street, Edinburgh EH1 1BL. Tel: 031-229 9292, ext. 4691.

PENICUIK TO BONNYRIGG CYCLEWAY
The 10km cycleway begins at Eskbridge Station at the foot of Kirkhill Road in Penicuik, following the old Edinburgh to Peebles railwayline. Lights might be advisable to negotiate the tunnel after Auchendinny Station.
Contact: Midlothian District Council, Recreational Leisure Dept. Tel: 031-440 0352.

RIVER ESK
A 5km route along the banks of River Esk.
Contact: Leisure, Recreation & Tourism Dept., East Lothian District Council. Tel: 031-665 3711.

STRATHCLYDE

GLASGOW TO KILLIN CYCLEWAY

The Glasgow-Loch Lomond-Killin cycleway takes you from the centre of Glasgow into the heart of the Scottish Highlands. There's a mixture of canal towpaths, quiet side roads, disused railways and forest tracks that take you 86 miles from Glasgow.

a. To Loch Lomond

Start at Scottish Exhibition Centre.
18 miles. Moderate.
Contact: Director of Planning, City of Glasgow Planning Dept., 231 George Street, Glasgow G1 1RX. Tel: 041-227 5701.

b. Balloch to Aberfoyle

27 miles long of which 13 miles are on way-marked tracks in Loch Ard Forest.

c. Aberfoyle to Callander

The route starts at Braeval just east of Aberfoyle. 5 miles.

d. Aberfoylde to Loch Ard to Callander

Utilises the quiet B829 to Stronachlacher and returns on the motor-free road down Strach Gartney (15 miles).

To Killin

At end of main street in Callander. Follow the old railway track past the Falls of Leny, Loch Lubnacy and on the Strathyre. Use the tiny back road to Balquhidder along the A84 and back onto the old railway. 26 miles.

PAISLEY TO GREENOCK CYCLEWAY

Despite the name this 10 mile route on the bed of an old railway goes as far as Kilmacolm, but should soon be extended to Greenock.
Contact: Director of Planning, Renfrew District Council, Municipal Buildings, Cotton Street, Paisley PA1 1BU. Tel: 041-889 5400.

GLASGOW TO IRVINE PEDESTRIAN/ CYCLE ROUTE

This is a shared facility, so consideration should be given to other users.

a. PAISLEY TO LOCHWINNOCH

The first 3 miles are shared which the Paisley to Greenock route. At mile marker 12 it veers south to Kilbarchan, then on to Lochwinnoch. 9 miles.
Contact: Cunninghame District Council, Cunninghame House, Irvine KA12 2AH. Tel: (0294) 74166.

b. LOCHWINNOCH TO KILWINNING

This 13 mile stretch is on minor roads for 7 miles, the rest on the old railway.
From Kilwinning you can do three miles on old railway to Irvine, or five and a half to Ardrossan.

CENTRAL

a. To Loch Lomond

Start at Scottish Exhibition Centre.
18 miles. Moderate.
Contact: Director of Planning, City of Glasgow Planning Dept., 231 George Street, Glasgow G1 1RX. Tel: 041-227 5701.

b. Balloch to Aberfoyle

27 miles long of which 13 miles are on way-marked tracks in Loch Ard Forest.

c. Aberfoyle to Callander

The route starts at Braeval just east of Aberfoyle. 5 miles.

d. Aberfoylde to Loch Ard to Callander

Utilises the quiet B829 to Stronachlacher and returns on the motor-free road down Strach Gartney (15 miles).

FIFE

Tentsmuir Forest
Contact: Forest Enterprise, Clentry, Kelty, Fife KY4 0JQ. Tel: (0383) 830240.
Close to Leuchars, between the estuaries of the Tay and Eden. Up to 12 miles on way marked routes, with other options available on the forest tracks and roads.
Car park. Public toilets. Picnic site.

TAYSIDE

Waymarked routes are available in Craigvinean (Dunkeld) and Drummond Hill (Kenmore) Forests.

Contact: Forest Enterprise, Queens View Centre, Loch Tummel, Perthshire. Tel: 0796 473123.

GRAMPIAN

Cyclists are free to use many miles of open forest roads, on Forestry Commission land within this region. Contact should be made with the local forester for information.
Buchan: Forest Enterprise, Buchan Forest District Office, Huntly. Tel: 0466 794161.
Kincardine: Forest Enterprise, Kincardine Forest District Office, Banchory. Tel: 033 044 537.

Bunzeach Cross Country Ski/Mountain Bike Trails
2 miles east of Strathdon on the A97.
Contact: Forest Enterprise, Buchan Forest District, Ordiquhill, Portsoy Road, Huntly, Aberdeenshire AB54 4SJ. Tel: 0466 794161.

Gartly Moor Cross Country Ski/Mountain Bike Trail
6 miles south east of Huntly. Two miles off the A96.
Contact: Forest Enterprise, Buchan Forest District, Ordiquhill, Portsoy Road, Huntly, Aberdeenshire AB54 4SJ. Tel: 0466 794161.

Pitfichie Cross Country Ski/Mountain Bike Trails
Near B993, north of Monymusk, 8 miles west of Inverurie.

Contact: Forest Enterprise, Buchan Forest District, Ordiquhill, Portsoy Road, Huntly, Aberdeenshire AB54 4SJ. Tel: 0466 794161.

HIGHLAND

Forestry Commission areas offer ideal opportunities to cycle on quiet, open forest roads. For further information contact the local forestry officer.
Dornoch: Forest Enterprise, Dornoch Forest District Tel: 0862 810359.
Easter Ross: Forest Enterprise, Dingwall. Tel: (0349) 62144.
Fort Augustus: Forest Enterprise, Fort Augustus Forest District, Fort Augustus. Tel: 0320 6322.
Inverness: Forest Enterprise, Inverness Forest District, Inverness Tel: 0463 791575.
Moray: Forest Enterprise, Moray Forest District, Balnacoul. Tel: 0343 820223.
Lorne: Forest Enterprise, Lorne Forest District, Oban. Tel: 0631 66155.

GUIDED MOUNTAIN BIKE TOURS

Leave from the Slochd on Saturday morning and arrive back on the following Friday

June 12th to 18th ● July 10th to 16th ● July 24th to 30th
Aug 7th to 14th ● Aug 21st to 27th ● Sept 11th to 17th

Contact: Ian Bishop, Wade Road Mountain Bikes, Slochd, Carrbridge, Inverness-shire PH23 3AY.
Tel: 047 984 666. Fax: 047 984 699.

SCOTTISH ISLANDS

ARRAN
Contact: Forest Enterprise, Brodick, Isle of Arran KA27 8BZ. Tel: (0770) 2218.
Varied routes on forest routes, many with car parks and picnic sites.

CONTACT ORGANISATIONS

Scottish Cyclist Union,
The Velodrome,
Meadowbank Stadium,
London Road,
Edinburgh EH7 6AD.
Tel: 031-652 0187.

Cyclists Touring Club,
69 Meadrow,
Godalming,
Surrey GU7 3HS.
Tel: (04868) 7217.

CANAL ROUTES

Scotland's canals, Highland or Lowland, provide easy, level cycling through some fine scenery with plenty of historical interest.

A permit is required for many sections. Contact should be made with the appropriate canal office.

CALEDONIAN CANAL – TOWPATH
Joining the east to the west coasts and linking Lochs Ness, Oich and Lochy, the banks of the Caledonian Canal offer fine views of the Great Glen at numerous points. Here are two attractive stretches.

Contact: Large groups contact Caledonian Canal Office, Clachnaharry Road, Inverness IV3 6RA. Tel: 0463 233140.

CRINAN CANAL – TOWPATH
Ardrishaig to Crinan. A83 Ardrishaig. Crinan B841. 9 miles/14.4km NW of Lochgilphead.

Contact: Crinan Canal Office, Pier Square, Ardrishaig PA30 8DZ. Tel: 0546 3210.

Canal towpath through conservation area (Bellanoch & Crinan). Superb views at Crinan end. Canal architecture of great charm and character. 10 miles/16km.

Open all year. Car park. Picnic areas.

FORTH & CLYDE CANAL
Take Bowling turn-off from A82 out of Glasgow, turn left at "Bowling Pottery" sign, cross railway bridge, bear left into car park or cross drawbridge on foot to gain access to towing path.

Contact: Forth & Clyde Canal Countryside Ranger, British Waterways Board, Canal House, Applecross Street, Glasgow G4 9SP. Tel: 041-332 6936.

Once connecting coast to coast via Bowling on the Clyde and Grangemouth on the Forth, this canal has recently undergone some renovation for recreational usage. Much of the canal offers interesting walking and the 33$^{1/2}$ miles/54km can be explored in convenient sections. These include Bowling-Dalmuir, Glasgow branch-Maryhill, around Cadder and Kirkintilloch, Twechar-Barrhill, Auchinstarry-Craigmarloch near Kilsyth, and other stretches towards Falkirk. Bowling to Kirkintilloch, Castlecary to Falkirk have surfaced towpaths. Features include industrial archaeology, historic monuments, varied plant and animal life, woodlands and the Roman remains along the parallel Antonine Wall (2-3 days).

Open all year. Car park. Picnic areas.

MONKLAND CANAL
Towpaths have now been reinstated from Calderbank to Drumpellier with plans to link with Summerlee Heritage Park.

Contact: Greater Glasgow Tourist Board, 35 St. Vincent Place, Glasgow G1 2ER. Tel: 041-204 4400

UNION CANAL – TOWPATH
The Union Canal once linked Edinburgh with Glasgow, joining the Forth-Clyde Canal at Falkirk. Like the Forth-Clyde Canal it has now been revitalised for recreational usage, though cut in a few places by new roads and other needs. It can be walked in convenient sections – for example Falkirk-Lathallan Road (A801) and then to Linlithgow, Broxburn, Ratho to Wester Hailes in Edinburgh. There is a city section from Wester Hailes to Fountainbridge. In addition to the peaceful rural locations, there is also much of industrial archaeological interest, particularly aqueducts and a tunnel section near Falkirk.

Contact: British Waterways Board, Countryside Ranger, Union Canal, Canal House, Applecross Street, Glasgow G4 9SP. Tel: 041-332 6936.

Canal side, tunnel, open country, contour canal (no locks, no hills). 5$^{1/2}$ miles/9km Falkirk-Lathallen Road (A801).

Open all year. Car park.

ACE

11 Church Street, Castle Douglas DG7 1EA. Tel: 0556 4542 (24 hrs)

CYCLE HIRE AND ADVICE. PLUS SALES, SERVICE, ACCESSORIES

We are situated in the middle of a town surrounded by great cycling country. There are miles of quiet country roads leading to interesting places, and several forests nearby with cycle trails.

Hire from our shop or book your bikes to be delivered at a location of your choice. We have both Mountain and Trail bikes available and also children's sizes. Rear seats can be fitted for infants.

Samples charges: £12.00 per bike for a 24 hour hire. £8.00 for hire within the working day. Reductions for groups. Travel may be charged for delivery. Guided rides available, ask for details. A deposit is required.

TROSSACHS CYCLE HIRE

for the BEST BIKES BEST TRAILS BEST SERVICE

TOP SPEC BIKES – £10 per day

NEW & EX-HIRE BIKES FOR SALE

Camping, Caravanning & Self Catering Accommodation

TROSSACHS HOLIDAY PARK ABERFOYLE • Tel: 08772 614

DAY TRIP OR MONTH'S HOLIDAY?

CENTRAL CYCLE HIRE

We have the widest range of town, touring and mountain bikes for hire in Scotland.

Also new bikes and lots of spares AND a rapid repair service.

031 228 6333

031 228 6363

LOCHRIN PLACE TOLLCROSS EDINBURGH

TRADES DESCRIPTIONS ACT

The accommodation mentioned in this holiday guide has not been inspected, and the publishers rely on information provided. The publishers have every confidence in their advertisers but cannot be held responsible for the accuracy of the descriptions published.

CYCLING/MOUNTAIN BIKING

Weekend and 6 night all-terrain mountain biking breaks for adult beginners. Guided half-day and full day tours for non-residential groups. Explore the Dark Peak along peaceful roads and traffic-free trails and bridle-ways, led by experienced enthusiasts. Superb scenic routes.

Safety-helmets and a mechanic-guide provided. Minibus support and recovery service included. Weekends from £59 fully inclusive, full board; 6 nights from £179. BAHA founder member.

Rock Lea Activity Centre,
Station Road, Hathersage, Peak National Park, via Sheffield S30 1DD.
Tel/Fax: (0433) 650345.
(See advertisement on inside back cover)

ADULTS - MULTI ACTIVITY

Superb weekend and 6-night multi-activity breaks for adults in the heart of the beautiful Peak National Park. Open all year. Highly acclaimed on BBC's Breakaway and Freewheeling programmes.

Action-filled 6-night breaks include sailing, cable-water-skiing, windsurfing, pony-trekking, orienteering, climbing, caving, abseiling, mountain biking, gorge-walking.

Prices from £99 for 2 nights full board, fully inclusive; £289 for 6 nights from Saturday, full board. BAHA founder member.

Rock Lea Activity Centre,
Station Road, Hathersage, Peak National Park, via Sheffield S30 1DD.
Tel/Fax: (0433) 650345.
(See advertisement on inside back cover)

FOLLOW THE COUNTRY CODE

AREA TOURIST BOARDS

Angus Tourist Board,
Tourist Information Centre,
Market Place,
Arbroath DD11 1HR.
Tel: Arbroath (0241) 72609/76680.

Aviemore & Spey Valley Tourist Board,
Grampian Road,
Aviemore PH22 1PP.
Tel: Aviemore (0479) 810363 (24 hrs).

Ayrshire Tourist Board,
Tourist Information Centre,
39 Sandgate,
Ayr KA7 1BG.
Tel: Ayr (0292) 284196 (24 hrs).

Ayrshire Tourist Board,
Tourist Information Centre,
62 Bank Street,
Kilmarnock KA1 1ER.
Tel: Kilmarnock (0563) 39090.

Ayrshire Tourist Board,
Tourist Information Centre,
The Promenade,
Largs KA30 8BG.
Tel: Largs (0475) 673765 (24 hrs).

Banff & Buchan Tourist Board,
Collie Lodge,
Banff AB45 1AU.
Tel: Banff (0261) 812789.

Caithness Tourist Board,
Tourist Office,
Whitechapel Road,
Wick, Caithness.
Tel: Wick (0955) 2596.

City of Aberdeen Tourist Board,
St. Nicholas House,
Broad Street,
Aberdeen AB9 1DE.
Tel: Aberdeen (0224) 632727.

City of Dundee Tourist Board,
4 City Square,
Dundee.
Tel: Dundee (0382) 27723.

Clyde Valley Tourist Board,
Horsemarket,
Ladyacre Road,
Lanark ML11 7LQ.
Tel: Lanark (0555) 662544.

Dumfries & Galloway Tourist Board,
Campbell House,
Bankend Road,
Dumfries DG1 4TH.
Tel: Dumfries (0387) 50434.

Dunoon & Cowal Tourist Board,
Tourist Information Centre,
7 Alexandra Parade,
DunoActivity centre,
Station Road, Hathersage, Peak National Park,
via Sheffield S30 1DD.
Tel/Fax: (0433) 650345.

East Lothian Tourist Board,
Brunton Hall,
Musselburgh,
East Lothian.
Tel: 031-665 6597.

Edinburgh Marketing,
Waverley Shopping Centre,
3 Princes Street,
Edinburgh 031-557 2727.

Fort William & Lochaber Tourism Ltd.,
Tourist Information Centre,
Cameron Centre,
Cameron Square,
Fort William PH33 6AJ.
Tel: Fort William (0397) 3781 (24 hrs).

Forth Valley Tourist Board,
Tourist Information Centre,
Burgh Halls, The Cross,
Linlithgow EH49 7AH.
Tel: Linlithgow (0506) 844600.

Greater Glasgow Tourist Board,
35-39 St. Vincent Place,
Glasgow.
Tel: 041-204 4400.

Inverness, Loch Ness & Nairn Tourist Board,
Castle Wynd,
Inverness IV2 3BJ.
Tel: Inverness (0463) 234353 (24 hrs).

Isle of Arran Tourist Board,
Tourist Information Centre,
Brodick Pier,
Brodick,
Isle of Arran.
Tel: Brodick (0770) 2140/2401.

Isle of Bute Tourist Board,
15 Victoria Street,
Rothesay,
Isle of Bute PA20 0AJ.
Tel: Rothesay (0700) 502151.

The Isle of Skye & South West Ross Tourist
Board,
Tourist Information Centre,
Meall House, Portree,
Isle of Skye IV51 9BZ.
Tel: Portree (0478) 2137.

Kincardine & Deeside Tourist Board,
45 Station Road,
Banchory AB31 3XX.
Tel: Banchory (033 02) 2066.

Kirkcaldy District Council,
Tourist Information Centre,
South Street,
Leven KY8 4NT.
Tel: Leven (0333) 429464.

Loch Lomond, Stirling & Trossachs Tourist
Board,
41 Dumbarton Road,
Stirling FK8 2QQ.
Tel: Stirling (0786) 475019 (24 hrs)

The West Highlands & Islands of Argyll
Tourist Board,
Area Tourist Office,
MacKinnon House,
The Pier, Campbeltown,
Argyll PA28 6EF.
Tel: Campbeltown (0586) 552056.

Moray District Tourist Board,
Tourist Information Centre,
17 High Street,
Elgin IV30 1EG.
Tel: Elgin (0343) 542666.

Oban, Mull & District Tourist Board,
Boswell House,
Argyll Square,
Oban.
Tel: Oban (0631) 63122.

Orkney Tourist Board,
Tourist Information Centre,
6 Broad Street,
Kirkwall,
Orkney KW15 1NX.
Tel: Kirkwall (0856) 872856.

Perthshire Tourist Board,
45 High Street,
Perth PH1 5TJ.
Tel: Perth (0738) 38353.

Ross & Cromarty Tourist Board,
Tourist Information Centre,
Achtercairn,
Gairloch,
Ross-shire IV21 2DN.
Tel: Gairloch (0445) 2130 (24 hrs).

St. Andrews & N.E. Fife Area Tourist Board,
Tourist Information Centre,
78 South Street,
St. Andrews KY16 9JX.
Tel: St. Andrews (0334) 72021.

Scottish Borders Tourist Board,
Tourist Information Centre,
Murray Green,
Jedburgh TD9 9LP.
Tel: Jedburgh (0835) 63435.

Shetland Islands Tourism,
Market Cross,
Lerwick,
Shetland ZE1 0LU.
Tel: Lerwick (0595) 3434.

Sutherland Tourist Board,
Area Tourist Office,
The Square,
Dornoch IV25 3SD.
Tel: Dornoch (0862) 810400.

Western Isles Tourist Board,
4 South Beach Street,
Stornoway,
Isle of Lewis PA87 2XY.
Tel: Stornoway (0851) 703088.

FOLLOW THE COUNTRY CODE

SET A GOOD EXAMPLE

AND TRY TO FIT IN WITH THE

LIFE AND WORK OF THE COUNTRYSIDE

RULES OF GOLF

Principal Changes introduced in the 1992 Code

DEFINITIONS

The terms "line of putt" and "line of play" are defined.

RULES

Rule 4–1e. Club Face

The restriction with regard to insets or attachments on metal clubs is eliminated.

Rule 4–4a. Selection and Replacement of Clubs

The addition or replacement of a club or clubs may not be made by borrowing any club selected for play by any other person playing on the course.

Rule 5–3. Ball Unfit for Play)
Rule 12–2. Identifying Ball)

If the player fails to carry out a part or parts of the procedure he is penalised only one stroke.

Rule 13–4. Ball Lying in or Touching Hazard

Expanded to state that if a ball lies in a hazard there is no penalty (provided nothing is done which constitutes testing the condition of the hazard or improves the lie of the ball) if the player touches the ground or water in a water hazard as a result of or to prevent falling, in removing an obstruction, in measuring or in retrieving or lifting a ball under any Rule.

Rule 24–2c. Ball Lost

There is an addition to the Rule to make provision for a ball lost in an immovable obstruction.

APPENDIX II

4–1a. General

Limited adjustability is permitted in the design of putters.

4–1c. Grip

If a putter has two grips, both of the grips must be circular in cross-section. However, putters which do not conform with this Rule may continue to be used until 31st December 1992.

MAP OF THE COURSES AND CLUBS

ISLANDS
(SHETLAND)

175

ISLANDS
(ORKNEY)

281

162

261

234

268

191

283

130

47

121

77

262

36

228

10   136

102

207

137

259

189

131

105

210

96

252

48

79

103   142   132

70

22   192   275

109   135   225   69

98

212

138   220

GRAMPIAN

123

59   35   211

90A

111

181

245

245A

256

ISLANDS
(WESTERN ISLES)

HIGHLAND

251

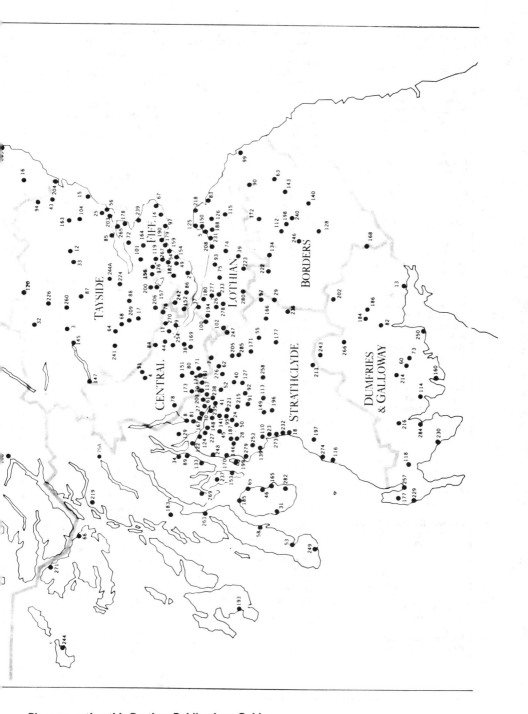

1 Aberdeen
Aberdeenshire

*Kings Links Golf Course
Contact Aberdeen District
Council, Aberdeen Leisure,
c/o Bon Accord Baths, Justice
Mill Lane, Aberdeen.
Tel: 0224 582700.
18 holes, length of course
6384m/5835 yds.
SSS 70
Charges: £4.95 round.
For reservations Tel: 632269.
Professional: Mr. R. McDonald,
Golf Shop, Golf Road, Aberdeen.
Tel: 0224 641577.

*Bon Accord Municipal Golf Club
19 Golf Road, Aberdeen.
Tel: 0224 633464.
18 holes, length of course 6384 yds.
SSS 70
Charges: Telephone Leisure &
Recreation, (0224) 642121.
Visitors are welcome but must be
accompanied by a member.
Secretary: James T. Burnett - Tel:
633464.
Professional: Ronnie McDonald -
Tel: 641577.

Caledonian Golf Club
20 Golf Road, AB2 1QB.
Tel: 0224 632443.
18 holes, length of course 6384 yds.
SSS 70
Charges: £4.80 (round).
For advance reservations Tel: 0224
632269.
Caddy cars, practice area and cater-
ing facilities are available.
Visitors are welcome all week.
Secretary: John A. Bridgeford - Tel:
0224 632443.

Westhill Golf Club (1977)
Westhill, Aberdeenshire.
Tel:0224 740159.
18 holes, length of course 5921 yds.
SSS 69
Charges: £8 round (Mon-Fri),
£11 (Sun & Public Holidays),
£10 day ticket, £13 (Sun
& Public Holidays).
Visitors are welcome all week
except Saturdays.
Secretary: J.L. Webster.
Professional: R. McDonald.

**Balgownie Golf Course
Royal Aberdeen Golf Club (2 courses),**
Balgownie, Bridge of Don.
Tel: 0224 702571 (Clubhouse).
Balgownie Links - 18 holes, length
of course 6372 yds.
Par 70
Silverburn Links - 18 holes, length
of course 4066 yds.
Par 60
Charges: Balgownie - £25 per
round, £30 daily. Silverburn -
£12.50 per round, £15 daily.
For advance reservations Tel: 0224
702221.
A practice area and full catering
facilities.
Visitors welcome - weekend restric-
tions. Letter of introduction
required.
Secretary: Mr. Fraser Webster - Tel:
0224 702571.
Professional: Mr. Ronnie MacAskill
- Tel: 0224 702221.

Murcar Golf Club
Bridge of Don,
Aberdeen AB2 8BD.
Tel: 0224 704345.
18 holes, length of course 6240 yds.
SSS 70
Charges: £12.50 round (before
11.30 a.m.), £20 daily, £50 weekly.
For advance reservations Tel:
Aberdeen 704354/704370.
Caddy cars and catering facilities
are available.
Visitors are welcome all week
except Saturdays, Sundays before
Noon and Wednesday afternoons.
Secretary: R. Matthews - Tel:
Aberdeen 704354.

Deeside Golf Club
Bieldside AB1 9DL.
Tel: 0224 869457.
18 holes, length of course 5972 yds.
SSS 69
Charges: £17 round, £19 daily, £50
weekly.
For advance reservations Tel: 0224
861041.
A practice area, caddy cars and
catering facilities are available.
Visitors are welcome Monday to
Friday.
Secretary: Dr. N.M. Scott - Tel:
0224 869457.
Professional: Frank Coutts - Tel:
0224 861041.

***Balnagask Golf Club
Nigg Bay Golf Club**
St Fittick's Road, Aberdeen.
Tel: 0224 871286.
18 holes, length of course 5521 m/
6042 yds.
SSS 69
Charges: £4.20 round.
A practice area is available.
Visitors are welcome all week.
Secretary: Harry Hendry – Tel:
0224 871286.

2 Aberdour
Fife

Aberdour Golf Club
Seaside Place, Aberdour,
Fife KY3 0TX,
Tel: 0383 860256.
18 holes, length of course
5460 yds.
SSS 67
Charges: Mon-Fri £13 round, £18
per day ticket.
For advance reservations Tel:
0383 860256.
Catering facilities are available.
Visitors are welcome all week.
Secretary: J.J. Train, Tel: 0383
860080.
Professional: Gordon MacCallum –
Tel: 0383 860256.

3 Aberfeldy
Perthshire

Aberfeldy Golf Club
Taybridge Road, Aberfeldy.
Tel: 0887 820535.
9 holes, length of course 5100m/
5577 yds.
SSS 67
Charges: £14 daily, £40 weekly.
A practice area, caddy cars and
catering facilities are available.
Secretary: A.M. Stewart – Tel:
Aberfeldy 820117.
Advance bookings at weekends in
June, July and August.

Kenmore Golf Course
Mains of Taymouth, Kenmmore,
Aberfeldy.
Tel: 0887 870 226.
9 holes, length of course
2751m/3026 yds.
18 holes, length of course
5502m/6052 yds.
SSS69
Charges: £10 adult, £7 juniors
round. £15 adult, £11 juniors daily.

£40 adult, £30 juniors weekly.
For advance reservations Tel: 0887 830226.
Practice area, caddy cars and catering facilities are available.
Visitors are welcome all week.
Secretary: Robin Menzies - Tel: 0887 830226.

4 Aberfoyle
Stirlingshire

Aberfoyle Golf Club
Braeval, Aberfoyle.
Tel: (Aberfoyle) 08772 493.
18 holes, length of course 4760m/ 5204 yds.
SSS 66
Charges: Weekday ticket £15, round £12; weekend ticket £20, round £15.
For advance reservations Tel: Mrs. C. Shackleton on Aberfoyle 531.
Visitors are welcome all week.
Secretary: R.D. Steele – Tel: Aberfoyle 638.

5 Aberlady
East Lothian

Luffness New Golf Club
The Clubhouse, Aberlady, EH32 0QA.
Tel: 0620 843336.
18 Holes, length of course 6122 yds.
SSS 69
Charges: On application.
For advance reservations Tel: 0620 843336.
A practice area and catering facilities are available.
Visitors are welcome weekdays only by introduction.
Secretary: Lt. Col. J.G. Tedford – Tel: 0620 843336.
Clubmaster: Tel – 0620 843376.

6 Aboyne
Aberdeenshire

Aboyne Golf Club
Formaston Park, Aboyne.
Tel: Aboyne 2328.
18 holes, length of course 5910 yds.
SSS 68
Charges: £17 daily, £13 round (Mon-Fri), £20 daily (Sat/Sun).
For advance reservations Tel: 03398 86755 (Secretary).
A practice area, caddy cars and catering facilities are available.

Visitors are welcome all week.
Secretary: Mrs. Mairi MacLean – Tel: 03398 87078.
Professional: I. Wright.

7 Airdrie
Lanarkshire

Airdrie Golf Club
Glenmavis Road,
Airdrie ML6 0PQ.
Tel: Airdrie 62195.
(Further details on application)

Easter Moffat Golf Club
Mansion House, Plains.
Tel: Caldercruix 842878.
18 holes, length of course 5690m/ 6222 yds.
SSS 70
Charges: £12 round, £18 daily.
For advance reservations Tel: Caldercruix 842878.
A practice area is available.
Visitors are welcome Monday to Friday.
Secretary: Mr. J.G. Timmons – Tel: (0236) 761440 or 441330.
Professional: Mr. B. Dunbar.

8 Alexandria
Dunbartonshire

Vale of Leven Golf Club
Northfield Road, Bonhill.
Tel: Alexandria 52351.
18 holes, length of course 5165 yds.
SSS 66
Charges: £7.50 round, £11 per day midweek; £10 per round, £15 per day weekends.
Catering facilities are available.
Visitors are welcome all week.
Discount for parties on application to secretary.
Secretary: W. McKinlay – Tel: Alexandria 52508.

9 Alloa
Clackmannanshire

Alloa Golf Club
Schaw Park, Sauchie,
By Alloa.
Tel: 0259 722745.
18 holes, length of course 6240 yds.
SSS 70
Charges: £12 round, £20 daily.
For advance bookings contact the Secretary.
A practice area, caddy cars and

catering facilities are available.
Visitors are welcome all week except weekends.
Secretary: A.M. Frame – Tel: 0259 50100.
Professional: Bill Bennett – Tel: 0259 724476.

10 Alness
Ross-shire

Alness Golf Club
Ardross Road, Alness, Ross & Cromarty.
Tel: (0349) 883877.
9 holes, length of course 4718 yds.
SSS 63
Par 66
Charges: £2.50 round/daily weekdays, £3.50 round/daily Sat-Sun. Juniors £1.25, O.A.P's £1.25.
Seniors £10, juniors £5 weekly.
For advance reservations Tel: 0349 883877.
A practice area and catering facilities are available.
Visitors are welcome all week.
Secretary: J.G. Miller – Tel: 0349 883877.

11 Alva
Clackmannanshire

Alva Golf Club
Beauclerc Street, Alva.
Tel: 0259 60431.
9 holes.
Charges: £5 per round (Mon-Fri), £8 per round (Sat/Sun).
A practice area and catering facilities are available.
Visitors are welcome all week.
Secretary: Mrs. Annette McGuire – Tel: 0259 60455.

12 Alyth
Perthshire

The Alyth Golf Club
Pitcrocknie, Alyth PH11 8JJ.
Tel: Alyth 2268.
18 holes, length of course 5689m/ 6226 yds.
SSS 70 (Boxes 68)
Charges: Weekdays £15 round, £20 daily. weekends £20 round, £25 daily.
For advance reservations Tel: Alyth 2268.
A practice area, caddy cars and catering facilities are available.
Visitors are welcome all week.

Secretary: Mr. H. Sullivan –
Tel: Alyth 2268.
Professional: Mr. Tom Melville –
Tel: Alyth 2411.

13 Annan
Dumfriesshire

Powfoot Golf Club
Powfoot, Annan.
Tel: Cummertrees 227.
18 holes, length of course 5465m/
5977 yds.
SSS 69
Charges: Day tickets Mon-Fri £23;
£14 per round Mon-Fri & Sun from
2.45pm.
For advance reservations Tel:
(0461) 202866/7.
A practice area, caddy cars and
catering facilities are available.
Visitors are welcome all week
except Saturdays and before 2.45pm
on Sundays.
Secretary: R.G. Anderson – Tel:
(0461) 202866/7.
Professional: Gareth Dick – Tel:
(04617) 327.

14 Anstruther
Fife

Anstruther Golf Club
Marsfield, Shore Road,
Anstruther.
Tel: Anstruther 310 956.
9 holes, length of course 4504m.
SSS 63
Charges: £10 weekdays, £14
Sat/Sun per round.
For advance reservations Tel:
Anstruther 310956.
Catering facilities are available.
Visitiors welcome.
Secretary: A.B. Cleary.

15 Arbroath
Angus

*Arbroath Golf Course (Public)
Arbroath Artisan Golf Club
(Playing over above)
Elliot, By Arbroath.
Tel: 0241 72069.
18 holes, length of course 6078 yds.
SSS 69
Charges: £5 round (Mon-Fri), £8
round (Sat/Sun), £7 daily (Mon-
Fri), £11 daily (Sat/Sun).
For advance reservations Tel: 0241
75837.

A practice area, caddy cars and
catering facilities are available.
Visitors are welcome all week.
Clubhouse facilities are not
available on Thursdays.
Secretary: David L. Langlands –
Tel: 0241 73853.
Professional: J. Lindsay Ewart –
Tel: 0241 75837.

Letham Grange Golf Club
Colliston, By Arbroath DD11 4RL
Tel: 024 189 373.
Old Course - 18 holes, length of
course Blue – 6939 yds: White –
6582 yds: Yellow – 6309 yds: Red -
5734 yds.
SSS 73
Charges: £17 round, £25.50 daily
(Mon-Fri); £22 round (Sat/Sun and
public holidays).
New Course - 18 holes, length of
course White - 5528 yds: Yellow -
5271 yds: Red - 4950 yds.
SSS 68
Charges: £10 per round, £15 daily
(Mon-Fri); £15 round (Sat/Sun and
public holidays).
1 round on each course - £23 week-
days; £32 weekends.
(1992 charges)
A practice area, powered buggies
and catering facilities are available.
Visitors are welcome all week.
Secretary: Heather A.C.
MacDougall – Tel: 024 189 373.
Professional: David Scott – Tel: 024
189 377.

16 Auchenblae
Kincardineshire

Auchenblae Golf Club
Auchenblae, Laurencekirk AB30
1AA.
Tel: Laurencekirk 8869.
9 holes, length of course 2174m.
SSS 30
Charges: Season ticket: Adult £35,
OAP £15, Junior £10. Day ticket
(Mon-Fri): Adult £5, OAP & Junior
£2.50. Saturday Ticket: Adult £6,
OAP & Junior £3. Sunday Ticket:
Adult £6.50, OAP & Junior £3.25.
Visitors are welcome all week apart
from Wednesday & Friday evenings
(5.30 pm-9 pm).
Secretary: A.I. Robertson – Tel:
Laurencekirk 8869.

17 Auchterarder
Perthshire

The Gleneagles Hotel Golf
Courses
King's Course
The Gleneagles Hotel,
Auchterarder PH3 1NF
Tel: 0764 63543. Telex: 76105
18 holes, length of course 6471 yds.
Par 70
Charges: On request.
Caddies, caddy car (on production
of a medical certificate), practice
area and catering facilities are avail-
able.
Golf available for residents and
members only.
Golf Manager: Contact the golf
office directly.
Professional: Ian Marchbank.

Queen's Course
Auchterarder, PH3 1NF.
Tel: 0764 63543. Telex 76105.
18 holes, length of course 5965 yds.
Par 68
Charges: On request.
Caddies, caddy car (on production
of a medical certificate), practice
area and catering facilities are avail-
able.
Golf available for residents and
members only.
Golf Manager: Contact the golf
office directly.
Professional: Ian Marchbank.

The Wee Course
Auchterarder, PH3 1NF.
Tel: 0764 63543. Telex: 76105.
9 holes, length of course 1,481 yds.
Par 27
Charges: On request.
Practice area and catering facilities
are available.
Golf available for residents and
members only.
Golf Manager: Contact the golf
office directly.
Professional: Ian Marchbank.

Auchterarder Golf Club
Orchil Road, Auchterarder.
Tel: Auchterarder 62804.
18 holes, length of course 5778 yds.
SSS 68
Charges: £12 round, £17 daily,
weekdays. £18 round, £25 daily,
weekends.
For advance reservations Tel:
Auchterarder 62804/63711.

Professional shop and catering facilities are available.
Secretary: Mr. W.M. Campbell –
Tel: Auchterarder 62804
(Office hrs. 9am-1pm).

18 Ayr
Ayrshire

*Belleisle Golf Course
Doonfoot Road, Ayr.
Tel: 0292 41258.
18 holes, length of course 6552 yds.
SSS 71
Charges: £12 round, £18 daily.
Weekly ticket £70 (This is a local authority owned course - charges are reviewed annually).
For advance reservations Tel: 0292 41258.
A practice area, caddy cars and catering facilities are available.
Visitors are welcome all week.
Professional: Mr. D. Gemmell –
Tel: 0292 41314.

*Dalmilling Municipal Golf Club
Westwood Avenue,
Ayr.
Tel: 0292 263893.
18 holes, length of course 5724 yds.
SSS 68
Charges: £9 round, £16 daily.
Weekly £70.
For advance reservations Tel: 0292 263893.
Caddy cars, practice area and catering facilities are available.
Visitors are welcome all week.
Secretary: Stewart D. Graham –
Tel: 0292 262468.
Professional: Phil Chenney.

19 Ballater
Aberdeenshire

Ballater Golf Club
Victoria Road, Ballater.
Tel: 03397 55567.
18 holes, length of course 5638 yds.
Par 67
Charges: On Application.
For advance reservations Tel: 03397 55567/55658.
A practice area, caddy cars and catering facilities are available.
Visitors are welcome Monday to Friday.

Secretary: A. Ingram –
Tel: 03397 55567.
Professional: J. Blair –
Tel: 03397 55658.

20 Balmore
Stirlingshire
Balmore Golf Club
Balmore, Torrance.
Tel: Balmore (03602) 240.
18 holes, length of course 5615 yds.
SSS 67
Charges: £10 round, £12 daily, £60 weekly.
For advance reservations Tel: 041 332 0392.
A practice area, caddy cars and catering facilities are available.
Visitors are welcome Monday - Friday with a member.
Secretary: G.P. Woolard – Tel: 041 332 0392.

21 Banchory
Kincardineshire

Banchory Golf Club
Kinneskie Road, Banchory.
Tel: Banchory 2365.
18 holes, length of course 5246 yds.
Charges: Mon-Fri £16.50 daily, Sat/Sun £18.50 daily.
For advance reservations Tel: Banchory 2447.
A practice area, caddy cars and catering facilities are available.
Golfing visitors are welcome.
Secretary: Mr. L. Buyers – Tel: Banchory 2365.
Professional Mr. D.W. Smart – Tel: Banchory 2447.

22 Banff
Bannfshire

Duff House Royal Golf Club
The Barnyards, Banff AB45 3SX.
Tel: 0261 812062.
18 holes, length of course 6161 yds.
SSS 69
Charges: £10 (weekday) round, £14 (weekend) round, £15 (weekday) daily, £20 (weekend) daily.
For advance reservations Tel: 0261 812062/812075.
A practice area, caddy cars and catering facilities are available.
Visitors are welcome all week (but within restricted times, as shown on Tee Booking sheets. Handicap Certificate preferred).

Secretary: K.T. Morrison –
Tel: 0261 812354.
Professional: R.S. Strachan –
Tel: 0261 812075.

23 Barassie
Troon, Ayrshire

Kilmarnock (Barassie) Golf Club
29 Hillhouse Road, Barassie, Troon KA10 6SY.
Tel: Troon 313920.
18 holes, length of course 5896m/6450 yds.
SSS 71
Charges: £35 daily (1992)
For advance reservations Tel: Troon 313920.
A practice area, caddy cars and catering facilities are available.
Visitors are welcome Mon/Tues/Thur/Fri.
Secretary: R.L. Bryce – Tel: Troon 313920.
Professional: W.R. Lockie – Tel: Troon 311322.

24 Barrhead
Renfrewshire

Fereneze Golf Club
Fereneze Avenue, Barrhead.
Tel: 041 881 1519.
(This is a Strictly Private Club)

25 Barry
Angus

Panmure Golf Club
Burnside Road, Carnoustie.
Tel: Carnoustie 53120.
18 holes, length of course 5761m/6302 yds.
SSS 70
Charges: On application.
For advance reservations Tel: Carnoustie 53120.
A practice area, caddy cars and catering facilities are available (except Mondays).
Visitors are welcome all week, except Saturdays.
Secretary: Captain J.C. Ray – Tel: Carnoustie 53120.
Professional: T. Shiel – Tel: Carnoustie 53120.

26 Bathgate
West Lothian

Bathgate Golf Course
Edinburgh Road, Bathgate, EH48
1BA.
Tel: Bathgate 52232.
18 holes, length of course 6325 yds.
SSS 70
Charges: £14 daily (Mon-Fri), £22
(Sat/Sun).
For advance reservations Tel:
Bathgate 630505.
A practice area, caddy cars and
catering facilities are available.
Secretary: Mr. W. Gray – Tel:
Bathgate 630505.
Professional: Sandy Strachan –
Tel: Bathgate 630553.

27 Bearsden
Dunbartonshire

Windyhill Golf Club
Windyhill, Bearsden G61 4QQ.
Tel: 041 942 2349.
18 holes, length of course 6254 yds.
SSS 70
Charges: £15 daily.
For advance reservations contact
the Secretary by letter.
A practice area, caddy cars and
catering facilities are available.
Visitors are welcome all week
except Sat/Sun, by prior
arrangement.
Secretary: Mr. A.J. Miller – Tel:
041 942 2349.
Professional: R. Collinson – Tel:
041 942 7157.

Douglas Park Golf Club
Hillfoot, Bearsden.
Tel: 041 942 2220.
18 holes, length of course
5444m/5957 yds.
SSS 69
Charges: £15 round, £20 daily.
For advance reservations Tel: 041
942 2220.
Caddy cars and catering facilities
are available.
Visiting parties by prior
arrangement are welcome
Wednesdays and Thursdays.
Secretary: D.N. Nicolson – Tel: 041
942 2220.
Professional: D. Scott – Tel: 041
942 1482.

Bearsden Golf Club
Thorn Road, Bearsden, Glasgow.
Tel: 041 942 2351.
9 holes, length of course 6014 yds.
SSS 69
Charges: On application.
Visitors are welcome, but must be
introduced by a member.
Secretary: Mr.J.R. Mercer – Tel:
041 942 2351.

28 Beith
Ayrshire

Beith Golf Club
Threepwood Road, Bigholm,
Beith.
Tel: Beith 3166.
(Further details on application)

29 Biggar
Lanarkshire

Biggar Golf Club
The Park, Broughton Road,
Biggar ML12.
Tel: 0899 20618.
18 holes, length of course 5416 yds.
SSS 66 Par 67
Charges: weekdays £8, weekends
£10. Juniors & OAP's £3 weekdays,
£5.50 weekends.
Advance reservations are essential
Tel: 0899 20319.
Caddy cars and catering facilities
are available.
Visitors are welcome all week.
Secretary: W.S. Turnbull – Tel:
0899 20566.

Leadhills Golf Course
Leadhills, Biggar, Lanarkshire.
Tel: 0659 74222.
9 holes, length of course 4150m.
SSS 62
Charges: Weekdays & weekends £4
daily/round.
Visitors are welcome all week.
Secretary: Mr. Harry Shaw – Tel:
0659 74222.

30 Bishopton
Renfrewshire

Erskine Golf Club
(Further details on application)

31 Blackwaterfoot
Isle of Arran

Shiskine Golf and Tennis Club
Blackwaterfoot, Isle of Arran.
Tel: Shiskine 226.
12 holes, length of course 3000 yds.
SSS 42
Charges: £8 round, £10 daily (Sept.-
June). £8 round (July-Aug.).
Weekly £30.
Reduced fees for juniors.
(All charges inc. V.A.T.).
Eating facilities available (June to
September inc.).
Visitors are welcome.
Secretary: Mrs. F. Crawford – Tel:
Shiskine 293.
Treasurer: E. Faulkner – Tel:
Shiskine 392.

32 Blair Atholl
Perthshire

Blair Atholl Golf Course
Golf Course Road, Blair Atholl.
Tel: 0796 481407.
9 holes.
SSS 69
Charges: £8 round Mon-Fri; £9
round Sat/Sun. £36 weekly.
For advance reservations Tel: 0796
481407.
A practice area, caddy cars and
catering facilities are available.
Visitors are welcome all week.
Secretary: J. McGregor.

33 Blairgowrie
Perthshire

**Blairgowrie Golf Club
Lansdowne Course,**
Golf Course Road, Rosemount
PH10 6LG.
Tel: 0250 872622.
18 holes, length of course 6895 yds.
SSS 73
Charges: On Application.
Caddies, caddy cars, practice area
and catering facilities are available.
Visiting societies are welcome:
Mon, Tues & Thurs.
Secretary: J.N. Simpson - Tel: 0250
872622.
Professional: Gordon Kinnoch -
Tel: 0250 873116.

Rosemount Course
Golf Course Road, Rosemount,
Blairgowrie PH10 6LG.
Tel: 0250 872622.
18 holes, length of course 6588 yds.
SSS 72
Charges: On Application.
For advance reservations Tel: 0250
87622.
Caddies, caddy cars, practice area
and catering facilities are available.
Visiting societies are welcome Mon,
Tues, Thurs.
Secretary: J.N. Simpson - Tel: 0250
872622.
Professional: Gordon Kinnoch -
Tel: 0250 873116.

Wee Course,
Golf Course Road, Rosemount,
Blairgowrie PH10 6LG.
Tel: 0250 872622.
9 holes, length of course 4614 yds.
SSS 65
Charges: On Application.
Secretary: J.N. Simpson - Tel: 0250
2622.
Professional: Gordon Kinnoch -
Tel: 0250 3116.

34 Blairmore
By Dunoon, Argyll

Blairmore & Strone Golf Course
Blairmore, By Dunoon.
Tel: Kilmun 676.
9 holes, length of course 1933m/
2112 yds.
SSS 62
Charges: £5 round, £5 daily, £25
weekly.
Visitors are welcome all week,
except Saturday afternoon.
Secretary: R.J.K. Dunlop - Tel:
Kilmun 260

35 Boat of Garten
Inverness-shire

Boat of Garten Golf Club
Tel: 047 983 351.
18 holes, length of course 5837 yds.
SSS 69
Charges: Mon-Fri £14 daily, Sat/
Sun £18 daily, £70 weekly.
For advance reservations Tel: 047
983 282 (starting sheet used
everyday).
Caddies, caddy cars and catering
facilities are available.
Visitors are welcome.
Secretary: J.R. Ingram.

36 Bonar Bridge
Sutherland

Bonar Bridge – Ardgay Golf Club
Bonar Bridge.
9 holes, length of course 4626 yds.
SSS Men 63, Ladies 66.
Charges: £6 daily, £30 weekly.
For advance reservations Tel: 08632
750 (Groups only).
Visitors are welcome all week.
Secretaries: A. Turner – Tel: 054
982 248.
J. Reid - Tel: 03632 750.

37 Bo'ness
West Lothian

West Lothian Golf Club
Airngath Hill, By Linlithgow.
Tel: Bo'ness 826030.
18 holes, length of course 6578 yds.
SSS 70
Charges: Midweek - £9 round, £12
daily. Weekends - £14 round, £18
daily.
For advance reservations Tel: Ian
Taylor, Linlithgow 842286.
Caddy cars, practice area and cater-
ing facilities are available.
Visitors are welcome mid-week at
all times. Weekend by arrangement.
Secretary: T.B. Fraser – Tel:
Bo'ness 825476.

38 Bonnybridge
Stirlingshire

Bonnybridge Golf Club
Larbert Road, Bonnybridge FK4
1NY.
Tel: 0324 812822.
9 holes, length of course 6058 yds.
SSS 69
Charges £8 round.
Practice area and catering facilities
are available.
Visitors welcome by arrangement.
Secretary: C.M.D. Munn – Tel:
0324 812822.

39 Bonnyrigg
Midlothian

Broomieknowe Golf Club
36 Golf Course Road, Bonnyrigg
EH19 2HZ.
Tel: 031 663 9317.
18 holes, length of course 5754 yds.

SSS 68
Charges: £14 round, £20 daily.
Sat/Sun £20 round.
For advance reservations Tel: 031
663 9317.
A practice area, caddy cars and
catering facilities are available.
Visitors are welcome Monday –
Friday.
Secretary: I.J. Nimmo – Tel:031
663 9317.
Professional: Mr. M. Patchett – Tel:
031 660 2035.

40 Bothwell
Lanarkshire
Bothwell Castle Golf Club
Blantyre Road, Bothwell, Glasgow
G71.
Tel: Bothwell 85 3177.
18 holes, length of course 5705m/
6240 yds.
SSS 70
Charges: £14 round, £21 daily.
For advance reservations Tel:
Bothwell 85 2052.
A practice area, caddy cars and
catering facilities are available.
Visitors are welcome Monday –
Friday.
Secretary: A.D.C. Watson – Tel:
Bothwell 85 2395.
Professional: Mr. W. Walker – Tel:
Bothwell 85 2052.

41 Braehead
(see under Paisley)

42 Braemar
Aberdeenshire

Braemar Golf Course
Cluniebank Road, Braemar.
Tel: 03397 41618.
18 holes, length of course 4916 yds.
SSS 64
Charges: £10 round; £15 daily; £50
weekly.
For advance reservations Tel:
Braemar 41618.
Caddy cars and catering facilities
are available.
Visitors are welcome all week.
Secretary: George A. McIntosh -
Tel: 0224 733836.

43 Brechin
Angus

Brechin Golf and Squash Club
Trinity, By Brechin DDH 7PD.
Tel: 035 62 2383.
18 holes, length of course 5287 yds.
SSS 66
Charges: On application.
Catering facilities available.
Visitors are welcome without reservation.
Secretary: A.B. May – Tel: Brechin 2326.
Professional: S. Crookston – Tel: Brechin 5270.

44 Bridge of Allan
Stirlingshire

Bridge of Allan Golf Club
Sunnylaw, Bridge of Allan, Stirling.
Tel: Bridge of Allan 832332.
9 holes, length of course 4508m/4932 yds.
SSS 65
Charges: £7 round. £10 on Sundays.
A practice area is available.
Visitors are welcome all week except Saturday and during Sunday competitions.
Secretary: A.M. Donoghue – Tel: Bridge of Allan 832007.

45 Bridge of Weir
Renfrewshire

Ranfurly Castle Golf Club Ltd
Golf Road, Bridge of Weir.
Tel: Bridge of Weir 612609.
(Further details on application)

46 Brodick
Isle of Arran

Machrie Bay Golf Club
46 Machrie, Machrie Bay, Brodick.
Tel: Shiskine 487.
9 holes, length of course 1904m/2082 yds.
SSS 31
Charges: £3 daily, £9 weekly, £12 fortnightly.
For advance reservations Tel: Machrie 267.
Catering facilities are available from June to September.
Secretary: Mr. R.B.H. Simpson – Tel: Shiskine 487.

Brodick Golf Club
Brodick, Isle of Arran.
Tel: 0770 2349.
18 holes, length of course 4405 yds.
SSS 62
Charges: £7 round, £8 (Sat/Sun).
£10 daily, £11 (Sat/Sun). Weekly £40.
For advance reservations Tel: 0770 2513.
A practice area, caddy cars and catering facilities are available.
Visitors are welcome; parties by advance reservation with secretary.
Secretary: Mr. H.M. MacRae.
Professional: Mr. P.S. McCalla – Tel: 0770 2513.

47 Brora
Sutherland

Brora Golf Club
Golf Road, Brora KW9 6QS.
Tel: Brora 21417.
18 holes, length of course 6110 yds.
SSS 69
Charges: £13 per day, £60 per week.
For advance reservations Tel: 0408 21417.
Caddy cars, practice area and catering facilities (May-August) are available.
Visitors are welcome all week.
Visitors can compete in any of our open competitions provided they have a current certificate of handicap with them.
Secretary: H. Baillie - Tel: 0408 21417.

48 Buckie
Banffshire

Strathlene Golf Club
Tel: Buckie 31798.
(Further details on application).

Buckpool Golf Club
Barhill Road, Buckie.
Tel: 0542 32236.
18 holes, length of course 6257 yds.
SSS 70
Charges: Per round after 3.30pm - £5 Mon-Fri; £7 Sat/Sun. Daily tickets - £9 Mon-Fri; £12 Sat/Sun. £30 weekly (Mon-Fri).
Juniors under-16 receive 50% reduction.
For advance reservations Tel: 0542 32236.
Catering facilities are available.

Visitors are welcome daily. Visiting parties are welcome by prior arrangement.

49 Burntisland
Fife

Burntisland Golf House Club
Dodhead, Burntisland.
Tel: 0592 874093.
18 holes, length of course 5391m/5897 yds.
SSS 69
Charges: £12.50 (weekday) round, £20
(Sat/Sun) round. £18 (weekday) daily, £28 (Sat/Sun) daily. Weekly by arrangement.
For advance reservations Tel: 0592 873247/874093.
A practice area, caddy cars and catering facilities are available.
Visitors are welcome all week.
Secretary: I. McLean – Tel: 0592 874093.
Professional: Mr. Jacky Montgomery – Tel: 0592 873247.

50 Caldwell
Renfrewshire

Caldwell Golf Club Ltd
Uplawmoor, Renfrewshire G78.
Tel: 050585 329.
18 holes, length of course 6046 yds.
SSS 69
Charges £12 round, £18 daily.
For advance reservations Tel: 050 585 616.
Caddy cars, practice area and catering facilities are available.
Vistors are welcome Mon to Fri.
Secretary: Donald McLean - Tel 041 333 9770.
Professional: Keith Baxter - Tel 050585 616.

51 Callander
Perthshire

Callander Golf Club
Aveland Road, Callander FK17 8EN.
Tel: 0877 30090.
18 holes, length of course 5125 yds.
Charges: Weekdays £12, weekends £16 (round). Weekdays £17, weekends £22 (daily).
For advance reservations Tel: Society Bookings 0877 30090.
Caddies, caddy cars, practice area

and catering facilities are available. Visitors welcome with Handicap Certificates or proof of recognised golf club on Wednesdays and Sundays.
Secretary: J. McClements – Tel: 0877 30090.
Professional: W. Kelly – Tel: 0877 30975.

52 Cambuslang
Glasgow

Cambuslang Golf Club
Westburn, Cambuslang.
Tel: 041 641 3130.
9 holes, length of course 6146 yds.
SSS 69
Visitors welcome when accompanied by member.
Secretary: William Lilly – Tel: 041 641 1498.

53 Campbeltown
Argyllshire

The Machrihanish Golf Club
Machrihanish, By Campbeltown.
Tel: Machrihanish 213.
18 and 9 holes, length of course 6228 yds.
SSS 70
Charges: Mon-Fri £13.50 (18), £4.50 (9) round.
£18 (18), £7 (9) daily Mon-Fri. £18 (18), £7 (9) daily Sat/Sun. Weekly £75 (18), £20 (9). Fortnightly £130 (18), £35 (9).
Children 14 years and under - half price on the 9 hole course.
For advance reservations Tel: Machrihanish 277.
A practice area, caddy cars and catering facilities are available.
Visitors are welcome all week.
Secretary: Mrs. A. Anderson – Tel: Machrihanish 213.
Professional: Mr. K. Campbell – Tel: Machrihanish 277.

54 Cardenden
Fife

Auchterderran Golf Club
Woodend Road, Cardenden.
Tel: Cardenden 721579.
9 holes, length of course 5250 yds.
SSS 66
Charges £6.60 daily, weekdays; £9.90 daily, weekends.

Visitors are welcome all week.
Secretary: Mr. Michael Doig – Tel: Cardenden 721877.

55 Carluke
Lanarkshire

Carluke Golf Club
Mauldslie Road, Hallcraig, Carluke ML8 5HG.
Tel: 0555 71 070.
18 holes, length of course 5308m/ 5805 yds. SSS 68
Charges: £10 round, £15 day ticket.
For advance reservations Tel: (Pro Shop) 0555 51 053.
A practice area and catering facilities are available.
Visitors are welcome all week, except Sat/Sun.
Secretary: J.H. Muir – Tel: 0555 70 620.
Professional: A. Brooks – Tel: 0555 51 053.

56 Carnoustie
Angus

Carnoustie Golf Club
3 Links Parade.
Tel: 0241 52480.
Secretary: D.W. Curtis – Tel: 0241 52480.

*Dalhousie Golf Club
Links Parade.
(Further details on application).

*Mercantile Golf Club
Links Parade.
Tel: 0241 52525.
(Further details on application).

*New Taymouth Golf Club
Taymouth Street.
Tel: 0241 52425.
(Further details on application).

Caledonia Golf Club
Links Parade.
Tel: 0241 52112.
(Further details on application).

*Carnoustie Golf Links Championship Course
Links Parade, Carnoustie DD7 7JE.
18 holes, length of course 6936 yds.
Charges: £31 round. 3–Day – £93; 5-Day - £124 (1992).
For advance reservations Tel: 0241 53789.
Caddies, caddy cars (no caddy cars

Nov - Apr incl.) and catering facilities are available.
Visitors are welcome all week, except Saturday morning and before 11.30 a.m. Sunday.
Secretary: Mr. E.J.C. Smith.

Carnoustie Golf Links Buddon Links Course
Links Parade, Carnoustie DD7 7JE.
18 holes, length of course 5420 yds.
SSS 68
Charges: £7 round (1992).
For advance reservations Tel: 0241 53789.
Caddies, caddy cars and catering facilities are available.
Visitors are welcome all week.
Secretary: Mr. E.J.C. Smith.

Carnoustie Golf Links Burnside Course
Links Parade, Carnoustie, DD7 7JB.
18 holes, length of course 6020 yds.
SSS 69
Charges: £12 round (1992).
For advance reservations Tel: 0241 53789.
Caddies, caddy cars (no caddy cars Nov - Apr Incl.) and catering facilities are available.
Visitors are welcome all week.
Secretary: Mr. E.J.C. Smith.

57 Carnwath
Lanarkshire

Carnwath Golf Course
1 Main Street, Carnwath.
Tel: Carnwath 251.
(Further details on application).

58 Carradale
Argyll

Carradale Golf Course
Carradale, Kintyre.
Tel: 05833 387.
9 holes, length of course 2387 yds.
SSS 63
Charges: £5 daily, £25 weekly.
For advance reservations
Tel: 05833 387.
Visitors are welcome all week.
Secretary: Dr. J.A. Duncan - Tel: 05833 387.

59 Carrbridge
Inverness-shire

*Carrbridge Golf Club
Carrbridge, Inverness-shire.
Tel: Carrbridge 623.
9 holes, length of course 5300 yds.
SSS 66
Charges: £7 Mon-Fri, £9 Sat/Sun
(1991).
For advance reservations Tel:
clubhouse 623.
Caddy cars, and light catering facilities available.
Visitors welcome all week.
Secretary: E.G. Drayson – Tel: 047
984 674.

60 Castle Douglas
Kirkcudbrightshire

Castle Douglas Golf Course
Abercromby Road, Castle Douglas.
Tel: Castle Douglas 2801.
9 holes, length of course 5408 yds.
SSS 66
Charges: £10 round/daily.
Visitors are welcome without reservation.
Secretary: A.D. Millar – Tel: 0556
2099.

61 Clydebank
Dunbartonshire

Clydebank & District Golf Club
Glasgow Road, Hardgate,
Clydebank G81 5QY.
Tel: Duntocher 73289.
18 holes, length of course
5326m/5825 yds.
SSS 68
Charges: £12 round.
For advance reservations Tel:
Professional (Duntocher 78686).
A practice area and catering
facilities are available.
Visitors are welcome Monday to
Friday.
Secretary: W. Manson – Tel:
Duntocher 72832.
Professional: David Pirie – Tel:
Duntocher 78686.

62 Coatbridge
Lanarkshire

Coatbridge Golf Club
Townhead Road, Coatbridge.
Tel: Coatbridge 28975.

18 holes, length of course 5877 yds.
SSS 68
Charges: £1.75 round.
For advance reservations Tel:
Coatbridge 21492.
A practice area, caddy cars and
catering facilities are available.
Visitors are welcome at all times,
except 1st Saturday of month.
Secretary: O. Dolan – Tel:
Coatbridge 26811.

Drumpellier Golf Club
Drumpellier Avenue, Coatbridge,
ML5 1RX.
Tel: 0236 28723.
18 holes, length of course 6227
yds.
SSS 70
Charges: £16 round, £22 daily.
For advance reservations Tel: 0236
23065/28538.
A practice area, caddy cars and
catering facilities are available.
Visitors are welcome Mondays
and Tuesdays.
Secretary: Mr. Wm. Brownlie –
Tel: 0236 23065.
Professional: Mr. K. Hutton – Tel:
0236 32971.

63 Coldstream
Berwickshire

Hirsel Golf Club
Kelso Road, Coldstream.
Tel: 0890 2678.
9 holes, length of course 5830 yds.
SSS 72 ladies
SSS 68 Men
Charges: Weekdays £10. Sat/Sun &
Public Hols. £15.
Caddy cars, practice area and catering facilities are available.
Visitors are welcome without reservation.
Secretary: Mr. J. Anderson, Bank
House, Coldstream. Tel: 0890 2789.

64 Comrie
Perthshire

Comrie Golf Club
c/o Secretary, 10 Polinard,
Comrie.
Tel: Comrie 70055.
9 holes, length of course 5962 yds.
SSS 69
Charges: £8 daily (£12 – weekends
and bank holidays), £30 weekly.
For advance reservations Tel:
Comrie 70544.

A practice area, caddy cars and
catering facilities are available.
Visitors are welcome all week,
except Monday evenings from
4.30 pm.
Secretary: Mr. D.G. McGlashan.

65 Corrie
Isle of Arran

Corrie Golf Club
Sannox, Isle of Arran.
Tel: Corrie 223.
9 holes, length of course 1948 yds.
SSS 61
Charges: £5 round/daily. £20
weekly. £30 fortnightly.
Catering facilities are available in
the Summer only.
Visitors are welcome all week
except Saturdays.
Secretary: R. Stevenson.

66 Craignure
Isle of Mull
Craignure Golf Club
Scallastle, Craignure, Isle of Mull.
Tel: 068 02 351.
9 holes, length of course 2218m.
SSS 32
Charges: On application.
Visitors are welcome all week.
Secretary: Sheila M. Campbell –
Tel: 068 02 370.

67 Crail
Fife

Crail Golfing Society
Balcomie Club House
Fifeness, Crail, Fife KY10 3XN.
Tel: 0333 50278.
18 holes, length of course 5720 yds.
SSS 68
Charges: £16 round, £24 daily,
weekday; £20 round, £30 daily,
weekend (1992).
Caddies, caddy cars, practice area
and catering facilities are possible.
Visitors are welcome. Advanced
bookings for parties are available,
except in latter half of July and first
half of August.
Secretary: Mrs. C.W. Penhale - Tel:
0333 50686.
Professional: G. Lennie – Tel: 0333
50278 and 0333 50960.

68 Crieff
Perthshire

Crieff Golf Club Ltd
Perth Road, Crieff PH7 3LR.
Tel: 0764 2397.
Ferntower Course:
18 holes, length of course 6402 yds.
SSS 71
Charges: On Application.
Dornock Course:
9 holes, length of course 2386 yds.
SSS 63
Charges: On Application.
For all reservations Tel: 0764 2909.
Buggies, caddy cars and catering
facilities are available.
Visitors are welcome all week (it is
advisable to book well in advance).
Secretary: L.J. Rundle – Tel: 0764
2397.
Professional: Mr. J. Stark - Tel:
0764 2909.

69 Cruden Bay
Aberdeenshire

Cruden Bay Golf Club
Aulton Road, Cruden Bay.
Tel: Cruden Bay 812285.
18 and 9 holes, length of course
5828 m/6370 yds.
SSS 71 (18), 62 (9)
Charges: £18.50 (18), £9.50 (9)
daily; £25.50 (18), £13.50 (9) weekends daily. £76 weekly; £130
fortnightly.
For advance reservations Tel: 0779
812285.
A practice area, caddy cars and
catering facilities are available.
Visitors are welcome all week but
restricted at weekends. No society
bookings at weekends.
Secretary: Ian A.D. McPherson –
Tel: 0779 812285.
Professional: Robbie Stewart – Tel:
0779 812414.

70 Cullen
Banffshire

Cullen Golf Club
The Links, Cullen, Buckie.
Tel: Cullen 40685.
(Further details on application).

71 Cumbernauld
Dunbartonshire

*Palacerigg Golf Club
Palacerigg Country Park,
Cumbernauld G67.
Tel: 6–734969.
18 holes, length of course
5894m/6444 yds.
SSS 71
Charges: £5 round/daily.
For advance reservations Tel:
6–721461.
A practice area and catering
facilities are available.
Visitors are welcome all week.
Secretary: John H. Dunsmore – Tel:
6–734969.

Westerwood Golf Club
Westerwood,
1 St. Andrews Drive,
Cumbernauld, Glasgow.
Tel: 0236 725281.
18 holes, length of course
6139m/6721 yds.
SSS 72
Charges: On application.
For advance reservations Tel: 0236
725 281.
Caddy cars, practice area and cater-
ing facilities are available.
Visitors are welcome all week.

72 Cupar
Fife

Cupar Golf Course
Cupar.
(Further details on application).

73 Dalbeattie
Kirkcudbrightshire

Colvend Golf Club
Sandyhills, Colvend, By
Dalbeattie.
Tel: Rockcliffe (Kirkcudbright)
398.
9 holes, length of course 2322 yds.
SSS 63
Charges: £10 daily, juniors half
price, except Sat/Sun.
Catering facilities are available.
Visitors are welcome - (Apr-Sept
course closed: Tues. from 2pm,
Thurs from 5.30pm.)
Secretary: Mr. J.B. Henderson, 9
Glenshalloch Road, Dalbeattie.
Tel - 0556 610878.

Dalbeattie Golf Club
(Further details on application).

74 Dalkeith
Midlothian

Newbattle Golf Club Ltd
Abbey Road, Dalkeith,
Midlothian.
Tel: 031 663 2123.
18 holes, length of course 5498m/
6012 yds.
SSS 69
Charges: £12 round, £20 daily.
For advance reservations Tel: 031
660 1631.
A practice area, caddy cars and
catering facilities are available.
Visitors are welcome all week,
except Weekends and Public
holidays.
Secretary: Mr. H.G. Stanners –
Tel: 031-663 1819.

75 Dalmahoy
Kirknewton EH27 8EB.

**Dalmahoy Hotel, Golf
and Country Club.**
Tel: 031-333 4105.
2 x 18 holes, length of courses East
6097m/6664 yds, West 5317 yds.
SSS East 72, West 66.
Charges: Green Fees. £30 round
East. £20 round West. £40 one
round each course.
Company/Society packages
available on request.
Visitors are welcome Monday-
Friday only (except residents).
Secretary: Jennifer Wilson.
Golf Professional: Scott Maxwell.

75A Dalmally
Argyllshire

Dalmally Golf Club
Dalmally, Argyll PA33 1AE.
9 holes.
SSS 62
Charges: £4 daily.
Visitors are welcome.
Secretary: A.J. Burke.
For Information Tel: 083 82
216/281/370.

76 Dollar
Clackmannanshire

Dollar Golf Course
Brewlands House, Dollar FK14
7EA.
Tel: 0259 42400.
18 holes, length of course 5144 yds.
SSS 66
Charges: £6 (Mon-Fri) round. £9
(Mon-Fri) daily, £12 (Sat/Sun)
daily.
For advance reservations Tel: 0259
42400.
Catering facilities are available.
Visitors are welcome all week.
Secretary: Mr. M.B. Shea – Tel:
0259 42400.

77 Dornoch
Sutherland

Royal Dornoch Golf Club
Golf Road, Dornoch.
Tel: 0862 810 219.
18 holes, length of course
6017m/6581 yds.
Charges: On request.
For advance reservations Tel: 0862
810219.
Caddies, caddy cars, practice area
and catering facilities are available.
Visitors are welcome all week.
Secretary: Ian C.R. Walker – Tel:
0862 810219.
Professional: W.E. Skinner – Tel:
0862 810902.

78 Drymen
Stirlingshire

Buchanan Castle Golf Club
Drymen.
Tel: 0360 60369/07/30.
18 holes, length of course 6086 yds.
SSS 69
Charges: £20 round, £30 daily.
For advance reservations Tel: 0360
60307.
Visitors are welcome by
arrangement.
Secretary: R. Kinsella – Tel: 0360
60307.
Professional: Mr. C. Demie – Tel:
0360 60330.

Strathendrick Golf Club
Drymen.
9 holes, length of course 4962 yds
(gents), 4518 yds (ladies).
SSS 65 (gents)

SSS 66 (ladies)
Charges: N/A.
Visitors accompanied by a member
are welcome all week, restrictions
on competition days.
Secretary: R.H. Smith - Tel: 0360
40582.

79 Dufftown
Banffshire

Dufftown Golf Club
Methercluny, Tomintoul Road,
Dufftown.
Tel: 0340 20325.
18 holes, length of course 5308 yds.
SSS 67
Charges: £7 (Mon-Fri), £8
(Sat/Sun). £25 weekly.
Bar and catering available daily.
Visitors are welcome all week.
Secretary: Mr. A. Stuart - Tel: 0340
20165.

80 Dullatur
Nr. Cumbernauld,
Dunbartonshire.

Dullatur Golf Club
Tel: Cumbernauld 723230.
18 holes, length of course 6229 yds.
SSS 70
Charges: £18 daily; £10 (after
1.30pm).
For advance reservations Tel:
Cumbernauld 723230.
Caddy cars, practice area and cater-
ing facilities are available.
Visitors are welcome Mon-Fri,
(except 1st Wed in month & public
holidays).
Secretary: W. Laing – Tel:
Cumbernauld 723230.
Professional: D. Sinclair – Tel:
Cumbernauld 723230.

81 Dumbarton
Dunbartonshire

Dumbarton Golf Course
Broadmeadow, Dumbarton.
Tel: Dumbarton 32830.
(Further details on application.)

Cardross Golf Club
Main Road, Cardross, Dumbarton
G82 5LB.
Tel: Cardross 841213.
18 holes, length of course 6469 yds.
SSS 71
Charges: £15 round, £25 day ticket.

For advance reservations Tel: 0389
841350.
Caddy cars, practice area and catering facilities are available.
Visitors welcome weekdays only.
Secretary: R. Evans C.A. – Tel:
0389 841754.
Professional: Robert Craig – Tel:
0389 841350.

82 Dumfries
Dumfriesshire

**Dumfries and County Golf
Club**
Edinburgh Road, Dumfries DG1
1JX.
Tel: 0387 53585.
18 holes, length of course 5928
yds.
SSS 68
Charges: £14, (Sun £17) daily - no
round ticket. £50 weekly.
A practice area, caddy cars and
catering facilities are available.
Visitors are welcome all week,
except Saturdays.
Secretary: J.K. Wells – Tel: 0387
53585.
Professional: Mr. G. Gray – Tel:
0387 68918.

83 Dunbar
East Lothian

Dunbar Golf Club
East Links, Dunbar EH42 1LP.
Tel: 0368 62317.
18 holes, length of course 5874m/
6426 yds.
SSS 71
Charges: Daily - £25 weekdays; £40
weekends & Specified holidays.
For advance reservations Tel: 0368
62317.
A practice area, caddies (if
reserved) and catering facilities are
available.
Visitors are welcome all week, after
9.30 am (except Thurs).
Secretary: Mr. Don Thompson –
Tel: 0368 62317.
Professional: Mr. D. Small –
Tel:
0368 62086.

*Winterfield Golf Club
North Road, Dunbar.
Tel: 0368 62280.
18 holes.
SSS 65
Charges: On Application.

For advance reservations Tel: 0368 63562.
Caddy cars and catering facilities are available.
Secretary: Mr. M. O'Donnell – Tel: 0368 62564.
Professional: Mr. K. Phillips - Tel: 0368 63562.

84 Dunblane
Perthshire

Dunblane New Golf Club
Perth Road, Dunblane.
Tel: Dunblane 823711.
18 holes, length of course 5371m/ 5874 yds.
SSS 68
Charges: £15 round (Mon-Fri), £22 (Sat/Sun), £22 daily.
(Charges subject to revision).
For advance reservations Tel: Dunblane 823711.
A practice area, caddy cars and catering facilities (by advance order) are available.
Visitors are welcome Monday to Friday.
Secretary: R.S. MacRae – Tel: Falkirk 21263.
Professional: R.M. Jamieson – Tel: Dunblane 823711.

85 Dundee
Angus

*Camperdown Golf Course
Camperdown Park, Dundee.
Tel: 0382 623398.
Visitors contact: Art & Recreation Division, Leisure Centre, Dundee.
Tel: 0382 23141 (ext. 413).
Secretary: K. McCreery - Tel: 0382 642925.
(Further details on application).

Downfield Golf Club
Turnberry Avenue, Dundee.
Tel: 0382 825595.
18 holes, length of course 6804 yds.
SSS 73
Charges: £22 round, £33 daily (1992).
Caddies, caddy cars, practice area and catering facilities available.
Weekday visitors are welcome with reservations. Saturday and Sunday call starter after 8am.
Secretary: Brian F. Mole – Tel: Dundee 825595.
Professional/Starter: C. Waddell – Tel: Dundee 89246.

86 Dunfermline
Fife

Dunfermline Golf Club
Pitfirrane Crossford, Dunfermline.
Tel: 0383 723534.
18 holes, length of course 6237 yds.
SSS 70
Charges: £15 round, £25 daily.
For advance reservations Tel: 0383 723534.
Caddy cars, practice area and catering facilities are available.
Visitors are welcome Mon. to Fri.
Secretary: H. Matheson – Tel: 0383 723534.

Canmore Golf Club
Venturefair, Dunfermline.
Tel: Dunfermline 724969.
(Further details from the Secretary on Dunfermline 726098).

Pitreavie (Dunfermline) Golf Club
Queensferry Road, Dunfermline KY11 5PR.
Tel: 0383 722591.
18 holes, length of course 5565m/ 6086 yds.
SSS 69
Charges: Weekdays £12 round, £17 daily. Weekends £22 daily, no round tickets. (1992).
For advance reservations –
Casual visitors Tel: 0383 723151,
Parties, Societies etc. Tel: 0383 722591.
A practice area, caddy cars and catering facilities are available.
Visitors are welcome all week.
Secretary: Mr. D. Carter – Tel: 0383 722591.
Professional: Mr. J. Forrester – Tel: 0383 723151.

87 Dunkeld
Perthshire

Dunkeld & Birnam Golf CLub
Fungarth, Dunkeld.
Tel: (0350) 727524.
9 holes, length of course 5264 yds.
SSS 66
Charges: On Application.
For advance reservations Tel: (0350) 727564.
Caddy cars and catering facilities are available.
Visitors are welcome all week without reservation.
Secretary: Mrs. W.A. Sinclair – Tel: (0350) 727564.

88 Dunning
Perthshire

Dunning Golf Club
Rollo Park, Dunning.
Tel: 398.
9 holes, length of course 4836 yds.
SSS 64
Charges: £5 round/daily, junior £2.50.
For Club/society bookings - Tel: 076484 312 (Secretary).
Caddy cars available.
No visitors after 5pm Mon-Fri, unless accompanied by member. No visitors before 4pm Saturday. No golf before 1pm on Sunday.
Secretary: Miss C. Westwood – Tel: 076484 312.

89 Dunoon
Argyll

Cowal Golf Club
Ardenslate Road, Dunoon.
Tel: Dunoon 5673.
18 holes, length of course 5716m/ 6251 yds.
SSS 70
Charges: £14 round (Mon–Fri), £18 round (Sat/Sun).
For advance reservations Tel: Dunoon 5673.
Caddy cars and catering facilities are available.
Secretary: Brian Chatham – Tel: Dunoon 5673.
Professional: R.D. Weir.

90 Duns
Berwickshire

Duns Golf Club
Hardens Road, Duns.
(Further details on application).

90A Durness
Sutherland

Durness Golf Club,
Durness, Sutherland.
9 holes, length of course 5545 yds /5040m.
SSS 68
Charges: £6 round/daily. £24 weekly.
For advance reservations Tel: Durness 364 or 351.
Caddy cars, practice area and catering facilities are available.
Visitors are welcome all week.

Secretary: Mrs. Lucy Mackay -
Tel: Durness 364.

91 Eaglesham
Renfrewshire

Bonnyton Golf Club
Eaglesham, Glasgow G76 0QA.
Tel: 03553 2781.
18 holes, length of course 6252 yds.
SSS 71
Charges: £25 daily.
Caddy cars, practice area and cater-
ing facilities are available.
Visitors welcome Monday to
Friday.
Secretary: A. Hughes – Tel: 03553
2781.
Professional: R. Crerar – Tel: 03553
2256.

92 East Kilbride
Lanarkshire

East Kilbride Golf Club
Nerston, East Kilbride, Glasgow
G74 4PF.
Tel: 03552 20913.
18 holes, length of course 6384 yds.
SSS 71
Charges: £14 round, £20 daily.
Visitors welcome weekdays only on
application if members of an official
club. Weekends, no visitors unless
accompanied by a member.
Secretary: W.G. Gray.
Professional: A.R. Taylor.

93 Edinburgh
Baberton Golf Club

Baberton Avenue, Juniper Green,
EH14 5DU.
Tel: 031-453 3361.
18 holes, length of course 6098 yds.
SSS 69
Eating facilities available by
arrangement.
Secretary: E.W. Horberry – Tel:
031-453 4911.
Professional: K. Kelly – Tel: 031-
453 3555.

*Braid Hills Golf Courses
Braid Hills Approach, Edinburgh
EH10.
(Further details on application).

**The Bruntsfield Links Golfing
Society**
32 Barnton Avenue, Davidsons
Mains, Edinburgh EH4 6JH.
Tel: 031-336 2006.
18 holes, length of course 6407 yds.
SSS 71
Charges: On Application.
For advance reservations Tel: 031-
336 1479.
A practice area, caddy cars and
catering facilities are available.
Secretary: Lt. Col. M.B. Hext – Tel:
031-
336 1479.
Professional: Brian MacKenzie –
Tel: 031-336 4050.

*Carrick Knowe Golf Club
27 Glen Devon Park, Edinburgh.
Tel: 031-337 2217.
(Further details on application).

*Craigentinny Golf Course
Craigentinny Avenue, Lochend,
Edinburgh.
Tel: 031-554 7501.
(Further details on application).

Portobello Golf Club
Stanley Street, Edinburgh EH15.
Tel: 031-669 4361.
9 holes, length of course 2167m/
2400 yds.
SSS 32
Charges: Weekdays & Sat & Sun £3
(9).
For advance reservations Tel: 031-
669 4361.
Visitors are welcome all week.
Secretary: Mr. Alistair Cook.

Duddingston Golf Club
Duddingston Road West,
Edinburgh.
Tel: 031-661 7688.
18 holes, length of course
6078m/6647 yds.
SSS 72
Charges: £18 round, £24 daily
(Mon-Fri). Societies - £15 round,
£21.50 day (Tue & Thurs only).
For advance reservations Tel: 031-
661 7688.
A practice area, caddy cars and
catering facilities are available.
Secretary: J.C. Small – Tel: 031-661
7688.
Professional: Mr. A. MacLean.

Kingsknowe Golf Club Ltd
326 Lanark Road, Edinburgh EH14
2JD.
Tel: 031-441 1145.

18 holes, length of course
5469m/5979 yds.
SSS 69
Charges £14 round, £18 daily, £50
weekly.
For advance reservations Tel: 031-
441 4030.
A practice area, caddy cars and
catering facilities are available.
Visitors are welcome.
Secretary: R. Wallace – Tel: 031-
441 1145.
Professional: W. Bauld – Tel: 031-
441 4030.

Lothianburn Golf Club
106a Biggar Road,
Edinburgh EH10 7DU.
Tel: 031-445 2206.
Visitors Welcome.
Secretary/Treasurer: W.F.A. Jardine
- Tel: 031-445 5067.
Professional: Paul Morton - Tel:
031-445 2288.
(Further details on application).

**Merchants of Edinburgh Golf
Club**
10 Craighill Gardens, Edinburgh
EH10 5PY.
Tel: 031-447 1219.
18 holes, length of course 4889 yds.
SSS 64
Charges: £8 round, £12 daily.
Reductions for arranged parties.
For advance reservations Tel: 031-
447 1219.
Catering facilities are available by
arrangement.
Visiting clubs welcome Monday to
Friday by request to the Secretary.
Secretary: A.M. Montgomery –
Tel: 031-447 7093.
Professional: Craig A. Imlah – Tel:
031-447 8709.

Mortonhall Golf Club
231 Braid Road, EH10 6PB.
Tel: 031-447 2411.
18 holes, length of course
5987m/6548 yds.
SSS 71
Charges: On application
Catering facilities available.
Visitors are welcome with introduc-
tion.
Secretary: Mr. P.T. Ricketts – Tel:
031-447 6974.
Professional: D. Horn.

**Prestonfield Golf Club
(Private)**
6 Priestfield Road North,
Edinburgh.

Tel: 031-667 1273.
18 holes, length of course
5685m/6216 yds.
SSS 70
Charges: On application.
For advance reservations Tel: 031-667 8597.
A practice area, caddy cars and catering facilities are available.
Secretary: M.D.A.G. Dillon
Professional: Mr. B. Commins

*Silverknowes Golf Club (Private)
Silverknowes Parkway, Edinburgh EH4 5ET.
Tel: 031-336 5359.
(Further details on application).

Ratho Park Golf Club
Ratho, Newbridge, Midlothian EH28 8NX.
Tel: 031-333 1252.
18 holes, length of course 5398m/5900 yds.
SSS 68
Charges: £16.50 round, £25 daily, £30 weekend.
For advance reservations Tel: 031-333 1406.
A practice area, caddy cars and catering facilities are available.
Visitors are welcome Tuesday, Wednesday and Thursday.
Secretary: Mr. J.C. McLafferty – Tel: 031-333 1752.
Professional: Mr. A. Pate – Tel: 031-333 1406.

Ravelston Golf Club
24 Ravelston Dykes Road, EH4 5NZ.
Tel: 031-315 2486.
9 holes, length of course 4754 m/5200 yds.
SSS 66 (men)
SSS 69 (ladies)
Charges: £10 daily for visitors.
Visitors are welcome (Mon. to Fri.)
Secretary: Mr. Frank Philip.

The Royal Burgess Golfing Society of Edinburgh
181 Whitehouse Road, Edinburgh EH4 6BY.
Tel: 031-339 2075.
18 holes, length of course 6494 yds.
SSS 71
Charges: On application.
For advance reservations Tel: 031-339 2075.
Trolley and catering facilities are available.
Visitors/parties are welcome Mon-Fri.
Secretary: John P. Audis –

Tel: 031-339 2075.
Professional: George Yuille – Tel: 031-339 6474.

Torphin Hill Golf Club
Torphin Road, Edinburgh EH13 0PL.
Tel: 031-441 1100.
18 holes, length of course 4597m/5020 yds.
SSS 66
Charges: £10 weekdays, £16 weekends daily.
For advance reservations Tel: 031-441 1100.
Practice area and catering facilities are available.
Visitors are welcome all week, except competition days (phone for details).
Secretary: E.H. Merchant - Tel: 031-441 1100.

94 Edzell
By Brechin, Angus

The Edzell Golf Club
High Street, Edzell DD9 7TF.
Tel: 035 64 235 (Clubhouse).
18 holes, length of course 6348 yds.
SSS 70
Charges: Weekday £15 round, weekend £20 round, weekday £22.50 daily, weekend £30 daily, £75 weekly.
For advance reservations Tel: 035 64 7283.
A practice area, caddy cars and catering facilities are available (Caddies by arrangement).
Visitors are welcome all week.
Secretary: J.M. Hutchison – Tel: 0356 647283.
Professional: A.J. Webster – Tel: 0356 648462.

95 Elderslie
Renfrewshire

Elderslie Golf Club
63 Main Road, Elderslie.
Tel: Johnstone 22835/23956.
18 holes, length of course 6031 yds.
SSS 69
Charges: £15.50 round, £21 daily.
For advance reservations Tel: Johnstone 23956.
A practice area and catering facilities are available. Plus P.G.A. professional shop etc.
Secretary: W. Muirhead – Tel: Johnstone 23956.

96 Elgin
Morayshire

Elgin Golf Club
Hardhillock, Birnie Road, Elgin IV30 3SX.
Tel: 0343 542338.
18 holes, length of course 5853m/6401 yds.
SSS 71
Charges: Weekdays: £13 round, £19 daily. Weekends: £18.50 round, £26.50 daily.
For advance reservations Tel: 0343 542338.
Caddies (by arrangement), caddy cars, and practice area. Catering facilities are available.
Visitors are welcome.
Secretary: Derek J. Chambers – Tel: 0343 542338.
Professional: Ian Rodger – Tel: 0343 542884.

97 Elie
Fife

Earlsferry Thistle Golf Club
Melon Park.
Tel: Anstruther 310053.
(Further details on application).

'The Golf House Club'
Elie, Fife KY9 1AS.
Tel: (0333) 330301.
18 holes, length of course 6241 yds.
SSS 70
Charges: Mon-Fri £20 round, £27.50 daily. Sat/Sun £30 round, £37.50 daily.
For advance reservations Tel: (0333) 330301.
Catering facilities are available.
Visitors are welcome midweek.
Secretary: A. Sneddon – Tel: (0333) 330301.
Professional: Robin Wilson – Tel: (0333) 330955.

98 Ellon
Aberdeenshire

McDonald Golf Club
Hospital Road, Ellon.
Tel: 0358 20576.
18 holes.
SSS 69
Charges: Mon-Fri £10, Sat £12, Sun
£15.
Catering facilities available on
request.
Secretary: Fred Chadwick –
Tel: 0358 21397.
Professional: Ronnie Urquhart –
Tel: 0358 22891.

99 Eyemouth
Berwickshire

Eyemouth Golf Club
(Further details on application).

100 Falkirk
Stirlingshire

Falkirk Golf Club
Stirling Road, Camelon, Falkirk.
Tel: 0324 611061/612219.
18 holes, length of course 6267 yds.
SSS 69
Charges: £8 round, £14 daily.
Advance reservations by
arrangement with starter Tel: 0324
612219.
A practice area and catering
facilities are available.
Visitors are welcome Monday to
Friday up to 4.00 pm, (Parties –
Mon/Tues/Thurs/Fri/Sun).
Secretary: J. Elliott – Tel: 0324
34118 (Home).

*Grangemouth Golf Course
Polmont Hill, By Polmont.
Tel: Polmont 711500.
(Further details on application).

101 Falkland
Fife

Falkland Golf Course
The Myre, Falkland.
Tel: Falkland 57404.
9 holes, length of course
2384m/2608 yds.
SSS 66 (18)
Charges: £5 daily (Mon-Fri), £7
(Sat/Sun).
Visitors are welcome. Parties are

welcome by prior arrangement.
Secretary: Mrs. C.R. Forsythe – Tel:
Falkland 57356.

102 Fauldhouse
West Lothian

Greenburn Golf Club
Greenburn, Bridge Street,
Fauldhouse.
Tel: 0501 70292.
(Further details on application).

103 Fochabers
Morayshire

**Garmouth & Kingston Golf
Club**
Garmouth, Fochabers.
Tel: 0343 87388.
18 holes, length of course 5656 yds.
SSS 67
Charges: Mon-Fri £10 round, £12
daily. Weekends £14 round, £18
daily. Reduced charges for parties
over 12.
For advance reservations Tel: 0343
87231.
Catering facilities are available.
Visitors are welcome all week.
Secretary: A. Robertson – Tel: 0343
87231.

104 Forfar
Angus

Forfar Golf Club
Cunninghill, Arbroath Road, Forfar
DD8 2RL.
Tel: 0307 62120.
18 holes, length of course
5497m/6108 yds.
SSS 69
Charges: £14 round (Mon-Fri), £20
daily. £25 daily Sat/Sun.
For advance reservations Tel: 0307
63773.
A practice area, caddy cars and
catering facilities are available.
Visitors are welcome all week.
Managing Secretary: W. Baird –
Tel: 0307 63773.
Professional: Mr. P. McNiven – Tel:
0307 65683.

105 Forres
Morayshire

Forres Golf Club
Muiryshade, Forres, IV36 0RD.
Tel: 0309 672949.
18 holes, length of course
5615m/6141 yds.
SSS 69
Charges: £12 daily, £17 weekends.
For advance reservations Tel:
Forres 672949.
Caddy cars, practice area and cater-
ing facilities are available.
Visitors are welcome all week.
Secretary: D.F. Black – Tel: Forres
672949.
Professional: Sandy Aird – Tel:
Forres 672250.

106 Fort Augustus
Inverness-shire

Fort Augustus Golf Club
Markethill, Fort Augustus.
Tel: Fort Augustus 6460.
9 holes (18 tees), length of course
5454 yds.
SSS 68
Charges: £4 daily.
For advance reservations Tel: Fort
Augustus 6460.
Caddy cars available.
Visitors are welcome all week,
except Saturday afternoons.
Secretary: I.D. Aitchison – Tel: Fort
Augustus 6460.

107 Fortrose
Ross-shire

**Fortrose & Rosemarkie Golf
Club**
Ness Road East, Fortrose IV10 8SE.
Tel: Fortrose 20529.
18 holes, length of course 5858 yds.
SSS 69
Charges: £10 per round Mon-Fri;
£15 per round Sat/Sun. £15 daily
Mon-Fri. £40 5-day ticket.
For advance reservations Tel:
Fortrose 20529 (parties only).
A practice area and caddy car avail-
able.
Visitors are welcome all week.
Secretary: Margaret Collier – Tel:
Fortrose 20529.

108 Fort William
Inverness-shire

Fort William Golf Club
North Road, Torlundy, Fort William.
Tel: 0397 704464.
18 holes, length of course 6217 yds.
SSS 71
Charges: £8 round, £10 daily.
Bar snacks available.
Visitors are welcome all week.
Secretary: Mr. J. Allan.

109 Fraserburgh
Aberdeenshire

Fraserburgh Golf Club
Philorth, Fraserburgh.
Tel: 0346 28287.
18 holes, length of course 6279 yds.
SSS 70
Charges: £10 daily (Mon-Fri), £14 (Sat/Sun), £40 weekly.
A practice area and catering facilities are available.
Secretary: Mr. J. Grant – Tel: 03465 2978.

110 Gailes
By Irvine, Ayrshire

Glasgow Golf Club
Gailes, Irvine.
Tel: 0294 311347.
18 holes, length of course 5937m/6493 yds.
SSS 71
Charges: £25 round, £30 daily (to be reviewed in December). 25% deposit required.
For advance reservations Tel: 041-942 2011.
A practice area, caddy cars and catering facilities are available.
Caddies available by prior arrangement.
Visitors are welcome Monday to Friday (Prior arrangement for parties of more than 8 players).
Professional: Mr. J. Steven – Tel: 041-942 8507.

111 Gairloch
Ross-shire

Gairloch Golf Club
Gairloch IV21 2BQ.
Tel: 0445 2407.
9 holes, length of course (18 holes)
4250 yds. SSS 63
Charges: £10 daily, £45 weekly. £5 daily for OAP's/juniors.
Caddy cars are available. Club hire.
Visitors are welcome all week.
Secretary: John M. Dingwall - Tel: 0445 2407.

112 Galashiels
Selkirkshire

Torwoodlee Golf Club
Edinburgh Road, Galashiels.
Tel: Galashiels 2260.
9 holes, length of course 5800 yds.
Charges: £12 round, £15 daily.
A practice area, caddy cars and catering facilities are available.
Visitors are welcome all week, except Saturdays to 5.00 pm and Thursdays after 2.00pm.
Secretary: A. Wilson – Tel: 0896 2260.

113 Galston
Ayrshire

Loudoun Gowf Club
Galston.
Tel: 0563 821993.
(Further details on application).

114 Gatehouse of Fleet
Kirkcudbrightshire

Gatehouse Golf Club
Gatehouse of Fleet.
Tel: Gatehouse 814459.
(Further details on application).

115 Gifford
East Lothian

Gifford Golf Club
c/o Secretary, Calroust, Tweeddale Avenue, Gifford EH41 4QN.
Tel: Gifford 267.
9 and 11 Tees, length of course 5613m.
SSS 69
Charges: £8 round/daily (Mon-Sun).
A small practice area is available.
Visitors welcome, except Tuesdays and Wednesdays from 4.00 pm, Saturdays and Sundays from 12 noon.
Course closed all day first Sunday each month - April to October.
Secretary: D.A. Fantom –
Tel: Gifford 267.

116 Girvan
Ayrshire

Girvan Golf Club
Golf Course Road, Girvan.
Tel: Girvan 4346.
18 holes, length of course 5095 yds.
SSS 65
Charges: £9 round. £16 daily.
Trolleys are available. Catering facilties can be arranged Tel: Girvan 4272.
Visitors are welcome all week.
Secretary: Mrs. R. Mitchell.

117 Glasgow

*Alexandra Park Golf Course

Alexandra Park, Denniston, Glasgow.
Tel: 041-556 3711.
9 holes, length of course 2870 yds.
Charges: Monday to Friday - Adults:£1.65, Juveniles: £0.85, Passport to recreation holders: £0.55. Sat & Sun - Adults: £1.95, Juveniles: £0.85, Passport to recreation holders: £0.55.
For advance reservations Tel: 041-556 3711.
A practice area and catering facilities are available.
Visitors are welcome all week.
Secretary: R. Watt.

Bishopbriggs Golf Club
Brackenbrae Road, Bishopbriggs, Glasgow.
Tel: 041-772 1810.
18 holes, length of course 6041 yds.
SSS 69
Charges: On application.
Catering facilities are available.
Parties are welcome with reservation, Tues, Weds & Thurs only (apply to secretary).
Secretary: John Magin – Tel: 041-772 8938.

Cathcart Castle Golf Club
Mearns Road, Glasgow G76 7YL.
Tel: 041-638 9449.
18 holes, length of course 5330m/5832 yds.
(Further details on application)

Cawder Golf Club
Cadder Road, Bishopbriggs.
2 x 18 holes, length of course
Cawder 5711m/6244 yds, Keir
5373m/5885 yds.
SSS 71 & 68
Charges: £18.50 daily.
For advance reservations Tel: 041-
772 5167.
A practice area, caddy cars and
catering facilities are available.
Visitors are welcome Monday to
Friday.
Secretary: G.T. Stoddart –
Tel: 041-772 5167.
Professional: K. Stevely –
Tel: 041-772 7102.

Cowglen Golf Club
301 Barrhead Road, Glasgow G43.
Tel: 041-632 0556.
(Further details on application).

Crow Wood Golf Club
Garnkirk Estate, Muirhead,
Chryston G69 9JF.
Tel: 041-779 2011.
(Further details on application).

*Deaconsbank Golf Course
Rouken Glen Golf Centre,
Stewarton Road, (Junction A726),
Thornliebank, Giffnock G46 7UZ.
Tel: 041-638 7044 or 041-620 0826.
18 holes, length of course 4800 yds.
SSS 63 (Par 64).
Charges: Mon-Fri £5.25, Sat/Sun
£6.50. Day ticket £7 & £11.
Catering facilities are available.
15 bay floodlit driving range, shop
facilities and hiring of clubs, etc.
Visitors are welcome.
Secretary: Christine Cosh.

Haggs Castle Golf Club
70 Dumbreck Road, Glasgow G41
4SN.
Tel: 041-427 1157.
18 holes, length of course 6464 yds.
SSS 71
Charges: £24 round, £36 daily.
For advance reservations Tel: 041-
427 1157.
A practice area, caddy cars and
catering facilities are available.
Visitors must be introduced by a
member. Parties only on
Wednesdays.
Secretary: Ian Harvey – Tel: 041-
427 1157.
Professional: J. McAlister – Tel:
041-427 3355.

Glasgow Golf Club
Killermont, Bearsden, Glasgow.
Tel: 041-942 2011.
18 holes, length of course
5456m/5968 yds.
SSS 69
Charges: On Application.
Visitors by member's introduction
on weekdays only.
Professional: Jack Steven – Tel:
041-942 8507.

Kings Park Golf Course
Carmunnock Road,
Glasgow G44.
9 holes
Charges: Monday to Friday -
Adults: £1.65, Juveniles: £0.85,
Passportto recreation holders: £0.55.
Sat & Sun - Adults: £1.95,
Juveniles: £0.85, Passport to
recreation holders: £0.55.
(For further information contact the
Golf Manager on 041-554 8274.)

*Knightswood Golf Course
Chaplet Avenue,
Glasgow G13.
Tel: 041-959 2131.
9 holes
Charges: Monday to Friday -
Adults: £1.65, Juveniles: £0.85,
Passport to recreation holders:
£0.55. Sat & Sun £1.95 all
categories.
(Further details on application).

*Lethamhill Golf Course
Hogganfield Loch,
Cumbernauld Road,
Glasgow G33 1AH.
Tel: 041-770 6220.
18 holes.
Charges: Monday to Friday -
Adults: £3.25, Juveniles: £1.85,
Passport to recreation holders:
£1.15. Sat & Sun £3.80 all
categories.
(Further details on application).

*Linn Park Golf Course
Simshill Road, Glasgow G44 5TA.
Tel: 041-637 5871.
18 holes.
Charges: Monday to Friday -
Adults: £3.25, Juveniles: £1.85,
Passport to recreation holders:
£1.15. Sat & Sun £3.80 all
categories.
For advance reservations Tel: 041-
637 5871.

*Littlehill Golf Course
Auchinairn Road, Glasgow G64 1OT.

Tel: 041-772 1916.
18 holes.
Charges: Monday to Friday -
Adults: £3.25, Juveniles: £1.85,
Passport to recreation holders:
£1.15. Sat & Sun £3.80 all
categories.

Mount Ellen Golf Club
Johnstone House, Johnstone Road,
Gartcosh.
Tel: Glenboig 872277.
18 holes, length of course 5525 yds.
SSS 68
Charges: £6 round, £16 daily (pack-
age deal). New offer to 'casual visi-
tor' Mon-Fri, £5.00 per round,
£8.00 per day (8.30 am-4.30 pm).
For advance reservations Tel:
Glenboig 872277.
Catering facilities are available.
Visitors are welcome all week.
Secretary: W.J. Dickson.

Pollock Golf Club
90 Barrhead Road, Glasgow.
Tel: 041-632 4351/1080.
(Further details on application).

*Ruchill Golf Course
Bilsland Drive,
Glasgow G22.
9 holes.
Charges: Monday to Friday -
Adults: £1.65, Juveniles: £0.85,
Passport to recreation holders:
£0.55. Sat & Sun - Adults: £1.95,
Juveniles: £0.85, Passport to
recreation holders: £0.55.
For further information contact the
Golf Manager on 041-554 8274.

118 Glenluce
Wigtownshire

**Wigtownshire County Golf
Club**
Mains of Park, Glenluce, Newton
Stewart.
Tel: Glenluce 420.
18 holes, length of course
5226m/5715 yds.
SSS 68
Charges: £11 per round, £14 daily
(weekdays); £13 per round, £16
daily (Sat/Sun).
For advance reservations Tel: 058
13 589.
Catering facilities are available.
Visitors are welcome all week
except Wednesdays after 5.30 pm.
Secretary: R. McCubbin – Tel: 058
13 589.

119 Glenrothes
Fife

Balbirnie Park Golf Club
Balbirnie Park, Markinch, By
Glenrothes, Fife.
Tel: (0592) 752006.
18 holes, length of course 6400 yds.
SSS 70
Charges: On Application.
For advance reservations Tel:
(0592) 752006.
Catering facilities by arrangement,
contact Ian Forbes.
Visitors are welcome all week.
Secretary: A.G. Grant - Tel. (0592)
757114.

Glenrothes Golf Club
Golf Course Road, Glenrothes.
Tel: 0592 758686.
Length of course 5984m/6444 yds.
SSS 71
Charges: £7.60 round, £13 daily
(weekday), £10 round, £15 daily
(weekend).
Starter: Tel: (0592) 750063.
For advance reservations Tel: 0592
754561 (Evenings), min. 12 players.
A practice area and catering
facilities are available.
Visitors are welcome all week.
Secretary: L.D. Dalrymple – Tel:
(0592) 754561.

120 Glenshee (Spittal o')
by Blairgowrie, Perthshire

Dalmunzie Golf Course
Tel: 025-085 224.
9 holes, length of course 2036
yards.
SSS 60
Charges: £7 daily. Under-14's half
price, under-7's free. Weekly family
ticket £55.
Catering and accommodation available.

121 Golspie
Sutherland

Golspie Golf Club
Ferry Road, Golspie.
Tel: 0408 633266.
18 holes, length of course
5337m/5836 yds.
SSS 68 (Gents)
SSS 71 (Ladies)
Charges: £14 daily, £70 weekly.

A practice area, caddy cars and
catering facilities are available.
Secretary: Mrs. Marie MacLeod.

122 Gourock
Renfrewshire

Gourock Golf Club
Cowal View, Gourock.
Tel: Gourock 31001.
18 holes, length of course
5936m/6492 yds.
SSS 71
Charges: On application.
A practice area and catering
facilities are available.
Visitors are welcome Monday to
Friday.
Secretary: Mr. C.M. Campbell –
Tel: Gourock 31001.
Professional: Mr. A. Green – Tel:
36834.

123 Grantown on Spey
Morayshire

Grantown on Spey Golf Club
The Clubhouse, Grantown-on-Spey.
Tel: 0479 2079.
18 holes, length of course 5631 yds.
SSS 67
Charges: £13 per day, £16
weekends, £50 weekly.
For advance reservations Tel: 0479
2715/2079.
Caddy cars, practice area and cater-
ing facilities are available.
Visitors are welcome all week.
Secretary: Dennis Elms – Tel: 0479
2715.

124 Greenock
Renfrewshire

Greenock Golf Club
Forsyth Street, Greenock
PA16 8RE.
Tel: 0475 20793.
27 holes, length of course 5888 yds.
SSS 68
Charges: £12 round, £15 daily.
For advance reservations Tel: 0475
87236.
A practice area, caddy cars and
catering facilities are available.
Visitors are welcome Tuesday,
Thursday and Sunday.
Secretary: E.J. Black – Tel: 0475
20793.

125 Gullane
East Lothian

Gullane No 1 Golf Course
East Lothian EH31 2BB.
Tel: 0620 842255.
18 holes, length of course
5913m/6466 yds.
SSS 71
Charges: £31 (Mon-Fri), £41
(Sat/Sun) round, £46 daily (Mon-
Fri). (1992 rates).
For advance reservations Tel: 0620
84 2255.
Caddy cars, caddies and catering
facilities are available.
Secretary: A.J.B. Taylor – Tel: 0620
842255.
Professional: J. Hume – Tel: 0620
843111.

Gullane No 2 Golf Course
East Lothian EH31 2BB.
Tel: 0620 842255.
18 holes, length of course 6233 yds.
SSS 70
Charges: £14 round (Mon-Fri), £17
(Sat/Sun). £21 daily (Mon- Fri), £27
(Sat/Sun) (1992 rates).
For advance reservations Tel: 0620
842255.
Caddy cars, caddies and catering
facilities are available.
Secretary: A.J.B. Taylor – Tel: 0620
842255.
Professional: J. Hume – Tel: 0620
843111.

Gullane No 3 Golf Course
East Lothian EH31 2BB.
Tel: 0620 842255.
18 holes, length of course 5166 yds.
SSS 65
Charges: £10 round (Mon-Fri), £12
(Sat/Sun). £14 daily (Mon-Fri), £17
(Sat/Sun) (1992 rates).
For advance reservations Tel: 0620
842255.
Caddy cars, caddies and catering
facilities are available.
Secretary: A.J.B. Taylor – Tel: 0620
842255.
Professional: J. Hume – Tel: 0620
843111.

**The Honourable Company of
Edinburgh Golfers**
Muirfield, Gullane, East Lothian
EH31 2EG.
Tel: 0620 842123.
18 holes, length of course 6601 yds.
SSS 73
Charges: £45 round, £60 daily (1992).

For advance reservations
Tel: 0620 84 2123.
Caddies, caddy cars, practice area and catering facilities are available. Visitors are welcome, but check with club.
Secretary: Group Captain J.A. Prideaux – Tel: 0620 84 2123.

126 Haddington
East Lothian

Haddington Golf Club
Amisfield Park, Haddington.
Tel: 062 082 3627/2727.
18 holes, length of course 5764m/6280 yds.
SSS 70
Charges: £9.25 round (Mon-Fri), £12 (weekends). £12.75 daily (Mon-Fri), £16 (weekends).
For advance reservations Tel: 062 082 2727.
A practice area, caddy cars and catering facilities are available. Visitors are welcome all week.
Secretary: A.S.F. Watt – Tel: 062 082 3627.
Professional: J. Sandilands – Tel: 062 082 2727.

127 Hamilton
Lanarkshire

Hamilton Golf Club
(Further details on application).

128 Hawick
Roxburghshire

Minto Golf Club
Denholm, Hawick.
Tel: 0450 87220.
18 holes, length of course 4992m/5460 yds.
SSS 68
Charges: £7 weekdays. £10 weekends.
For advance reservations Tel: 0450 72180.
A practice area, caddy cars and catering facilities are available. Visitors are welcome all week.
Secretary: Mrs. E. Mitchell – Tel: 0450 72180.

129 Helensburgh
Dunbartonshire

Helensburgh Golf Club
25 East Abercromby Street, Helensburgh.
Tel: Helensburgh (0436) 74173.
(Further details on application).

130 Helmsdale
Sutherland

Helmsdale Golf Club
Golf Road, Helmsdale KW8 6JA.
Tel: 043 12 240.
9 holes, length of course 3338m/3650 yds (2 x 9 holes).
SSS 62
Charges: £3 round £5 daily, £15 weekly.
For advance reservations Tel: 043 12 240.
Visitors are welcome all week.
Secretary: Mr. J. Mackay – Tel: 043 12 240.

131 Hopeman
Morayshire

Hopeman Golf Club
Hopeman, Elgin, Morayshire.
Tel: (0343) 830578.
18 holes, length of course 5003m/5474 yds.
SSS 67
Charges: Daily (Mon-Fri), £10, after 3pm £7. (Sat-Sun), £15, after 3pm £10. 5-day ticket (Mon-Fri) £28, 7-day consecutive ticket £35.
For advance reservations Tel: 0343 830578.
A small practice area and catering facilities are available. Visitors are welcome all week.
Secretary: W.H. Dunbar - Tel: (0343) 830687.

132 Huntly
Aberdeenshire

Huntly Golf Club
Cooper Park, Huntly.
Tel: 0466 792643.
18 holes, length of course 5399 yds.
SSS 66.
Charges: £10 (weekdays) £12 (weekends) daily.
Catering facilities are available.
Secretary: G. Alexander.

133 Innellan
Argyllshire

Innellan Golf Club
Innellan.
Tel: Innellan 242.
9 holes, length of course 18 holes 4246m/4642 yds.
Charges: £4 (Mon-Sat), £5 Sun per round. £4 (Mon-Sat), £5 Sun daily. Weekly £12.
Catering facilities are available. Visitors are welcome all week, except Mon, Tues and Wed from 5 pm.
Secretary: Jeff Arden – Tel: Dunoon 3546.

134 Innerleithen
Peeblesshire

Innerleithen Golf Club
Leithen Water.
9 holes, length of course 5318m/5820 yds.
SSS 68
Charges: £7 daily Mon-Fri, £9 daily weekends.
Secretary: S.C. Wyse – Tel: Innerleithen 830071.

135 Inverallochy
Aberdeenshire

Inverallochy Golf Course
24 Shore Street, Cairnbulg.
Tel: Inverallochy 2324.
18 holes, length of course 5137 yds.
Par 64.
(Further details on application).

136 Invergordon
Ross-shire

Invergordon Golf Club
(Further details on application).

137 Inverness
Inverness-shire

Inverness Golf Club
Culcabock Road, Inverness IV2 3XQ.
Tel: 0463 239882.
18 holes, length of course 5694m/6226 yds.
SSS 70
Charges: £14 round (weekdays), £20 round (Sundays and public holi-

days), £50 weekly.
For advance reservations Tel: 0463 231989.
A practice area, caddy cars, caddies and catering facilities are available.
Visitors are welcome all week.
Professional: A.P. Thomson – Tel: 0463 231989.

138 Inverurie
Aberdeenshire

Inverurie Golf Club
Davah Wood, Blackhall Road, Inverurie.
Tel: Inverurie 20207/24080.
18 holes, length of course 5096 yds.
SSS 66
Charges: £8 daily (Mon-Fri), £12 (Sat/Sun).
A practice area (for members only), caddy cars and catering facilities are available.
Administrator: Mrs. A. Gerrard – Tel:
Inverurie 24080.

139 Irvine
Ayrshire

The Irvine Golf Club
Bogside, Irvine.
Tel: 0294 75979.
18 holes, length of course 5858m/6408 yds.
SSS 71
Charges: £23 round, £28 daily.
For advance reservations Tel: Bogside 75979.
A practice area, caddy cars and catering facilities are available (Caddies by arrangement).
Visitors are welcome by arrangement.
Secretary: Mr. Andrew Morton – Tel: 0294 75979.
Professional: Mr. Keith Erskine – Tel: Irvine 75626.

*Ravenspark Golf Course
Kidsneuk.
Tel: Irvine 79550.
(Further details on application).

140 Jedburgh
Roxburghshire

Jedburgh Golf Club
Dunion Road, Jedburgh.
Tel: 0835 63587.
9 holes, length of course

2746m/5492 yds.
SSS 67
Charges: £10 daily.
For advance reservations Tel: 0835 63587 (evenings).
Catering facilities are available.
Visitors are welcome all week.
Secretary: R. Strachan.

141 Johnstone
Renfrewshire

Cochrane Castle Golf Club
Craigston, Johnstone PA5 0HF.
Tel: 0505 20146.
18 holes, length of course 6226 yds.
SSS 70
Charges: £10 (round), £15 (daily).
Advance reservations by letter only.
Caddy cars, a practice area and catering facilities are available.
Visitors are welcome Monday to Friday.
Secretary: J.C. Cowan - Tel: 0505 20146.
Professional: Stuart H. Campbell - Tel: 0505 28465.

142 Keith
Banffshire

Keith Golf Course
Fife Park.
Tel: Keith 2469.
(Further details on application).

143 Kelso
Roxburghshire

Kelso Golf Club
Racecourse Road, Kelso.
Tel: 0573 23009.
(Further details on application).

144 Kemnay
Aberdeenshire

Kemnay Golf Club
Monymusk Road, Kemnay.
Tel: 0467 42225.
9 holes.
SSS 67
Charges: £8 daily, £10 weekends.
For advance reservations Tel: 0467 42225.
Limited Catering available from the bar.
Visitors are welcome Sundays, depending on starting times.
Secretary: Mr. D.W. Imrie – Tel: 0467 43047.

145 Kenmore
Perthshire

Taymouth Castle Golf Course
Kenmore, Tayside PH15 2NT.
Tel: 0887 830228.
18 holes, length of course 6066 yds.
Mens Medal Tees SSS 69
Yellow Tees SSS 67
Ladies SSS 72
Charges: Weekday £14, weekend & Bank Hols. £18 (round). Weekdays £22 (daily).
For advance reservations - Mike Mulcahey Tel: 0887 830228.
Caddy cars, a practice area and catering facilities are available.
Visitors are welcome all week with reservations.
Professional: Alex Marshall - Tel: 0887 820910.

146 Kilbirnie
Ayrshire

Kilbirnie Place Golf Club
Largs Road, Kilbirnie.
Tel: Kilbirnie 683398.
18 holes, length of course 5500 yds.
SSS 67
Charges: £10 weekday, £17.50 Sunday (round). £15 weekday (daily).
Catering facilities are available.
Visitors are welcome, except Saturdays.
Secretary: J.C. Walker - Tel Kilbirnie 682998.

147 Killin
Perthshire

Killin Golf Club
Killin Golf Course
Killin.
Tel: Killin 312.
9 holes, length of course 2410 yds.
SSS 65
Charges: weekday round £6.50, weekend round £8.50.
Caddy cars and catering facilities are available.
Visitors are welcome all week.
Secretary: Mr. A. Chisholm – Tel: 08383 235.

148 Kilmacolm
Renfrewshire

Kilmacolm Golf Club
Porterfield Road, Kilmacolm.
Tel: Kilmacolm 2139.
18 holes, length of course 5890 yds.
SSS 68
Charges: £15 per round, £20 daily.
Caddy cars, a practice area and
catering facilities are available.
Visitors are welcome on weekdays.
Professional: D. Stewart - Tel 2695.

149 Kilmarnock
Ayrshire

*Caprington Golf Club
Ayr Road, Kilmarnock.
Tel: Kilmarnock 21915.
(Further details on application).

150 Kilspindie
East Lothian

Kilspindie Golf Club
Aberlady, East Lothian EH32 0QD.
Tel: Aberlady 216 or 358.
18 holes, length of course
4957m/5410 yds.
SSS 66
Charges: £16 round (Mon–Fri), £20
(Sat/Sun), £20 daily (Mon–Fri), £26
(Sat/Sun).
A practice area, caddy cars and
catering facilities are available.
Visitors are welcome Monday to
Friday.
Secretary: H.F. Brown – Tel:
Aberlady 358.

151 Kilsyth
Stirlingshire

Kilsyth Lennox Golf Club
Tak-Ma-Doon Road, Kilsyth, G65
0HX.
Tel: Kilsyth 822190.
9 holes, length of course 5934 yds.
SSS 69
Charges: £6 round, £10 daily.
Catering facilities are available.
Visitors are welcome all week with
reservation.
Secretary: A.G. Stevenson

152 Kincardine on Forth
Fife

Tulliallan Golf Club
Alloa Road, Kincardine-on-Forth.
Tel: Kincardine-on-Forth 30396.
18 holes, length of course
5459m/5965 yds.
SSS 69
Charges: £13 round (Mon–Fri), £15
(Sat/Sun), £17 daily (Mon–Fri), £21
(Sat/Sun).
For advance reservations Tel: 0259
30798.
Caddy cars and catering facilities
are available.
Visitors are welcome by prior
arrangement.
Secretary: J.S. McDowall – Tel:
0324 485420.
Professional: Steve Kelly – Tel:
0259 30798.

153 Kingarth
Isle of Bute

Bute Golf Club
Kingarth.
9 holes, length of course
2284m/2497 yds.
SSS 64
Charges: Adults £5 daily, £15
weekly. Juniors (under-17 yrs) £1
daily, £5 pa + £5 joining fee.
Secretary: J. Burnside.

154 Kinghorn
Fife

Kinghorn Municipal Golf Club
c/o Kirkcaldy District Council,
Leisure & Direct Services Division,
Kinghorn.
Tel: (0592) 645000.
18 holes, length of course
4544m/4969 yds.
SSS 67
(Par 65)
Charges: £7.60 round (Mon–Fri),
£10 (Sat/Sun) (1992).
Catering facilites through
Clubmistress Tel: Kinghorn
890345.
Secretary: J.P. Robertson – Tel:
(0592) 203397.

155 Kingussie
Inverness-shire

Kingussie Golf Club
Gynack Road, Kingussie.
Tel: Clubhouse - Kingussie 661374
Sec. Office - Kingussie 661600.
18 holes, length of course
5079m/5555 yds.
SSS 67
Charges: Weekdays £10 round, £13
daily; Sat/Sun £12 round, £16 daily.
£45 weekly (1992).
For advance reservations Tel:
Kingussie 661600/661374.
Caddy cars and catering facilities
are available.
Visitors are welcome all week.
Secretary: W.M. Cook – Tel:
Kingussie 661600.

156 Kinnesswood
Kinross-shire

Bishopshire Golf Course
(Further details on application).

157 Kinross
Kinross-shire

Green Hotel Golf Courses
Green Hotel.
Tel: 0577 63467.
Red Course - 18 holes, length of
course 5719m/6257 yds.
SSS 73
Blue Course - 18 holes, length of
course 5905m/6456 yds.
SSS 74
Charges (both courses): £11 round
Mon-Fri, £15 Sat/Sun. £15 daily
Mon-Fri, £20 Sat/Sun (1991).
For advance reservation Tel: Green
Hotel.
Caddy cars and catering facilities
are available.
Secretary: S.M. Stewart.

158 Kintore
Aberdeenshire

Kintore Golf Club
Balbithan Road, Kintore.
Tel: Kintore 32631.
18 holes, length of course 5974 yds.
SSS 69
Charges: £8 daily, £12 weekends.
£6 after 6pm all week.
For advance reservations Tel:
Kintore 32631.

Visitors are welcome all week except between 4pm-7pm Mon, Wed and Fri.
Secretary: J.D. Black – Tel: Kintore (0467) 32214.

159 Kirkcaldy
Fife

*Dunnikier Park Golf Course
Dunnikier Way, Kirkcaldy, Fife.
Tel: Kirkcaldy 261599.
18 holes, length of course 6036m/6601 yds.
SSS 72
Charges: £7.60 round, £13 daily (Mon-Fri); £10 round, £15 daily (Sat/Sun).
A practice area, caddy cars and catering facilities are available.
Secretary: Mr. R.A. Waddell.
Kirkcaldy Golf Club
Balwearie Road, Kirkcaldy, Fife.
Tel: Kirkcaldy 260370.
18 holes, length of course 6004 yds.
SSS 70
Charges: £12 round (weekdays), £15 (weekends), £18 daily (weekdays), £21 daily (weekends).
For advance reservations Tel: Kirkcaldy 205240/203258.
A practice area, caddy cars and catering facilities are available.
Visitors are welcome all week, except Tuesdays and Saturdays.
Secretary: J.I. Brodley – Tel: Kirkcaldy 205240/263316 (home).
Professional: Mr. Paul Hodgson – Tel: Kirkcaldy 203258.

160 Kirkcudbright
Kirkcudbrightshire

Kirkcudbright Golf Club
Stirling Crescent, Kirkcudbright.
Tel: 0557 30314.
18 holes, length of course 5121m/5598 yds.
SSS 67
Charges: £12 round, £15 daily, £50 weekly.
For advance reservations Tel: 0557 30314.
Visitors are welcome all week.
Secretary: Mr. A.G. Gordon – Tel: 0557 30542.

161 Kirkintilloch
Dunbartonshire

Hayston Golf Club
Campsie Road, Kirkintilloch G66 1RN.
Tel: 041-776 1244.
18 holes, length of course 5808m/6042 yds.
SSS 69
Charges: £12 round, £20 daily.
For advance reservations Tel: 041-775 0882.
A practice area, caddy cars and catering facilities are available.
Secretary: J.V. Carmichael - Tel: 041-775 0723
Professional: Mr. S. Barnett – Tel: 041-775 0882.

Kirkintilloch Golf Club
Todhill, Campsie Road.
Tel: 041 776 1256.
(Further details on application).

162 Kirkwall
Orkney

Orkney Golf Club
Grainbank.
Tel: Kirkwall 872487.
18 holes, length of course 5406 yds.
SSS 68
Charges: £8 daily, £30 weekly.
A practice area is available.
Visitors are welcome all week.
Secretary: L.F. Howard – Tel: 0856 874165.

163 Kirriemuir
Angus

Kirriemuir Golf Club
Northmuir, Kirriemuir.
Tel: 0575 72144.
18 holes, length of course 5553 yds.
SSS 66
Charges: £12 round, £17.50 daily, £60 weekly (1992).
Practice area, caddy cars and catering facilities are available.
Visitors are welcome weekdays.
Professional: Mr. A. Caira – Tel: 0575 73317.

164 Ladybank
Fife

Ladybank Golf Club
Annsmuir, Ladybank, Fife.
Tel: 0337 30814/30725.
18 holes, length of course 6641 yds.
SSS 72
Charges: Nov/April - £14 per round, £20 daily. May & Oct. - £17 per round, £24 daily. June/Sept. - £23 per round, £31 daily. Weekly £90.
For advance reservations Tel: 0337 30814.
Caddy cars, a practice area and catering facilities are available.
Visitors are welcome all week, except Saturdays.
Secretary: A.M. Dick - Tel: 0337 30814.
Professional: M. Gray - Tel: 0337 30725.

165 Lamlash
By Brodick, Isle of Arran
Lamlash Golf Club
Tel: Lamlash 296.
18 holes, length of course 4611 yds.
SSS 63
Charges: £8 daily Mon-Fri, £10 Sat/Sun daily; senior citizen £6. 3-day weekend £26; week £50; Fortnightly £70 (1992).
Secretary: J. Henderson – Tel: Lamlash 272.

166 Lanark
Lanarkshire

Lanark Golf Club
The Moor, Whitelees Road, Lanark.
Tel: Lanark 3219.
18 hole and 9 hole, length of course 6423 yds.
SSS 71 (18 hole)
Charges: £16 round, £25 daily.
For advance reservations Tel: Lanark 2349.
A practice area, caddy cars and catering facilities are available (Caddies if requested).
Visitors are welcome Monday to Friday.
Secretary: G.H. Cuthill – Tel: Lanark 3219.
Professional: R. Wallace – Tel: Lanark 61456.

167 Langbank
Renfrewshire

The Gleddoch Club
Langbank, Renfrewshire PA14 6YE.
Tel: 0475 54 304.
18 holes, length of course 6332 yds.
SSS 71
Charges: £20 for visitors (day ticket)
For advance reservations Tel: 0475 54304.
Trolleys, practice area, hire or clubs and catering facilities are available.
Visitors are welcome all week.
Secretary: Tel: 0475 54 304.
Professional: Tel: 0475 54 704.

168 Langholm
Dumfriesshire

Langholm Golf Course
Whitaside, Langholm, Dumfriesshire.
9 holes, length of course 5744 yds.
SSS 68
Charges: £8 round/daily, £30 weekly.
Practice area is available.
Visitors are welcome all week.
Secretary: C.A. Edgar - Tel: 03873 80878.

169 Larbert
Stirlingshire

Falkirk Tryst Golf Club
86 Burnhead Road, Stenhousemuir, Larbert FK5 4BD.
Tel: 0324 562415.
18 holes, length of course 5533m/6083 yds   SSS 69
Charges: £10 round, £15 daily.
For advance reservations Tel: (0324) 562054.
Caddy cars, practice area and catering facilities are available.
No unintroduced visitors on Saturdays/Sundays.
Secretary: R.D. Wallace - Tel: (0324) 562415/562054.
Professional: Steven Dunsmore - Tel: (0324) 562091.

Glenbervie Golf Club
Stirling Road, Larbert FK1 4SJ.
Tel: Larbert 562605.
18 holes, length of course 6469 yds.
SSS 71
Charges: £20 round, £28 daily.
For advanced reservations Tel: Larbert 562605 (visiting parties).

A practice area, caddy cars and catering facilities are available.
Visitors are welcome Monday to Friday.
Secretary: Mrs. M. Purves – Tel: Larbert 562605.
Professional: Mr. J. Chillas – Tel: Larbert 562725.

170 Largs
Ayrshire

Largs Golf Club
Irvine Road, Largs KA30 8EV.
Tel: 0475 673594.
18 holes, length of course 6220 yds.
SSS 70
Charges: £18 round, £24 daily.
For advance reservations Tel: 0475 686192.
A practice area, caddy cars and catering facilities are available.
Visitors are welcome all week.
Parties - Tues & Thur.
Secretary: F. Gilmour – Tel: 0475 672497.
Professional: R. Collinson – Tel: 0475 686192.

171 Larkhall
Lanarkshire

*Larkhall Golf Course
(Further details on application).

172 Lauder
Berwickshire

*Lauder Golf Club
Lauder.
Tel: Lauder 526.
9 holes, length of course 6002 yds.
SSS 70
Charges: £5 weekdays, £6 weekends.
Practice area is available.
Visitors are welcome all week (some restrictions before noon on Sundays).
Secretary: David Dickson - Tel: 05782 526.

173 Lennoxtown
Stirlingshire

Campsie Golf Course
Crow Road.
Tel: Lennoxtown 310244.
(Further details on application).

174 Lenzie
Lanarkshire

Lenzie Golf Club
19 Crosshill Road.
Tel: 041 776 1535.
(Further details on application).

175 Lerwick
Shetland

The Shetland Golf Club
Dale Golf Course
P O Box 18.
Tel: Gott 369.
18 holes, length of course 5279m/5776 yds.
SSS 70
Charges: £5 daily.
Visitors are welcome.
Secretary: Mr. Hunter.

176 Leslie
Fife

Leslie Golf Club
Balsillie Laws, Leslie, Glenrothes.
9 holes, length of course 4516m/4940 yds.
SSS 64
Charges: £5 day ticket. £8 Sat./Sun.
Bar facilities from 7.30 pm – 11.00 pm.
Visitors are welcome all week.
Secretary: M.G. Burns – Tel: 0592 741449.

177 Lesmahagow
Lanarkshire

*Hollandbush Golf Club
Acretophead, Lesmahagow.
Tel: Lesmahagow 893484.
(Further details on application).

178 Leuchars
Fife

St. Michael's Golf Club
Tel: Leuchars 365.
9 holes, length of course (18 holes) 5100m/5578 yds.
SSS 68, (Par 70).
Charges: £10 day ticket, under-16's £5.
For Society reservations Tel: 0334 53156.
Caddy cars, bar and catering facilities are available.

Visitors are welcome all week but
not before 1 pm on Sundays.
Secretary: Dr. G.G.W. Bennet –
Tel: 0334 53156 (Home).

179 Leven
Fife

Leven Links Golf Course
The Promenade,
Leven KY8 4HS.
Tel: 0333 428859.
18 holes, length of course
5800m/6400 yds.
SSS 71
Charges: £18 round (weekdays),
£24 (weekends). £26 daily
(weekdays), £36 (weekends).
For advance reservations Tel: 0333
428859.
Catering facilities are available.
Visitors are welcome Sunday to
Friday.
Secretary: B. Jackson, Esq – Tel:
0333 428859.

Leven Thistle Golf Club
Balfour Street, Leven.
Tel: Leven 26397.
18 holes, length of course
5800m/6434 yds.
SSS 71
Charges: £13 round, £18 daily.
For advance reservations Tel: Mr.
B. Jackson – Leven 28859.
A practice area, caddy cars and
catering facilities are available.
Visitors are welcome Monday to
Friday (Small Parties – weekend).
Secretary: J. Scott – Tel: Leven
26397.

*Scoonie Golf Club
North Links, Leven, KY8 4SP.
Tel: 27057.
18 holes, length of course 4967m.
SSS 66
Charges: £7 round, £10 daily week-
days; £9.40 round, £12 daily
weekends. Reduction for OAPs.
Caddy cars and full catering
facilities are available.
Visitors are welcome, except
Thursdays & Saturdays.
Secretary: Bill Stevenson - Tel:
0333 25301.

180 Linlithgow
West Lothian

Linlithgow Golf Club
Braehead, Linlithgow.
Tel: Linlithgow 842585.
18 holes, length of course
5239m/5729 yds.
SSS 68
Charges: £10 round, £14 daily
(Mon-Fri). £14 round, £17 daily
(Sun).
For advance reservations Tel: 0506
842585.
A practice area, caddy cars and
catering facilities are available.
Visitors are welcome all week
except Wednesdays and Saturdays.
Secretary: Mrs. A. Bird – Tel:
Linlithgow 842585.
Professional: Mr. D. Smith – Tel:
Linlithgow 844356.

181 Lochcarron
By Strathcarron, Ross-shire

Lochcarron Golf Club
Lochcarron, Wester Ross.
Tel: 05202 257.
9 holes, length of course 1733 yds.
SSS 60
Charges: £5 (round), £8 (daily), £18
(weekly).
Visitors are welcome all week.
Secretary: G. Weighill –
Tel: 05202 257.

182 Lochgelly
Fife

Lochgelly Golf Course
Lochgelly Golf Club
Cartmore Road.
Tel: Lochgelly 780174.
(Further details on application).

183 Lochgilphead
Argyllshire

Lochgilphead Golf Club
Blarbuie Road, Lochgilphead.
Tel: 0546 602340.
(Further details on application).

184 Lochmaben
By Lockerbie, Dumfriesshire

Lochmaben Golf Club
Back Road, Lochmaben, Lockerbie
DG11 1NT.
Tel: (0387) 810552.
9 holes, length of course
4616m/5304 yds.
SSS 66
Charges: £8 round/daily
(weekdays), £10 round/daily (weekends).
A practice area is available.
Catering facilities by special
arrangement for visiting parties.
Visitors are welcome weekdays
before
5 pm and weekends, except when
competitions are in progress.
Secretary: K. Purves – Tel: Annan
3379.

185 Lochranza
Isle of Arran

Lochranza Golf Course
Isle of Arran KA27 8HL.
Tel: 077083 273 (1993 Tel No: will
be 0770830 273).
9 Holes, length of course 5600 yds.
Par 69
(Further details on application).

186 Lockerbie
Dumfriesshire

Lockerbie Golf Club
Corrie Road, Lockerbie.
Tel: Lockerbie 3363.
18 holes, length of course 5418 yds.
SSS 66
Charges: £10 Mon-Fri; £12 Sat/Sun
daily.
For advance reservations Tel:
Lochmaben 810352.
A practice area, and catering
facilities by arrangement are
available.
Visitors are welcome all week.
Secretary: A. Graham – Tel: 05762
2165.

187 Lochwinnoch
Renfrewshire

Lochwinnoch Golf Club
Burnfoot Road, Lochwinnoch.
Tel: Lochwinnoch 842153.
length of course 6202 yds.

SSS 70
Charges: £13 round/daily
For advance reservations write to secretary.
A practice area, caddy cars and catering facilities are available.
Visitors are welcome mid week.
Secretary: Mrs. E. McBride – Tel: 842153.
Prrofessional: Gerry Reilly – Tel: 843029.

188 Longniddry
East Lothian

Longniddry Golf Club
Links Road, Longniddry EH32 ONL.
Tel: Longniddry 52141.
18 holes, length of course 6219 yds.
SSS 70
Charges: £20 round (Mon–Fri), £30 daily (Mon–Fri).
For advance reservations Tel: 0875 52141.
A practice area, caddy cars and catering facilities are available.
Visitors are welcome Mon to Fri.
Secretary: G.C. Dempster – Tel: 0875 52141.
Professional: W.J. Gray – Tel: 0875 52228.

189 Lossiemouth
Morayshire

Moray Golf Club
Stotfield, Lossiemouth.
Tel: Lossiemouth 2018.
18 holes both courses.
Charges: On request.
Caddy cars, practice area and catering facilities are available.
visitors are welcome without reservation.
Secretary: J. Hamilton - Tel: Lossiemouth 2018.
Professional: A. Thomson - Tel: Lossiemouth 3330.

190 Lundin Links
Fife

Lundin Golf Club
Golf Road, Lundin Links, Leven.
Tel: 0333 320202.
18 holes, length of course 6377 yds.
SSS 71
Charges: £18 per round (Mon-Fri).
£25 (Sats). £27 daily. £80 weekly

ticket.
For advance reservations Tel. 0333 320202.
Caddy cars, practice area and catering facilities are available.
Visitors are welcome all week, except on Saturdays they cannot play before 2.30pm.
Secretary: A.C. McBride - Tel: 0333 320202.
Professional: D.K. Webster - Tel: 0333 320051.

Lundin Ladies Golf Club
Woodlielea Road, Lindin Links, Leven KY8 6AR.
9 holes, length of course 2365 yds.
SSS 67
Charges: £6 weekdays (18 holes), £7.50 weekends (18 holes).
For advance reservations Tel: 0333 320832 (Clubhouse) or write to secretary.
A few caddy cars are available.
Visitors are welcome all week.
Secretary: Miss Lynn Herbert.

191 Lybster
Caithness

Lybster Golf Club
Main Street, Lybster, Caithness.
9 holes, length of course 1807 yds.
SSS 62
Charges: Daily, £4; juniors £2.
Weekly £10.
Advance reservations are not necessary.
Visitors are welcome all week.
Secretary: F. Marshall Bowman.

192 Macduff
Banffshire

Royal Tarlair Golf Club
Buchan Street, Macduff.
Tel: 0261 32897.
18 holes, length of course 5866 yds.
SSS 68
Charges: £10 weekdays, £12 weekends (daily); £40 (Adult), £10 (Juniors) weekly.
For advance reservations Tel: 32897.
Caddies, caddy cars and catering facilities are available.
Visitors are welcome all week.
Secretary: Mrs. T. Watt - Tel: 02615 221.

193 Machrie
Port Ellen, Isle of Islay
The Machrie Golf Club
The Machrie Hotel & Golf Club, Port Ellen, Islay PA42 7AN.
Tel: 0496 2310.
(Further details on application)

194 Maddiston
By Falkirk, Stirlingshire

Polmont Golf Club Ltd
Manuel Rigg, Maddiston, Falkirk FK2 0LS.
Tel: Polmont 711277.
9 holes, length of course 6603 yds.
SSS 70
Charges: Daily - £5 (Mon-Fri), £10 Sunday.
Catering facilities are available.
Visitors are welcome all week, except after 5pm and Saturdays.
Secretary: Ian Gilchrist - Tel: 0324 711253.

195 Mallaig
Inverness-shire

Traigh Golf Club
(Further details on application).

196 Mauchline
Ayrshire

Ballochmyle Golf Club
Mauchline KA5 6LE.
Tel: 0290 50469.
18 holes, length of course 5847 yds.
SSS 69
Charges: On application.
Catering facilities are available.
Visitors are welcome with reservation.
Secretary: D.G. Munro - Tel: 0290 50469.

197 Maybole
Ayrshire

*Maybole Golf Course
(Further details on application).

198 Melrose
Roxburghshire

Melrose Golf Club
The Clubhouse, Dingleton Road, Melrose.
Tel: Melrose 2855.
(Further details on application).

199 Millport
Isle of Cumbrae

Millport Golf Club
Golf Road, Millport, Isle of Cumbrae KA28.
Tel: 0475-530-311.
Length of course 5831 yds.
SSS 68
Charges: Weekly, daily and round tickets are available.
Full catering facilities are available.
Visitors are welcome all week without introduction.
Secretary: W.D. Patrick - Tel: 0475-530-308.

200 Milnathort
Kinross-shire

Milnathort Golf Club Ltd
South Street, Milnathort.
Tel: 0577 864069.
9 holes, length of course 5669 yds.
SSS 69
Charges: £10 daily (weekdays), £15 daily (weekends).
For advance reservations Tel: 0577 64069.
A practice area is available.
Catering facilities are only available with prior booking.
Visitors are welcome all week.
Captain: R. Wallace – Tel: 0577 863855.

201 Milngavie
Dunbartonshire

Hilton Park Golf Club
Stockmuir Road, Milngavie, G62 7HB.
Tel: 041 956 4657.
2 Ù 18 hole courses, length of courses 6007 and 5374 yds.
SSS 70 and 67
Charges: On application.
Caddy cars, practice area and catering facilities are available.
Visitors are welcome by prior

arrangement Monday-Thursday, except 2nd and 4th Tuesdays of each month.
Secretary: Mrs. J.A. Dawson - Tel: 041– 956 4657.
Professional: Mr. Wm. McCondichie - Tel: 041 956 5125.

Dougalston Golf Course
Strathblane Road, Milngavie, Glasgow.
Tel: 041–956 5750.
(Further details on application).
Golf Manager: W. McInnes - Tel: 041 956 5750.

Milngavie Golf Club
Laighpark, Milngavie, Glasgow G62.
Tel: 041–956 1619.
18 holes, length of course 5818 yds.
SSS 68
A practice area and catering facilities are available.
Visitors are welcome if introduced by a member.
Secretary: Mrs. A.J.W. Ness - Tel: 041–956 1619.

202 Moffat
Dumfriesshire

The Moffat Golf Club
Coatshill, Moffat DG10 9SB.
Tel: 0683 20020.
18 holes, length of course 5218 yds.
SSS 66
Charges: Weekdays £11, weekends £17, daily. £35 weekly.
For advance reservations Tel: Moffat 20020.
Caddy cars, practice area and catering facilities are available.
Visitors are welcome without reservations, except Wednesday after 12 noon.
Secretary: T.A. Rankin – Tel: Moffat 20020.

203 Monifieth
Angus

Broughty Golf Club
6 Princes Street, Monifieth, Dundee.
Tel: Monifieth 532147.
For advance reservations Tel: 0382 532767.
A practice area, caddy cars and catering facilities are available.
Visitors are welcome all week and after 2 pm on Saturdays.
Secretary: Samuel J. Gailey –

Tel: 0382 730014.
Professional: Ian McLeod –
Tel: 0382 532945.

Medal Course
The Links, Monifieth.
Tel: 0382 532767.
18 holes, length of course 6657 yds.
SSS 72
Charges: £17 round, £25 daily.
Sundays £19 round, £28 daily.
Weekly £55.
For party reservations Tel: 0382 78117.
Caddy cars and catering facilities are available.
Visitors are welcome Monday to Friday after 9.30am, Saturday after 2pm and Sunday after 10am.
Secretary: H.R. Nicoll - Tel: 0382 535553.
Professional: Ian McLeod – Tel: 0382 532945.

Ashludie Golf Course
The Links, Monifieth.
Tel: 0382 532767.
18 holes, length of course 5123 yds.
SSS 64
Charges: £11 round, £16 daily. Sun £12 round, £17.50 daily. Weekly £35 (1992).
For party reservations Tel: 0382 78117.
Caddy cars and catering facilities are available.
Visitors are welcome Monday to Friday after 9.30am. Saturday after 2 pm and Sundays after 10 am.
Secretary: H.R. Nicoll - Tel: 0382 535553.
Professional: Ian McLeod – Tel: 0382 532945.

204 Montrose
Angus

Mercantile Golf Club
East Links, Montrose.
Tel: Montrose 72408.
(Further details on application).

205 Motherwell
Lanarkshire

Colville Park Golf Club
Jerviston Estate, Merry Street, Motherwell.
Tel: Motherwell 63017.
18 holes, length of course 5724m/6265 yds. SSS 70 (par 71)
Charges: £14 daily.

For advance reservations Tel: Motherwell 63017.
A practice area and catering facilities are available.
Visitors are welcome by prior arrangement Monday to Friday.
Secretary: Scott Connacher – Tel: Motherwell 65378 (after 5pm).

206 Muckhart
By Dollar, Clackmannanshire

Muckhart Golf Club
Tel: Muckhart 423.
18 holes, length of course 6134 yds.
SSS 70
Charges: £12.50 round (Mon-Fri), £18 (Sat/Sun), £18 daily (Mon-Fri), £24 (Sat/Sun).
Caddy cars and catering facilities are available.
Secretary: A.B. Robertson.
Professional: Mr. K. Salmoni.

207 Muir of Ord
Ross-shire

Muir of Ord Golf Club
Great North Road, Muir of Ord IV6 7SX.
Tel: 0463 870825.
18 holes, length of course 5129 yds.
SSS 65
Charges: April/Sept £10 daily (weekdays), £12 (Sat/Sun).
Oct/March £7 daily (weekdays), £8 (Sat/Sun). Summer £40 weekly.
For advance reservations Tel: 0463 870825.
A practice area and catering facilities are available.
Visitors are welcome all week.
Administrator: Mrs. C. Moir – Tel: 0463 870825.
Professional: Mr. G. Vivers – Tel: 0463 871311.

208 Musselburgh
East Lothian

The Musselburgh Golf Club
Monktonhall, Musselburgh.
Tel: 031 665 2005/7055.
18 holes, length of course 6614 yds.
SSS 72.
Charges: On application.
Catering facilties are available except Tuesdays.
Visitors are welcome with reservation.
Secretary: G.A. McGill.
Professional: Mr. T. Stangoe.

209 Muthill
Perthshire

Muthill Golf Club
Peat Road, Muthill,
Crieff PH5 2AD.
(Further details on application).

210 Nairn

Nairn Golf Club

Seabank Road, Nairn.
Tel: 0667 53208.
18 holes, length of course 6556 yds.
SSS 71
Charges: £23 round (Mon-Fri), £28 (Sat/Sun); £33 daily (Mon-Fri), £38 (Sat/Sun).
For advance reservations Tel: 0667 53208.
A practice area, caddies, caddy cars and catering facilities are available.
Visitors are welcome all week.
Secretary: Mr. J.G. Somerville – Tel: 0667 53208.
Professional: Mr. R. Fyfe – Tel: 0667 52787.

Nairn Dunbar Golf Club
Lochloy Road, Nairn IV12 5AE
Tel: 0667 52741.
18 holes, length of course 6431 yds.
SSS 71
Charges: £15 daily (Mon-Fri), £20 (Sat/Sun).
A practice area and caddy cars are available.
Secretary: Mrs. S.J. MacLennan.
Professional: Brian Mason.

211 Nethybridge
Inverness-shire

Abernethy Golf Club
Tel: Nethybridge 305.
(Further details on application).

212 Newburgh-on-Ythan
Aberdeenshire

Newburgh-on-Ythan Golf Club
51 Mavis Bank, Newburgh, Ellon, AB4 0FB.
Tel: Newburgh 89438.
9 holes, length of course 6300 yds.
SSS 70
Charges: £10 daily (weekdays), £12 daily, (weekends).

For advance reservations Tel: Udny 2070 (Mr. J. Stewart – Match Sec.).
A practice area is available.
Visitors are welcome all week but club competitions every Tuesday evening.
Secretary: Mr. A.C. Stevenson - Tel: Newburgh 89438.

213 New Cumnock
Ayrshire

New Cumnock Golf Club
(Further details on application).

214 New Galloway
Kirkcudbrightshire

New Galloway Golf Club
New Galloway, Kirkcudbrightshire DG7 3RN.
9 holes, length of course 2313m/2529 yds.
SSS 65
Charges: £8 per day.
Visitors are welcome.
Secretary: Mr. A.R. Brown - Tel: (06443) 455.

215 Newton Mearns
Renfrewshire

The East Renfrewshire Golf Club
Pilmuir.
Tel: Loganswell 258.
(Further details on application).

Eastwood Golf Club
Muirshield, Loganswell, Newton Mearns, Glasgow G77 6RX.
Tel: Loganswell 261.
18 holes, length of course 5886 yds.
SSS 68
Charges: £12 round, £18 daily.
(Subject to prior application and approval).
For advance reservations Tel: Loganswell 280.
Caddy cars and catering facilities are available.
Visitors are welcome all week.
Secretary: C.B. Scouler – Tel: Loganswell 280 (a.m. only).
Professional: S. Campbell – Tel: Loganswell 285.

216 Newton Stewart
Wigtownshire

Newton Stewart Golf Club
Kirroughtree Avenue, Minnigaff,
Newton Stewart.
Tel: 0671 2172.
9 holes, length of course
5160m/5646 yds. SSS 67
Charges £9 per round/daily; £14
weekends; £50 weekly (1993).
For advance reservations Tel: 0671
2172.
Catering facilities are available.
Visitors are welcome all week.
Secretary: D.C. Matthewson - Tel:
0671 3236.

217 Newtonmore
Inverness-shire

Newtonmore Golf Club
Tel: 05403 328
Charges: £9 daily mid-week, £12
weekends; £36 weekly.
Secretary: R.J. Cheyne - Tel: 05403
591.
(Further details on application).

218 North Berwick
East Lothian

*Glen Golf Club
East Links, Tantallon Terrace,
North Berwick EH39 4LE.
Tel: 0620 2221.
18 holes, length of course 6079 yds.
SSS 69
Charges: On application
Catering facilities available during
the season (Apr-Oct) and at
weekends throughout the year.
Secretary: D.R. Montgomery -
Tel: Starter's box 0620 2726.
Professional (shop only) R. Affleck.

219 Oban
Argyllshire

Glencruitten Golf Course
Glencruitten Road, Oban.
Tel: Oban 62868.
18 holes, length of course 4452 yds.
SSS 63
Charges: £6.50 round, £8 daily, £30
weekly.
For advance reservations Tel: 0631
62868.
A practice area and catering
facilities are available.

Visitors are welcome Mon, Tues,
Wed, Fri and Suns.
Secretary: C.M. Jarvie – Tel: 0631
62308.

220 Old Meldrum
Aberdeenshire

Old Meldrum Golf Club
Kirk Brae, Old Meldrum.
Tel: 06512 2648.
18 holes, length of course 5988 yds.
SSS 69 (Par 70) Medal Tees
SSS 66 (Par 68) Forward Tees
Charges: Per round/daily - £10
Mon-Fri, £15 Sat/Sun, weekly
(Mon-Fri) £35.
For reservations Tel: 06512 2648.
Visitors and visiting parties
welcome.
A practice area and bar facilities are
available.
Secretary: D. Petrie - Tel: 06512
2383.

221 Paisley
Renfrewshire

*Barshaw Golf Club
Barshaw Park, Paisley.
Tel: 041-889 2908.
18 holes, length of course 5703 yds.
SSS 67
Charges: £5.90 round;
juniors/OAP's/unemployed £3.
Visitors are welcome all week.
Secretary: Mr. W. Collins – Tel:
041-884 2533.

The Paisley Golf Club
Tel: 041-884 2292.
18 holes, length of course
5857m/6424 yds.
SSS 71
Charges: £14 round, £19 daily.
A practice area and catering
facilities are available.
Secretary: W.J. Cunningham – Tel:
041-884 3903.
Professional: G.B. Gilmour - Tel:
041-554 4114.

222 Peebles
Peeblesshire

Peebles Golf Club
Kirkland Street, Peebles.
Tel: Peebles 20197.
18 holes, length of course
5612m/6137 yds.
SSS 69

Charges: On application.
A practice area, buggies, caddy cars
and catering facilities are available.

223 Penicuik
Midlothian

Glencorse Golf Club
Milton Bridge, Penicuik EH26
0RD.
Tel: Penicuik 676939.
18 holes, length of course 5205 yds.
SSS 66
Charges: £15 round, £20 daily.
(Subject to review).
For advance reservations Tel:
Penicuik 677189 (Clubs/Societies
only).
Caddy cars and catering facilities
are available.
Visitors are welcome on, Tues, Wed
and Thurs.
Secretary: D.A. McNiven – Tel:
Penicuik 677189.
Professional: Mr. C. Jones – Tel:
Penicuik 676481.

224 Perth
Perthshire

**The Craigie Hill Golf Club
(1982) Ltd**
Cherrybank, Perth.
18 holes, length of course 5379 yds.
SSS 66
Charges: £9 round (Mon-Fri), £14
daily (Mon-Fri), £18 daily (Sun).
For advance reservations Tel: 0738
22644.
A practice area, caddy cars and
catering facilities are available.
Visitors are welcome all week
except Saturdays.
Secretary: Mr. W.A. Miller – Tel:
0738 20829.
Professional: Mr. F. Smith – Tel:
0738 22644.
King James VI Golf Club
Moncreiffe Island, Perth.
Tel: Perth 25170/32460.
18 holes, length of course
5177m/5664 yds.
SSS 68
Charges: £11.50 round, £17 daily
(Mon-Fri), £23 (Sun) (1992).
For advance reservations Tel: Perth
32460.
A practice area, caddy cars and
catering facilities are available.

Murrayshall Golf Club,
Murrayshall Country House
Hotel & Golf Course,
Scone, Perthshire PH2 7PH.
Tel: 0738 51171.
18 holes, length of course
5901m/6460 yds.
SSS 71
Charges: On Application
For advance reservations Tel: 0738
51171.
Caddies, caddy cars, buggies,
practice area and catering facilities
are available.
Visitors are welcome all week.
Professional: Neil MacIntosh - Tel:
0738 52784.

225 Peterhead
Aberdeenshire

Craigewan Golf Course
Peterhead Golf Club
Craigewan Links, Peterhead.
Tel: Peterhead 72149.
(Further details on application).

226 Pitlochry
Perthshire

Pitlochry Golf Course Ltd.,
Pitlochry.
Tel: Pitlochry 2792 (bookings).
18 holes, length of course 5811 yds.
SSS 68.
Charges: (Weekday day tickets, 1st
Apr to 31st Oct): Adult £13, Junior
£3. (Saturday day tickets, 1st Apr to
31st Oct) Adult £16, Junior £5.
(Sunday day tickets, 1st Apr to 31st
Oct) Adult/Junior £16. Restricted
course: (1st Nov to 31st Mar) day
ticket, any day: Adult £6, Junior
£1.50.
Caddy cars, tuition and catering
facilities are available.
Visitors are welcome all week.
Secretary: D.M. McKenzie.
Professional: George Hampton -
Tel: Pitlochry 2792.

227 Port Glasgow
Renfrewshire

Port Glasgow Golf Club
Devol Road, Port Glasgow.
Tel: 0475 704181.
18 holes, length of course
5592m/5712 yds.
SSS 68
Charges: £10 round, £15 daily.
Weekly by arrangement.

For advance reservations Tel: 0475
704181.
A practice area and catering
facilities are available.
Visitors are welcome uninvited
before 3.55 pm, not on Saturdays
and invited only Sundays.
Secretary: N.L. Mitchell – Tel: 0475
706273.

228 Portmahomack
Ross-shire

Tarbat Golf Club
Portmahomack.
Tel: 0862 87 236.
(Further details on application).

229 Portpatrick
By Stranraer, Wigtownshire

**Portpatrick (Dunskey) Golf
Club**
Tel: 0776 81 273.
18 holes, (9 hole, par 3).
Charges: £12 round, £18 daily
(Mon-Fri), £15 round, £22 daily
(Sat/Sun). £60 weekly. 9 hole
course: Adult £4 round, £8 daily 7
days. Juniors (under 18) half stated
price.
Secretary: J.A. Horberry - Tel: 0776
81231

230 Port William
Wigtownshire

St Medan Golf Club
Monreith, Port William.
Tel: Port William 358.
9 holes, length of course 2277 yds.
SSS 62
Charges: £6 round, £9 daily, £30
weekly.
Catering facilities are available.
Visitors are welcome all week.
Secretary: D. O'Neill – Tel:
Whithorn 555.

231 Prestonpans
East Lothian

Royal Musselburgh Golf Club
Preston Grange House, Prestonpans.
Tel: (0875) 810276.
18 holes, length of course 6255 yds.
SSS 70
Charges: £15 (round) weekdays,
£25 (daily). £25 (round) weekends
(1992).

Advance reservations in writing
preferable.
Caddy cars, practice area and catering facilities are available.
Visitors are welcome weekdays,
except Friday afternoons.
Secretary: T.H. Hardie - Tel: (0875)
810276.
Professional: J. Henderson - Tel:
(0875) 810139.

232 Prestwick
Ayrshire

Prestwick Golf Club
2 Links Road, Prestwick.
Tel: Prestwick 77404.
18 holes, length of course 6544 yds.
SSS 72
Charges: On application.
Caddies, caddy cars, practice area
and catering facilities are available.
Visitors are welcome Mon, Tues,
Wed, Fri 8-9 am, 10 am-12.30 pm
and 2.45-4.00 pm Thursday 8-11
am.
Secretary: D.E. Donaldson.
Professional: F.C. Rennie.

**Prestwick St. Cuthbert Golf
Club**
East Road, Prestwick KA9 2SX.
Tel: 0292 77101.
18 holes, length of course 6470 yds.
SSS 71
Charges: £18 round, £24 daily.
For advance reservations Tel: 0292
77101.
Catering facilities (except
Thursdays) are available.
Visitors are welcome Monday to
Friday (not on weekends or public
holidays).
Secretary: R.Morton – Tel: 0292
77101.

**Prestwick St. Nicholas Golf
Club**
Grangemuir Road,
Prestwick KA9 1SN.
Tel: 0292 77608.
18 holes, length of course
5441m/5952 yds.
SSS 69
Charges: £18 round (after 2 pm),
£28 daily.
For advance reservations Tel: 0292
77608.
Caddy cars and catering facilities
are available.

Visitors are welcome Monday to Friday only.
Secretary: J.R. Leishman – Tel: 0292 77608.
Professional: S. Smith – Tel: 0292 79755.

233 Pumpherston
West Lothian

Pumpherston Golf Club
Drumshoreland Road, Pumpherston, Livingston EH53 0LF.
Tel: 0506 32869.
9 holes, length of course 4712m/5154 yds.
SSS 65
Restricted practice area and catering facilities are available.
Visitors are welcome all week, only with a member.
Secretary: A.H. Docharty - Tel: 0506 854652.

234 Reay
By Thurso, Caithness

Reay Golf Club
Tel: Reay 288.
18 holes, length of course 5372m/5876 yds.
SSS 68
Charges: £10 round/daily, £30 weekly.
A practice area is available.
Secretary: Miss P. Peebles – Tel: Reay 537.

235 Renfrew
Renfrewshire

Renfrew Golf Club
Blythswood Estate, Inchinnan Road, Renfrew.
Tel: 041 886 6692.
18 holes, length of course 6231m/6818 yds.
SSS 73
Charges: £16 round, £25 daily.
Catering services are available.
Secretary: A.D. Brockie – Tel: 041 886 6692.

236 Rigside
Lanarkshire

Douglas Water Golf Club
Ayr Road, Rigside.
9 holes   SSS 69
Charges: £4 daily, £6 Sat/Sun.

Please write for advance reservations.
A practice area is available.
Visitors are welcome all week.
Secretary: Robert W. McMillan.

237 Rothesay
Isle of Bute

*Port Bannatyne Golf Club
Bannatyne Mains Road, Port Bannatyne.
Tel: 0700 502009.
13 holes, length of course 4256m/4654 yds.
SSS 63
Charges: £7 daily, including weekends. £28 weekly.
For advance reservations Tel: 0700 502009.
Visitors are welcome all week.
Secretary: Mr. I.L. MacLeod – Tel: 0700 502009.

Rothesay Golf Club
Canada Hill, Rothesay, Isle of Bute.
Tel: Clubhouse 0700 502244.
18 holes, length of course 5370 yds.
Charges: On Application (day tickets only).
Pre-booking essential for Saturday/Sunday.
Catering facilities available.
Secretary: J. Barker - Tel: 0700 503744.
Professional: J. Dougal - Tel: 0700 503554.

238 Rutherglen
Lanarkshire

Blairbeth Golf Club
Fernhill, Rutherglen.
Tel: 041 634 3355.
(Further details on application).

239 St. Andrews
Fife

Royal & Ancient Golf Club
Tel: St. Andrews 72112/3.
(Further details on application).

St. Andrews Old Course
18 holes, length of course 6566 yds.
SSS 72
Charges: £40 round all week (closed Sunday).
For advance reservations Tel: St. Andrews 75757.
Caddies are available.

A Handicap Certificate or letter of introduction is required from visitors.
Executive Secretary: A. Beveridge – Tel: St. Andrews 75757.

St. Andrews New Course
18 holes, length of course 6039m/6604 yds.
SSS 72
Charges: £20 round, all week: £100 7 day ticket (unlimited play).
For advance reservations Tel: St. Andrews 75757.
Caddies and caddy cars are available.
Executive Secretary: A. Beveridge – Tel: St. Andrews 75757.

St. Andrews Eden Course
18 holes, length of course 5588m/6112 yds.
SSS 70
Charges: £15 round, all week: £100 7 day ticket (unlimited play).
For advance reservations Tel: St. Andrews 75757.
Caddies and caddy cars are available.
Executive Secretary: A. Beveridge – Tel: St. Andrews 75757.

St. Andrews Jubilee Course
18 holes, length of course 6805 yds.
SSS 73
Charges: £20 round, all week: £100 7 day ticket (unlimited play).
For advance reservations Tel: St. Andrews 75757.
Caddies and caddy cars available.
Executive Secretary: A. Beveridge – Tel: St. Andrews 75757.

St. Andrews Balgove Course
9 holes beginners' course. 18 holes.
Charges: £4 per round.
Visitors are welcome without reservation.
Executive Secretary: A. Beveridge – Tel: St. Andrews 75757.

240 St. Boswells
Roxburghshire

St. Boswells Golf Club
St. Boswells, Roxburghshire.
Tel: 0835 22359.
9 holes, length of course 5250 yds.
SSS 65
Charges: £8 round (Mon–Fri), £10 round (Sat/Sun), £8 daily (Mon–Fri), £10 daily (Sat/Sun).

For advance reservations
Tel: 0835 22359.
Visitors are welcome all week.
Secretary: G.B. Ovens – Tel: 0835
22359.

241 St. Fillans
Perthshire

St. Fillans Golf Club
South Lochearn Road, St. Fillans.
Tel: St. Fillans 312.
9 holes, length of course
4812m/5628 yds.
SSS 68
Charges: £8 round, £12 day ticket
(Mon-Fri); £10 round, £14 day
ticket (Sat/Sun).
Caddy cars and limited catering
facilities are available.
Visitors are welcome all week.
Visiting clubs by arrangement.
Secretary: J. Allison – Tel: Comrie
70951.

242 Saline
Fife

Saline Golf Club
Kinneddar Hill, Saline, Fife.
Tel: 0383 852 591.
9 holes, length of course 5302 yds.
SSS 66
Charges: £8 weekdays, £10
weekends.
For advance reservations Tel:
Clubhouse 0383 852 591.
Practice area. Catering facilities are
available by prior arrangement.
Visitors are welcome all week,
except Saturdays.
Secretary: R. Hutchison - Tel: 0383
852 344.

243 Sanquhar
Dumfriesshire

Euchan Golf Course
Sanquhar.
Tel: 0659 50577.
9 holes, length of course 5144m.
SSS 68
Charges: £6 round, £8 daily (Mon-
Fri), £10 (Sat/Sun).
For advance reservations Tel: 0659
58181.
Catering facilities (advance notice
by parties) are available.
Visitors are welcome all week.
Secretary: Mrs. J. Murray – Tel:
0659 58181.

244 Scarinish
Isle of Tiree

Vaul Golf Club
(Further details on application).

245 Sconser
Isle of Skye

Isle of Skye Golf Club
(Formerly Sconser Golf Club)
Sconser, Isle of Skye.
9 holes, length of course
4385m/4798 yds.
SSS 63
Charges: £7 round, £20 weekly; £14
per 3-days.
Visitors are welcome all week.
Advance reservations are only
required for large parties Tel:
Secretary – 0478 2277.
Secretary: J. Stephen – Tel: 0478
2000.

245A Skeabost Bridge
Isle of Skye

Skeabost Golf Club
Skeabost House Hotel,
Skeabost Bridge,
Isle of Skye IV51 9NP.
Tel: 047-032-215
9 holes, length of course 1597 yds.
SSS 29
Charges: £6 per daily.
For advanced reservations
Tel. 047-032-215
Catering facilities are available.
Visitors are welcome all week.
Secretary: John Stuart -
Tel: 047 032 322.

246 Selkirk
Selkirkshire

Selkirk Golf Club
Selkirk Hills, Selkirk.
Tel: 0750 20621.
9 holes, length of course 5636 yds.
Charges: £8 daily.
Visitors are welcome without reser-
vation.
Secretary: R. Davies - Tel: 0750
20427.

247 Shotts
Lanarkshire

Blairhead Golf Course
Shotts Golf Club
Blairhead, Shotts.
Tel: Shotts 20431.
(Further details on application).

248 Skelmorlie
Ayrshire

Skelmorlie Golf Course
Belthglass Road, Upper Skelmorlie,
Cunningham.
Tel: Wemyss Bay 5201520.
13 holes, length of course 5056m.
SSS 65
Charges: Mon-Fri £5.50 round, £8
daily. £22 weekly. Sun £7.50 round,
£11 daily.
A practice area and catering
facilities are available.
Visitors are welcome all week
except Saturdays.
Secretary: Mr. P. Griffin – Tel:
0475 520152.

249 Southend
By Campbeltown, Argyllshire

Dunaverty Golf Club
Southend, by Campbeltown, Argyll.
Tel: 0586 83 677.
18 holes, length of course 4799 yds.
SSS 64
Charges: £7 round, £10 daily, £30
weekly.
For advance reservations Tel: 0586
83 698/677.
Catering facilities are available.
Visitors are welcome all week with-
out reservation, but check for club
competitions.
Secretary: J. Galbraith - Tel: 0586
83 698.

250 Southerness
Kirkcudbrightshire

Southerness Golf Club
Southerness, Dumfries DG2 8AZ.
Tel: 0387 88 677.
18 holes, length of course 6564 yds.
SSS 72
Charges: £20 daily, £26 (weekend),
£80 weekly (Mon-Fri).
For advance reservations Tel:
038788 677.
A practice area, caddy cars and
catering facilities are available.

Visitors – members of recognised golf clubs only are welcome all week.
Secretary: W.D. Ramage – Tel: 038788 677.

251 South Uist
Western Isles

Links-Land Golf Course Askernish Golf Club
Askernish.
Tel: Lochboisdale 541.
(Further details on application).

252 Spey Bay
Morayshire

Spey Bay Golf Club
Spey Bay Hotel, Spey Bay, Fochabers IV32 7JP.
Tel: 0343 820424.
18 holes, length of course 6059 yds.
SSS 69
Charges: Mon-Sat £5.50 per round, Sun £7 per round.
Caddy cars, practice area and catering facilities available at the hotel.
Visitors and golf outings welcome.
(Enquiries to hotel manager).

253 Stevenston
Ayrshire

Ardeer Golf Club
Greenhead, Stevenston.
Tel: 0294 64542.
18 holes, length of course 6630 yds.
SSS 72
Charges: £10 (Mon-Fri), £12 (Sun), round; £18 (Mon-Fri), £24 (Sun) daily.
For advance reservations Tel: 0294 64542/601327.
Caddy cars, practice area and catering facilities are available.
Visitors are welcome all week, except Saturdays.
Secretary: W.F. Hand - Tel: 0294 63538.
Starter/Shop: R. Rodgers - Tel: 0294 601327.

254 Stirling
Stirlingshire

Stirling Golf Club
Queen's Road, Stirling FK8 3AA.
Tel: Stirling 73801.
18 holes, length of course 6409 yds.

SSS Medal 71, Front Tee 69.
Charges: £15.50 round, £21.50 daily.
A practice area, caddy cars and catering facilities are available.
Visitors are welcome week-days only.
Secretary: Mr. W.C. McArthur - Tel: Stirling 64098/61348.
Professional: Mr. I. Collins – Tel: Stirling 71490.

255 Stonehaven
Kincardineshire

Stonehaven Golf Club
Cowie, Stonehaven AB3 2RH.
Tel: 0569 62124.
18 holes, length of course 4669m/5103 yds.
SSS 65
Charges: £13 daily (Mon-Fri), £18 (Sat/Sun), £50 weekly, £70 fortnightly.
For advance reservations Tel: Stonehaven 62124.
A practice area, catering & full licensing facilities are available.
Visitors are welcome Monday to Friday. Late afternoon and evening on Saturday and Sunday.
Secretary: Mr. R.O. Blair – Tel: Stonehaven 62124.

256 Stornoway
Isle of Lewis

Stornoway Golf Course
Tel: Stornoway 2240.
(Further details on application).

257 Stranraer
Wigtownshire

*Stranraer Golf Club
Creachmore, By Stranraer.
Tel: Leswalt 245.
18 holes, length of course 5760m/6308 yds.
SSS 71
Charges: £15 round (Mon-Fri), £20 round (Sat/Sun), £20 daily (Mon-Fri), £25 daily (Sat/Sun).
A practice area, caddy cars and catering facilities are available.
Secretary: Mr. W.I. Wilson – Tel: Stranraer 3539.

258 Strathaven
Lanarkshire

Strathaven Golf Club
Overton Avenue, Glasgow Road, Strathaven.
Tel: Strathaven 20421.
18 holes, length of course 5696m/6226 yds.
SSS 70
Charges: £17 round, £24 daily.
For advance reservations Tel: Strathaven 20421.
A practice area, caddy cars and catering facilities are available.
Secretary: Mr. A.W. Wallace – Tel: Strathaven 20421.
Professional: Mr. M. McCrorie – Tel: Strathaven 21812.

259 Strathpeffer
Ross-shire

Strathpeffer Spa Golf Club
Strathpeffer IV14 9AS.
Tel: 0997 421219.
18 holes, length of course 4000m/4792 yds.
SSS 65
Charges: Weekdays - £10 round, £15 daily; (Sat/Sun) £12 round, £18 daily.
For advance reservations Tel: 0997 421219.
A practice area, caddy cars and catering facilities are available.
Visitors are welcome all week.
Secretary: Mr. N. Roxburgh – Tel: 0997 421396.

260 Strathtay
By Aberfeldy, Perthshire

Strathtay Golf Club
Tel: Strathtay 367.
9 holes, length of course 4082 yds (18 holes).
SSS 63
Charges: £6 (weekdays) daily, £8 Sats/Suns, £25 weekly tickets.
For advance reservations Tel: Strathtay 367.
Visitors are welcome all week, except Sun 12-5 and Mon 6-9.
Secretary: J. Armstrong–Payne – (All Correspondence – Tighanoisinn, Grantully, By Aberfeldy, PH15 2QT) – Tel: Strathtay 367.

261 Stromness
Orkney

Stromness Golf Club
Ness, Stromness.
Tel: Stromness 850593.
(Further details on application).

262 Tain
Ross-shire

Tain Golf Club
Tain, Ross-shire.
Tel: 0862 892314.
Length of course 6238 yds.
SSS 70
Charges: £10 round, £15 daily
(Mon-Fri); £15 round, £20 daily
(Sat/Sun).
For advance reservations Tel: 0862
892314.
Full catering facilities are available.
Visitors are welcome.
Secretary: Mrs. K.D. Ross.

263 Tarbert
Argyllshire

Tarbert Golf Club
Kilberry Road, Tarbert.
Tel: 0880 820565.
9 holes, length of course 4744 yds.
SSS 64
Charges: £4 (9 holes), £6 (18 holes).
£8 daily; £25 weekly.
Licensed clubhouse available.
Visitors are welcome without reservation.
Secretary: Peter Cupples –
Tel: 0880 820 536.

264 Tarland
Aberdeenshire

Tarland Golf Club
Aberdeen Road, Tarland.
Tel: 03398 81413.
9 holes, length of course
5386m/5888 yds.
SSS 68 (18 holes)
Charges: £10 (Mon-Fri), £12 (Sat-Sun), £40 weekly, £70 fortnightly.
For advance reservations Tel: 03398
81413 (no reservations at
weekends).
Caddy cars and practice area are
available.

Visitors are welcome all week, but
advise 'phoning regarding
weekends.
Secretary: J.H. Honeyman - Tel:
0224 323111.

265 Tayport
Fife

Scotscraig Golf Club
Golf Road, Tayport DD6 9DZ.
Tel: 0382 552515.
18 holes, length of course 6496 yds.
SSS 71
Charges: On Application.
Caddies by arrangement, caddy
cars, practice area and catering
facilities are available.
Visitors are welcome on weekdays,
or on weekends by prior
arrangement.
Secretary: K. Gourlay.

266 Thornhill
Dumfriesshire

Thornhill Golf Club.
Thornhill.
Tel: 0848 30546.
18 holes, length of course 6011 yds.
SSS 69
Par 71
Charges: £12 weekdays, £18 weekends.
For advance reservations tel: 0848
30546 (Club Steward).
A practice area and catering
facilities are available.
Visitors are welcome all week.

267 Thornton
Fife

Thornton Golf Club
Station Road, Thornton, KY1 4DW.
Tel: 0592 771111.
18 holes, length of course
5560m/6177 yds.
SSS 69
Charges: £12 weekdays, £18 weekends per round; £18 weekdays, £27
weekends daily. Juniors 50% off
adult rate.
For advance reservations Tel: 0592
771111.
Practice area and catering facilities
are available.
Visitors are welcome all week.
Secretary: Neil Robertson – Tel:
0592 771111.

268 Thurso
Caithness
Thurso Golf Club
Newlands of Geise, Thurso.
Tel: Thurso 63807.
(Further details on application).

269 Tighnabruaich
Argyllshire

Kyles of Bute Golf Club.
Copeswood,
Tighnabruaich PA21 2BE.
Tel: 0700 811 601.
9 holes, length of course 2389 yds.
SSS 64
Charges: £5 daily.
Secretary: Mr. J.A. Carruthers.

270 Tillicoultry
Clackmannanshire

Tillicoultry Golf Course
Alva Road, Tillicoultry.
9 holes, length of course
4518m/5266 yds.
SSS 66
Charges: £7 round Mon-Fri (18
holes), £10 after 4pm. (Sat-Sun);
£12 round.
For advance reservations Tel:
Tillicoultry 50124.
A practice area and catering
facilities are available.
Visitors are welcome all week
(except competition days).
Secretary: Mr. R. Whitehead – Tel:
0259 50124.

271 Tobermory
Isle of Mull

Tobermory Golf Club
Tobermory.
9 holes, length of course
4474m/4921 yds.
SSS 64
Charges: £7.50 daily, £25 weekly,
£40 fortnightly. Juniors half price.
For advance reservations Tel: 0688
2020.
Visitors are welcome.
Secretary: Dr. W.H. Clegg – Tel:
0688 2013.

272 Torphins
Aberdeenshire

Torphins Golf Club
Tel: 03398 82115.
9 holes, length of course 4660 yds.
SSS 63
Charges: £8 daily. £10 daily (weekends). £15 weekly.
Members evening from 5pm
Tuesdays.
Secretary: Mrs. Sue Mortimer – Tel:
03398 82563.

273 Troon
Ayrshire

Royal Troon Golf Club
Old Course, Craigend Road, Troon
KA10 6LD.
Tel: 0292 311555.
18 holes, length of course 7097 yds.
SSS 74
Charges: £65 daily (includes 1
round on both courses. (No ladies or
under-18's).
Caddies and catering facilities
(please advise 1 week beforehand)
are available
Visitors are welcome Mon-Thurs
only with advance reservations.
Secretary: J.D. Montgomerie.
Professional: R. Brian Anderson.

Royal Troon Golf Club
Portland Course, Crosbie Road,
Troon KA10 6EP.
Tel: Troon 311555.
18 holes, length of course 6274 yds.
SSS 71
Charges: £37 daily (composite fee).
Catering facilities are available
Visitors are welcome Mon-Thurs
only with advance reservations.
Secretary: J.D. Montgomerie.
Professional: R. Brian Anderson.

*Lochgreen Golf Course
Harling Drive, Troon KA10 6NF.
c/o Kyle & Carrick District Council,
30 Miller Road, Ayr.
Tel: Troon 312464.
18 holes, length of course 6765 yds.
SSS 72
Charges: £4.80 round (Mon–Fri),
£5.80 (Sat/Sun), £7.60 daily
(Mon–Fri), £9.20 (Sat/Sun), £28.40
weekly.
Postal bookings only.
A practice area, caddy cars and
catering facilities are available.
Visitors are welcome all week.

Secretary: Starters Office – Tel:
Troon 312464.
Professional: Gordon McKinlay –
Tel: Troon 312464.

*Darley Golf Course
Harling Drive, Troon, KA10 6NF.
c/o Kyle & Carrick District Council,
30 Miller Road, Ayr.
Tel: Troon 312464.
18 holes, length of course 6327 yds.
SSS 70
Charges: £12.00 round; £18.00
daily ticket; 5-day tickets £50.00.
Postal bookings only.
A practice area, caddy cars and
catering facilities are available.
Visitors are welcome all week.
Secretary: Starters Office – Tel:
Troon 312464.
Professional: Gordon McKinlay –
Tel: Troon 312464.

*Fullarton Golf Course
St Meddans Golf Club
Harling Drive, Troon KA10 6NF.
c/o Kyle and Carrick District
Council, 30 Miller Road, Ayr.
Tel: Troon 312464.
18 holes, length of course 4784 yds.
SSS 63
Charges: £8.00 per round; £14.00
daily ticket; 5-day ticket £50.00.
Postal bookings only.
A practice area, caddy cars and
catering facilities are available.
Visitors are welcome all week.
Secretary: Starters Office – Tel:
Troon 312464.
Professional: Gordon McKinlay –
Tel: Troon 312464.

274 Turnberry
Ayrshire

Ailsa & Arran
Tumberry Hotel & Golf Courses
Tel: 0655 31000.
2 x 18 holes, length of course Ailsa
6408 yds., Arran 6276 yds.
SSS Ailsa 72, Arran 70.
A practice area, caddies, trolleys
and catering facilities are available.
Clubhouse Manager: Mr. R.L.
Hamblett
Professional: Mr. R.S. Jamieson

275 Turriff
Aberdeenshire

Turriff Golf Club
Rosehall, Turriff.
Tel: 0888 62982.
18 holes, length of course 6145 yds.
SSS 69
Charges: £10 round (Mon-Fri), £13
(Sat/Sun); £13 daily (Mon- Fri), £16
(Sat/Sun).
For advance reservations Tel: 0888
63025.
A small practice area, clubs, caddy
cars and
catering facilities are available.
Visitors are welcome all week and
after 10 am Sat/Sun.
Secretary: Mr. J.D. Stott – Tel: 0888
62982.
Professional: Mr. R. Smith – Tel:
0888 63025.

276 Uddingston
Lanarkshire

Calderbraes Golf Club
57 Roundknowe Road, Uddingston.
Tel: Uddingston 813425.
(Further details on application).

277 Uphall
West Lothian

Uphall Golf Club
Tel: 0506 856404.
(Further details on application).

278 West Calder
West Lothian

Harburn Golf Club
West Calder EH55 8RS.
Tel: 0506 871256.
18 holes, length of course
5340m/5843 yds.
SSS 68
Charges: £11 (Mon-Fri), £16
(Sat/Sun) round; £16 (Mon-Fri),
£22 (Sat/Sun) daily.
For advance reservations
Tel: 0506 871256.
Caddy cars, practice area and catering facilities are available.
Visitors are welcome all week.
Secretary: F. Vinter - Tel: 0506
871131.
Professional: S. Crookston - Tel:
0506 871582.

279 West Kilbride
Ayrshire

West Kilbride Golf Club
Fullerton Drive, West Kilbride
KA23 9HT.
Tel: 0294 823128.
18 holes, length of course 6247 yds.
SSS 70
Charges: On Application.
For advance reservations Tel: 0294
823042.
A practice area, caddy cars and
catering facilities are available.
Visitors are welcome Monday to
Friday.
Secretary: E.D. Jefferies – Tel:
0294 823911.
Professional: G. Howie – Tel: 0294
823042.

280 West Linton
Peeblesshire

West Linton Golf Club
West Linton.
Tel: 0968 660463.
18 holes, length of course
5607m/6132 yds.
SSS 69
Charges: £13 round (Mon-Fri), £20
(Sat/Sun), £18 daily (Mon-Fri).
For advance reservations Tel: 0968
660256.
A practice area and catering
facilities are available.
Visiting parties welcome Mon-Fri,
casual visitors welcome also, at
weekend after 1pm.
Secretary: G. Scott – Tel: 0968
660970 (Office), 0968 675843
(Home).

281 Westray
Orkney

Westray Golf Club
(Further details on application).

282 Whiting Bay
Isle of Arran

Whiting Bay Golf Club
Tel: 07707 487.
(Further details on application).

283 Wick
Caithness

Wick Golf Club
Reiss,
Caithness KW1 4RW.
Tel: (0955) 2726.
18 holes, length of course 5976 yds.
SSS 69
Charges: Weekdays £10 daily;
weekends £12 daily; weekly £40;
juniors £3; fortnightly £50.
Visitors welcome without
reservations.
Society meetings catered for.
Secretary: Mrs. M.S.W. Abernethy -
Tel: 0955 2702.

284 Wigtown
Wigtownshire

**Wigtown & Bladnoch Golf
Club**
Wigtown, Newton Stewart.
Tel: 09884 3354.
9 holes, length of course 2521m.
SSS 67
Charges: £7 daily weekdays; £10
round Sat/Suns.
Visitors are welcome all week.
Secretary: J.R. Bateman - Tel: 098
884 650.

285 Wishaw
Lanarkshire

Wishaw Golf Club
55 Cleland Road, Wishaw.
Tel: Wishaw 372869.
18 holes, length of course 6160 yds.
SSS 69
Charges: £15 daily; midweek per
round £12. £20 (Sun).
A practice area, caddy cars and
catering facilities are available.
Secretary: D.D Gallacher.
Professional: J Campbell.

USEFUL ADDRESSES

British Tourist Authority,
Thames Tower,
Blacks Road,
Hammersmith,
London W6 9EL.
Tel: 081-846 9000.

British Waterways,
Canal House,
1 Applecross Street,
Glasgow G4 9SP.
Tel: Glasgow 041-332 6936.

Scottish Natural Heritage,
Battleby House,
Redgorton,
Perth PH1 3EW.
Tel: Perth (0738) 27921.

Cyclists Touring Club,
69 Meadrow,
Godalming,
Surrey GU7 3HS.
Tel: (0483) 417217.

Forest Enterprise,
Information Office,
231 Corstorphine Road,
Edinburgh EH12 7AT.
Tel: 031-334 0303.

Highlands and Islands Enterprise,
Bridge House,
20 Bridge Street,
Inverness IV1 1QR.
Tel: Inverness (0463) 234171.

Historic Scotland,
20 Brandon Street,
Edinburgh EH3 5RA.
Tel: 031-244 3101.

Mountaineering Council of Scotland,
Rahoy Bridge,
Gallanach Road,
Oban PA34 4PD.

National Trust for Scotland,
5 Charlotte Square,
Edinburgh EH2 4DU.
Tel: 031-226 5922.

Scottish Natural Heritage,
12 Hope Terrace,
Edinburgh EH9 2AS.
Tel: 031-447 4784.

(North Scotland Region),
Forest Enterprise,
21 Church Street,
Inverness IV1 1EL.
Tel: Inverness (0463) 232811.

Royal Society for the Protection of Birds,
17 Regent Terrace,
Edinburgh EH7 5BN.
Tel: 031-557 3136.

Scottish Cyclists Union,
The Velodrome,
Meadowbank Stadium,
London Road,
Edinburgh EH7 6AD.
Tel: 031-652 0187.

Scottish Sports Council,
Caledonia House,
South Gyle,
Edinburgh EH12 9DQ.
Tel: 031-317 7200.

Scottish Tourist Board,
23 Ravelston Terrace,
Edinburgh EH4 3EU.
Tel: 031-332 2433.

Scottish Tourist Board (London Office),
19 Cockspur Street,
London SW1Y 5BL.
Tel: 071-930 8661/2/3.

Scottish Wildlife Trust,
Cramond House, Kirk Cramond,
Cramond Glebe Road,
Edinburgh EH4 6NS.
Tel: 031-312 7765.

Scottish Youth Hostels Association,
7 Glebe Crescent,
Stirling FK8 2JA.
Tel: Stirling (0786) 451181.

(South Scotland Region),
Forest Enterprise,
Greystone Park,
55 Moffat Road,
Dumfries DG1 1NP.
Tel: Dumfries (0387) 69171.

ACTIVITY HOLIDAYS
A PASTIME PUBLICATION

I/We have seen your advertisement and wish to know if you have the following vacancy: —

Name_____

Address_____

_____

_____

Dates from pm _____

Please give date and day of week in each case

To am _____

Number in Party _____

Detail of Children _____

Please remember to include a stamped addressed envelope with your enquiry.

ACTIVITY HOLIDAYS
A PASTIME PUBLICATION

I/We have seen your advertisement and wish to know if you have the following vacancy: —

Name_____

Address_____

_____

_____

Dates from pm _____

Please give date and day of week in each case

To am _____

Number in Party _____

Detail of Children _____

-------CUT ALONG HERE-------

-------CUT ALONG HERE-------

MAPS

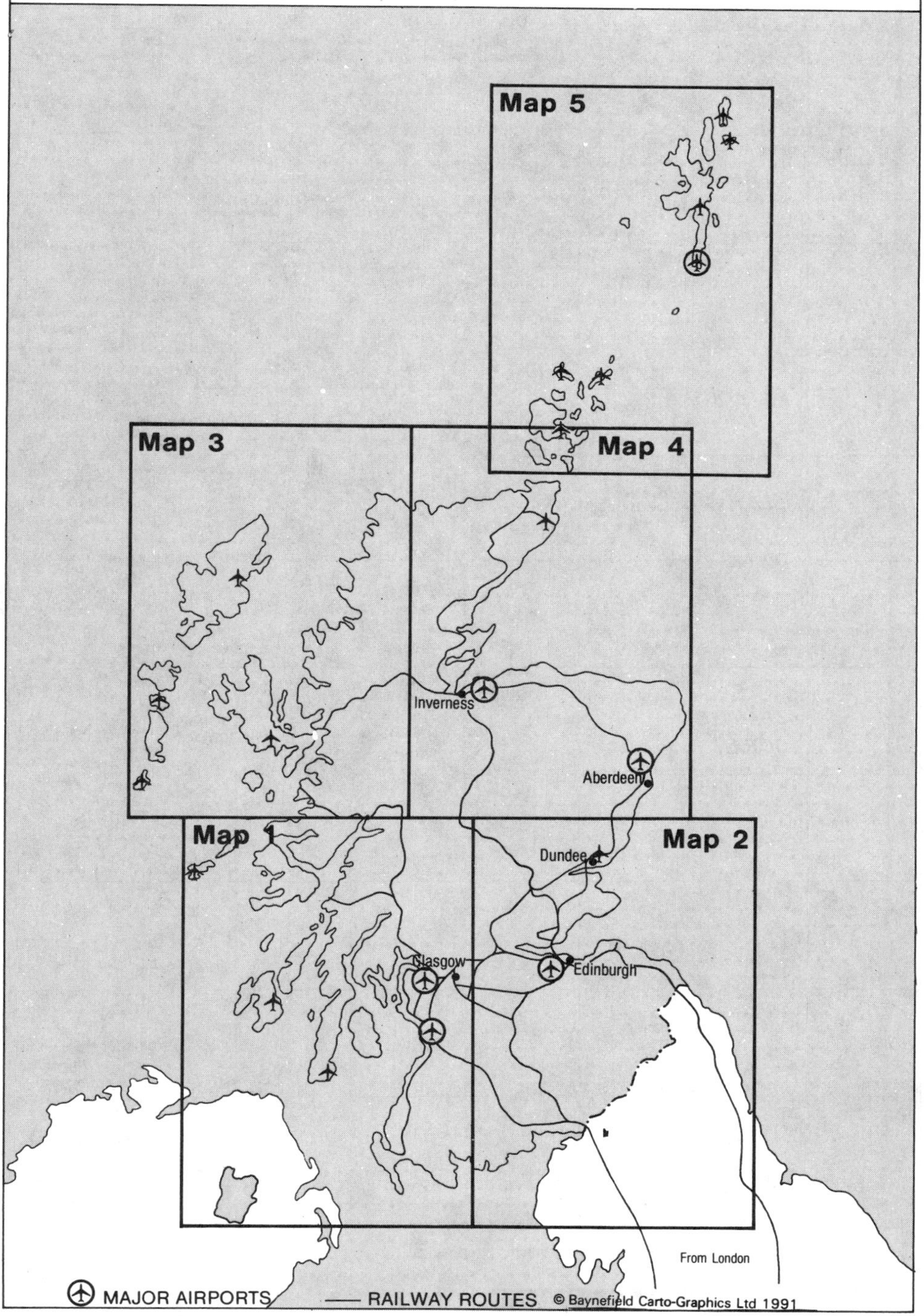

Map 5

Map 3

Map 4

Inverness

Aberdeen

Map 1

Map 2

Dundee

Glasgow

Edinburgh

From London

✈ MAJOR AIRPORTS   —— RAILWAY ROUTES   © Baynefield Carto-Graphics Ltd 1991

MAP 1

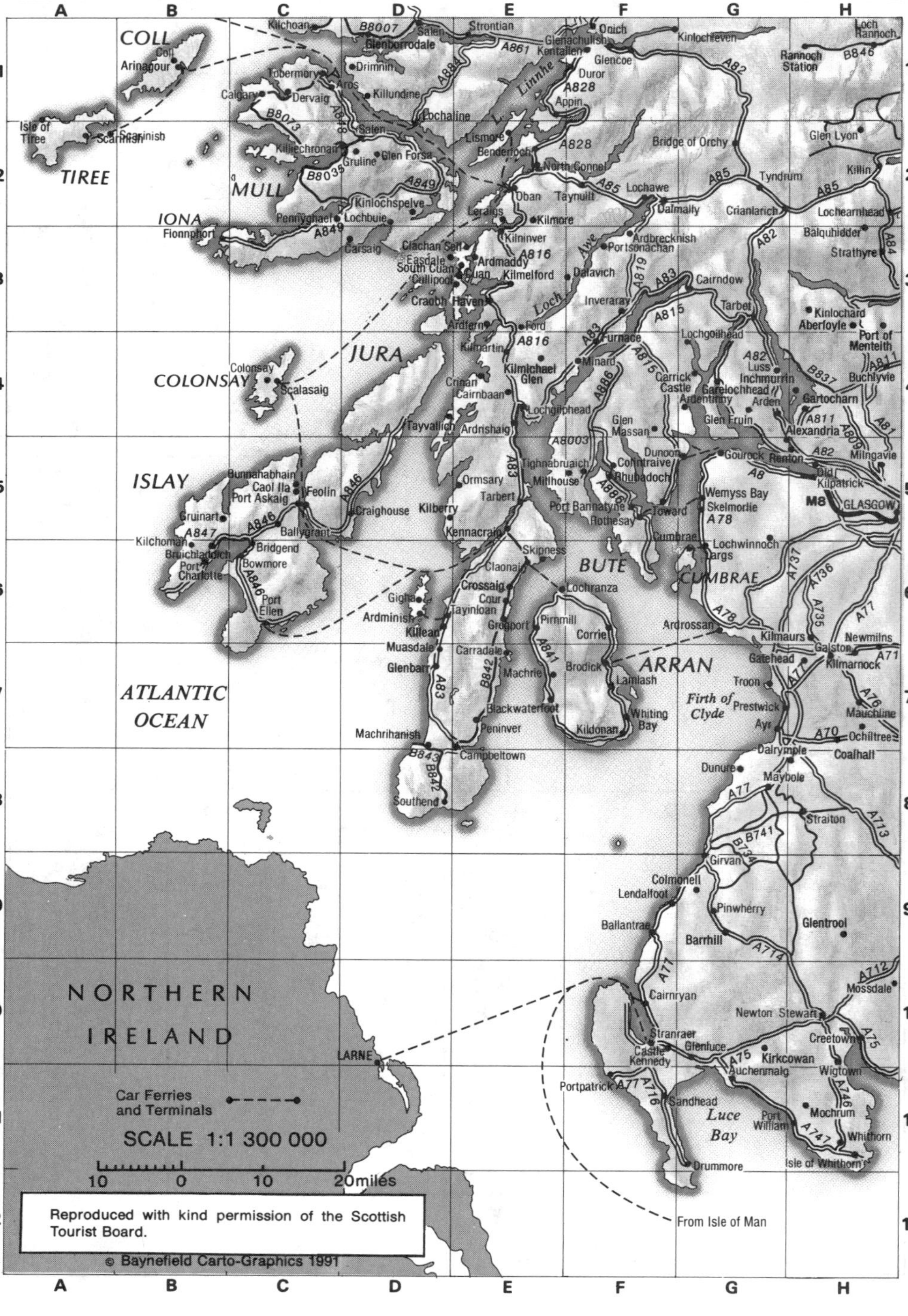

Map of western Scotland showing the following regions and place names, with grid references A–H (columns) and 1–12 (rows).

Islands and regions: COLL, TIREE, MULL, IONA, COLONSAY, JURA, ISLAY, BUTE, CUMBRAE, ARRAN, NORTHERN IRELAND

Ocean: ATLANTIC OCEAN, Firth of Clyde, Loch Rannoch, Loch Linnhe, Luce Bay

Place names (selected): Kilchoan, Blenborrodale, Salen, Strontian, Glenachulish, Onich, Kinlochleven, Rannoch Station, Loch Rannoch, Tobermory, Drimnin, Killundine, Lochaline, Glencoe, Duror, Appin, Glen Lyon, Coll, Arinagour, Calgary, Dervaig, Aros, Glen Forsa, Lismore, Benderloch, North Connel, Bridge of Orchy, Tyndrum, Killin, Isle of Tiree, Scarinish, Kilichronan, Salen, Gruline, Oban, Taynuilt, Lochawe, Crianlarich, Lochearnhead, Pennyghael, Lochbuie, Kinlochspelve, Lerags, Kilmore, Dalmally, Balquhidder, Strathyre, Carsaig, Clachan Seil, Kilninver, Ardbrecknish, Portsonachan, Cairndow, Kinlochard, Aberfoyle, Port of Menteith, Buchlyvie, Easdale, South Cuan, Cuan, Ardmaddy, Kilmelford, Delavich, Inveraray, Tarbet, Lochgoilhead, Craobh Haven, Ardfern, Ford, Kilmartin, Furnace, Carrick Castle, Gairlochhead, Ardentinny, Arden, Inchmurrin, Luss, Gartocharn, Alexandria, Milngavie, Crinan, Cairnbaan, Minard, Glen Massan, Dunoon, Cairndow, Gourock, Renton, Old Kilpatrick, Tayvallich, Ardrishaig, Tighnabruaich, Colintraive, Rhubodach, Wemyss Bay, Skelmorlie, Lochwinnoch, GLASGOW, Ormsay, Millhouse, Port Bannatyne, Toward, Cumbrae, Largs, Kilberry, Tarbert, Rothesay, Kennacraig, Skipness, Lochranza, Kilmaurs, Newmilns, Galston, Claonaig, Crossaig, Cour, Tayinloan, Gigha, Ardminish, Killean, Muasdale, Glenbarr, Carradale, Machrie, Pirnmill, Corrie, Brodick, Lamlash, Ardrossan, Gatehead, Kilmarnock, Blackwaterfoot, Peninver, Kildonan, Whiting Bay, Troon, Prestwick, Ayr, Mauchline, Ochiltree, Machrihanish, Campbeltown, Dunure, Dalrymple, Coalhall, Southend, Maybole, Straiton, Colmonell, Lendalfoot, Girvan, Pinwherry, Glentrool, Ballantrae, Barrhill, Mossdale, Cairnryan, Newton Stewart, Creetown, LARNE, Stranraer, Glenluce, Kirkcowan, Wigtown, Portpatrick, Castle Kennedy, Auchenmalg, Sandhead, Port William, Mochrum, Drummore, Luce Bay, Isle of Whithorn, Whithorn

Roads: A82, A85, A83, A84, A819, A815, A811, A78, A77, A70, A71, A713, A714, A712, A75, A746, A747, A716, A849, A846, A847, A861, A828, A816, A8, A8003, B846, B837, B807, B8007, B8035, B8073, B741, B842, B843, B844, B8024, B8025

Car Ferries and Terminals

SCALE 1:1 300 000

10   0   10   20 miles

Reproduced with kind permission of the Scottish Tourist Board.

© Baynefield Carto-Graphics 1991

From Isle of Man

MAP 2

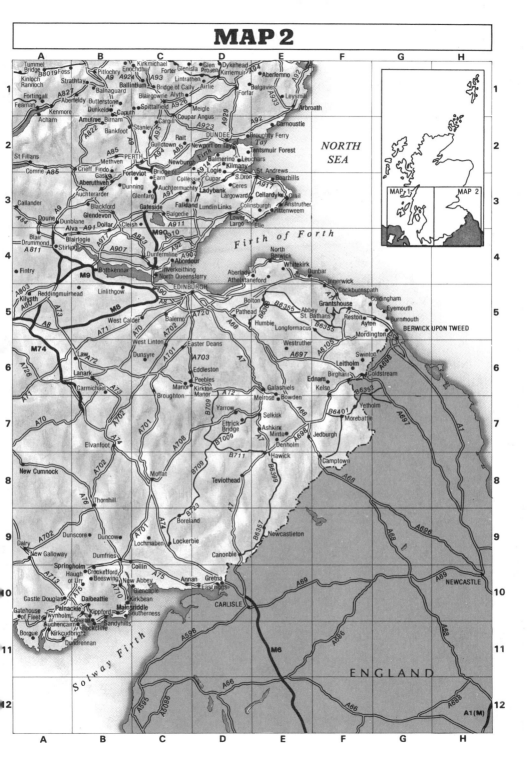

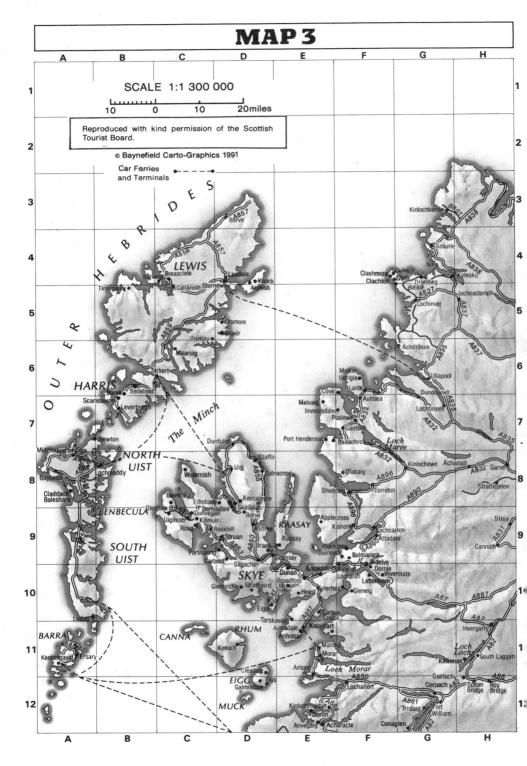

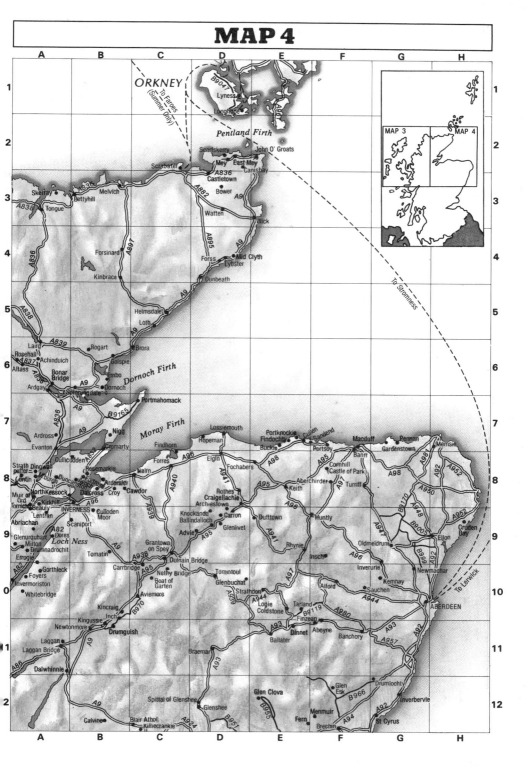

MAP 5

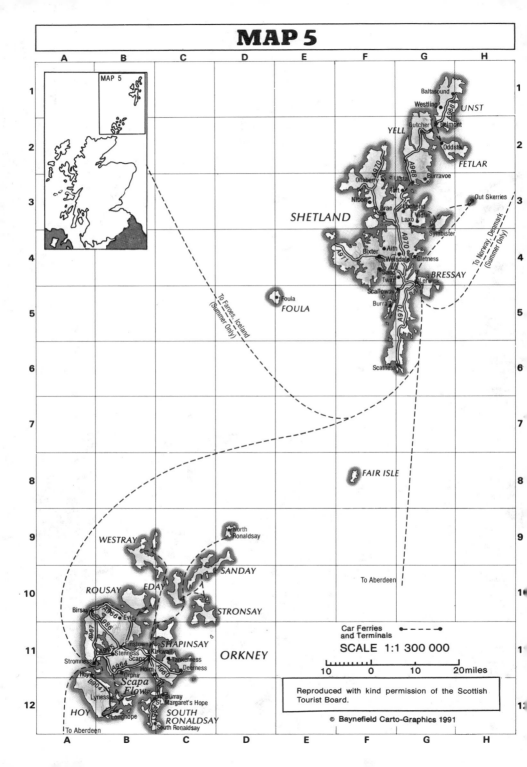

MAP 5

Baltasound
Westling
UNST
YELL
Gutcher Belmont
Oddsta
FETLAR
Burravoe
Out Skerries
Ollaberry Ulsta
Nibon Toft
SHETLAND
Niboo Lochend
Brae Vidlin
Laxo
Symbister
Bixter Aith
Weisdale Celtness
Sand BRESSAY
Scalloway Lerwick
Burra Twatt

To Faroes, Iceland
(Summer Only)
To Norway, Denmark
(Summer Only)

Foula
FOULA

Scatness

FAIR ISLE

North
Ronaldsay

WESTRAY
SANDAY

To Aberdeen

ROUSAY EDAY
STRONSAY

Birsay Evie
ORKNEY

Car Ferries
and Terminals

SCALE 1:1 300 000

10   0   10   20miles

Stromness Finstown
Stenness Kirkwall
Scapa Tankerness
Hoy Orphir Deerness
Holm

Reproduced with kind permission of the Scottish
Tourist Board.

Lyness
Scapa
Flow

Burray
St. Margaret's Hope

HOY
SOUTH
RONALDSAY

Longhope
South Ronaldsay

To Aberdeen

© Baynefield Carto-Graphics 1991